Europe and the Management of Globalization

European politicians often speak of their efforts to 'manage globalization'. At one level, this is merely a rhetorical device to make globalization more palatable to citizens and prove that policy-makers are still firmly in control of their country's fate. This volume argues that the advocacy of managed globalization goes beyond rhetoric and actually has been a primary driver of major European Union (EU) policies in the past twenty years. The EU has indeed tried to manage globalization through the use of five major mechanisms: 1) expanding policy scope; 2) exercising regulatory influence; 3) empowering international institutions; 4) enlarging the territorial sphere of EU influence; and 5) redistributing the costs of globalization. These mechanisms are neither entirely novel, nor are they always effective but they provide the contours of an approach to globalization that is neither ad hoc deregulation, nor old-style economic protectionism.

The recent financial crisis may have seemed initially to vindicate the European efforts to manage globalization, but it also represented the limits of such efforts without the full participation of the US and China. The EU cannot rig the game of globalization, but it can try to provide predictability, oversight, and regularity with rules that accommodate European interests.

This book was based on a special issue of *Journal of European Public Policy*.

Wade Jacoby is Professor of Political Science and Director of the Center for the Study of Europe at Brigham Young University in Provo, Utah. Jacoby has published articles in *World Politics, Comparative Political Studies, Politics and Society, The Review of International Political Economy, The Review of International Organizations*, and many other journals. Jacoby received the DAAD Prize for his scholarship on Germany and the EU in 2006 and was a Fernand Braudel Fellow at the European University Institute in 2009-2010.

Sophie Meunier is a Research Scholar in Public and International Affairs at the Woodrow Wilson School, Princeton University, and the Co-Director of the European Union Program at Princeton. She is the author of *Trading Voices: The European Union in International Commercial Negotiations* (Princeton University Press, 2005); and the co-editor of *Making History: European Integration and Institutional Change at Fifty* (Oxford University Press, 2007).

Journal of European Public Policy Series
Series Editor: Jeremy Richardson is a Professor at Nuffield College, Oxford University

This series seeks to bring together some of the finest edited works on European Public Policy. Reprinting from Special Issues of the 'Journal of European Public Policy,' the focus is on using a wide range of social sciences approaches, both qualitative and quantitative, to gain a comprehensive and definitive understanding of Public Policy in Europe.

To Idir and Ines Aitsahalia, who have managed to become global citizens and to Taylor, Mackenzie, and Kendall Jacoby, who are globally unmanageable

Europe and the Management of Globalization

Edited by

Wade Jacoby and Sophie Meunier

Routledge
Taylor & Francis Group

LONDON AND NEW YORK

First published 2011
by Routledge
2 Park Square, Milton Park, Abingdon, Oxon, OX14 4RN

Simultaneously published in the USA and Canada
by Routledge
270 Madison Avenue, New York, NY 10016

Routledge is an imprint of the Taylor & Francis Group, an informa business

This book is a reproduction of the *Journal of European Public Policy*, vol. 17, issue 3. The Publisher requests to those authors who may be citing this book to state, also, the bibliographical details of the special issue on which the book was based.

Typeset in Times New Roman by Taylor & Francis Books
Printed and bound in Great Britain by MPG Books Group, UK

British Library Cataloguing in Publication Data
A catalogue record for this book is available from the British Library

ISBN13: 978-0-415-59213-0

Disclaimer
The publisher would like to make readers aware that the chapters in this book are referred to as articles as they had been in the special issue. The publisher accepts responsibility for any inconsistencies that may have arisen in the course of preparing this volume for print.

Contents

Notes on Contributors

Rawi Abdelal is the Joseph C. Wilson Professor of Business Administration at Harvard Business School.

Brian Burgoon is an Associate Professor in the Department of Political Science at the University of Amsterdam.

Orfeo Fioretos is Assistant Professor of Political Science, Temple University.

Nicolas Jabko is Associate Professor at Johns Hopkins University and at Sciences Po-Paris.

Wade Jacoby is Professor of Political Science and Director of the Center for the Study of Europe at Brigham Young University.

R. Daniel Kelemen is Associate Professor of Political Science and Director of the Center for European Studies at Rutgers University.

Sophie Meunier is Research Scholar in Public and International Affairs at the Woodrow Wilson School, Princeton University, and Co-Director of the EU Program at Princeton.

Elliot Posner is Associate Professor at the Peterson Institute for International Economics.

Alberta Sbragia is Jean Monnet Chair ad personam and the Mark A. Nordenberg University Chair at the University of Pittsburgh, USA, where she directs the European Union Center of Excellence and the European Studies Center.

Nicolas Véron is Senior Fellow at Bruegel, Belgium, and Visiting Fellow at the Peterson Institute for International Economics.

Europe and the management of globalization

Wade Jacoby and Sophie Meunier

ABSTRACT   European policy-makers often speak of their efforts to 'manage globalization'. We argue that the advocacy of managed globalization is more than a rhetorical device and indeed has been a primary driver of major European Union (EU) policies over the past 25 years. We sketch the outlines of the concept of managed globalization, raise broad questions about its extent, and describe five major mechanisms through which it has been pursued: (1) expanding policy scope; (2) exercising regulatory influence; (3) empowering international institutions; (4) enlarging the territorial sphere of EU influence; and (5) redistributing the costs of globalization. These mechanisms are neither entirely novel, nor are they necessarily effective, but they provide the contours of an approach to globalization that is neither ad hoc deregulation nor old-style economic protectionism.

INTRODUCTION

Globalization – defined here as the increased flows of goods, services, capital, people, and information across borders – has been the source of many worries in Europe over the past decade, way before the global financial meltdown that began in 2008. In many European countries, globalization is perceived more as a threat than an opportunity. Some see a narrow threat to their jobs, others to their broader social welfare, and yet others to their entire way of life. At the same time, globalization promises opportunities, especially to those who can serve new markets or existing markets with cheaper inputs. This blend of threat and opportunity – combined with a sense that globalization may simply be too powerful to be resisted outright – has led many European policy-makers to speak of what we term 'globalization with adjectives'. Typically, the adjective injects a note of caution that suggests the embrace of globalization is a conditional one – whether globalization is to be 'humanized', 'tamed', 'harnessed', or 'managed'.

In this introduction, we adopt the term 'managed globalization' as a short cut for all attempts to make globalization more palatable to citizens. We define managed globalization as the attempt by public or private actors to ensure that the liberalization of rules about international flows of goods and services, capital, and labor goes hand in hand with formal practices to bind market

1

players and their governments. This collection traces a set of debates that culminated in the concept of managed globalization – debates that go back to the early 1980s and the policies to reform European economies in light of widespread discontent in the 1970s (Jacoby and Meunier 2009). This period saw the first sustained efforts to use common European tools to manage not just regional economic integration but rather to help set the rules for global exchanges.

The phrase 'managed globalization' emerged only after a long gestation and experimentation with a basket of mechanisms discussed below. As Rawi Abdelal and Sophie Meunier recall in their contribution, the concept was originally launched into the broader public debate by Frenchman Pascal Lamy in 1999 when he was European Trade Commissioner and has been perpetuated during his tenure as head of the World Trade Organization (WTO) (Lamy 2004). The term was used somewhat less under Lamy's immediate successor Peter Mandelson, but this idea has mainly been strengthened by the ongoing economic crisis. Broadly, the widespread perception that the crisis involves a failure of regulation is likely to increase the legitimacy of the concept in the eyes of many European voters and already in the eyes of many analysts (Cohen-Tanugi 2009; Cooper *et al.* 2007; Sapir 2007). For example, highly visible European figures like Mario Monti have recently spoken of the dangers of 'ungoverned globalization' (Monti 2009).

That said, this introduction tries to separate rhetoric from reality. What did this idea of 'managed globalization' do for Europe? Was it only political rhetoric for domestic political consumption, or instead was it a source of real policies with an international impact? Have demands for the management of globalization been met by the EU? What kinds of management strategies have European leaders supplied? How well are those strategies working? We argue that the will to manage globalization has been a primary driver of major European Union (EU) policies over the past 25 years. This introduction sketches the outlines of the concept of managed globalization, raises broad questions about its extent, and describes five major mechanisms through which it has been pursued. The rest of this book fleshes out these five mechanisms and supplies concrete example of managed globalization in action (and, sometimes, inaction).

MANAGED GLOBALIZATION: RHETORIC OR POLICY?

Just because politicians talk about managed globalization does not mean they actually try to implement it. Is the talk just empty rhetoric, designed to appease a public worried about globalization, or is it also a real driver of policies? Hay (2007) suggests that European publics have so internalized the necessities of deregulation that they have come to 'hate politics', which is unable to offer them any defense. At minimum, managed globalization is a rhetorical effort to suggest there is something European leaders can do. We and our contributors ask: Is it also something more? Does it lead to policy innovation?

One possibility is that globalization with adjectives is purely rhetorical. 'Managing' means altering the existing course of things and reorganizing them for a purpose. Political leaders often imply that citizens are safer in their hands than they would otherwise be because they are 'managing' globalization, instead of merely letting it happen. It shows the voters that politicians are firmly in control, that they still have a margin of maneuver, that they have not abdicated policy-making in the face of external forces. French politicians, in particular, have a well-deserved reputation for promising voters relief from the direct onslaught of market forces. 'Managing globalization' means tinkering with free-market outcomes, which in France accords with *dirigiste* habits of centrally managing the economy (Abdelal and Meunier 2010).

If globalization with adjectives is merely a rhetorical trope, however, it is certainly a widespread one. Lamy is far from alone in having promised to manage globalization. Other prominent EU officials have talked of managing globalization, including Romano Prodi, former Commission President,[1] and John Bruton, former EU Ambassador to the United States.[2] Nor is this a purely EU discourse. Building on the debate about 'fair trade' that went back to the 1980s, an International Labor Organization report spoke of 'fair globalization' as early as 1994, and the WTO often refers to the need to 'harness globalization'.[3]

National politicians have their own variants of globalization with adjectives. While still Chancellor of the Exchequer, Gordon Brown argued that 'some critics say the issue is whether we should have globalization or not. In fact, the issue is whether we manage globalization well or badly, fairly or unfairly'.[4] German Chancellor Angela Merkel speaks often of 'shaping globalization' (*Globalisierung gestalten*),[5] as does External Relations Commissioner Benita Ferrero-Waldner.[6] While few Spanish commentators speak of *globalización gestionada*, Conservative politician Ana Pastor promises *globalización económica responsable*,[7] and Javier Moreno, Socialist MEP and Secretary-General of the Partido Socialista Obero Español (PSOE) Europe, has spoken up for 'social globalization'.[8]

All of this says nothing about the content, if any, of managed globalization or the other variants. Perhaps this family of concepts is merely the European answer to ubiquitous American tropes like the 'electronic herd' and 'golden strait-jacket' of a world that is 'flat' (Friedman 2000, 2007). To many Europeans, the notion of a 'flat' world is threatening. Our central argument, however, is that the advocacy of managed globalization is not purely a rhetorical device but is instead often accompanied by policy substance.

Our overarching finding is that there is a real effort afoot in Europe to manage globalization. How well these policies work, on the other hand, is quite a mixed story. Individual contributions develop specific arguments on the basis of empirical investigations drawn from areas such as rules for capital flows, the environment, trade dislocation policies, and enlargement. That said, our contributors also acknowledge many European failures to manage globalization in other ways, including the largely unsatisfying course of the Lisbon Process designed explicitly to help European economies face globalization. Perhaps nowhere are European difficulties in managing globalization so striking as in the context of the financial crisis, where EU actors have been relatively slow off the mark.

Elliott Posner and Nicolas Véron (2010) show that there are areas of regulation for which intensive regulatory harmonization did not amount to an effort to manage globalization. Indeed, EU policy-makers largely followed American and British approaches in their attempts to forge an integrated regional financial system. In between come mixed results, above all in the area of trade.

We focus here explicitly on the EU, which has been portrayed as actually or potentially playing a crucial role in managing globalization. This introduction is open towards a variety of theoretical perspectives and substantive insights into how the EU 'really works'. Thus, rather than favoring a particular model of EU decision-making, we treat the EU as something of a 'black box' insofar as the pressures and processes that result in particular decisions are a matter for each author to treat as a consequence of his or her own analytical choices. This means that individual contributions emphasize the source of novel policies in several ways: through intergovernmental bargaining in the Council of Ministers (Jabko 2010; Posner and Véron 2010), through corporate and/or civil society actors (Jacoby 2010; Kelemen 2010), through public opinion (Burgoon 2010), and through Commission entrepreneurialism (Abdelal and Meunier 2010; Fioretos 2010; Sbragia 2010) as the ultimate source of policy demand.

There is no doubt that many Europeans expect the EU to do something about globalization. According to a 2007 *Financial Times*/Harris poll, the majority of Europeans surveyed in Britain, France, Italy, and Spain believe that globalization is having a negative effect on their countries. The largest supporters of globalization (36 per cent) were found in Germany, then the world's leading exporter.[9] To the question 'Should the European Union do more to protect people from the adverse effects of globalization?', a vast majority support an activist, protective EU: 94 per cent in Spain, 93 per cent in Italy, 89 per cent in France and in Germany, and 64 per cent in Great Britain. In addition, as Brian Burgoon's contribution points out, EU-27 citizens surveyed tend to trust the EU more than their own nation states, non-government organizations (NGOs), international institutions, or any other actors named in the survey to 'get the effects of globalization under control' (Eurobarometer 2004).

We argue that the EU has attempted to implement policies designed to manage globalization by using five main mechanisms: expanding policy scope, exercising regulatory influence, empowering international institutions, enlarging the territorial sphere of EU influence, and redistributing the costs of globalization. Rather than more specific policies, we focus on these broader functional mechanisms that represent fundamental ways of coping with major strategic problems. These mechanisms are neither entirely novel, nor are they necessarily effective; but they provide the contours of an approach to globalization that is neither ad hoc deregulation, nor old-style economic protectionism.

BETWEEN PROTECTIONISM AND AD HOC GLOBALIZATION

In simplest terms, we see managed globalization as an orientation to economic liberalization that may be located on a continuum between two other approaches to globalization. The first is old-fashioned protectionism, in which actors seek to limit competitive pressures by excluding products and services from their markets. Advocates of managed globalization generally see such measures as either politically illegitimate or economically unwise. This does not, of course, mean that protectionist policies do not retain ample support in Europe (and elsewhere), but rather that they should be analytically distinct from policies we cluster under the rubric of managed globalization. Some managed globalization policies began as purely regional instruments and may, in that regional context, have had a protectionist effect. Nevertheless, with the passage of time, European actors used these policies also to affect global markets (Bach and Newman 2007).

We call the second alternative ad hoc globalization. It is somewhat harder to define, since one might get the impression that it is 'globalization without rules'. Yet liberalization is rarely entirely without rules. For example, most of the substantial economic liberalization of the first three decades after the second world war occurred in a rule-laden context known by the shorthand 'Bretton-Woods'. Each successive wave of globalization has had rules, and we think it is axiomatic that all future waves of globalization will as well (whether and how they are enforced is a separate question). Our central point is that some actors try to shape those rules while others do not. The former are aspirant managers of globalization. The latter are simply players (who may or may not play by those rules, e.g. they may comply or cheat). Thus a company, however large, that simply tried to negotiate, say, a particular tax break with a political jurisdiction as a quid quo pro for investing would not be engaged in a management effort so long as it made no effort to extend that condition to other firms. For a long time, European officials focused on managing regional integration and thought little about how globalization might better be managed in Europe's interest. This is now changing, albeit slowly and incompletely.

Thus, managed globalization means going beyond the simple removal of regulations and making some effort to shape and regularize the competitive order. Many variations are possible. Sometimes, this shaping occurs in domains where EU-based competitors enjoy prominent market positions that they seek to defend, while in other cases it occurs in domains where EU-based competitors hold weak positions that they seek to expand. Some of these management strategies are executed at national and even subnational levels. In the past decade, however, the EU has been, within Europe, the principal developer of the concept and rhetoric of managed globalization, as well as the principal actor responsible for its operationalization and implementation.[10]

INTERNAL CHALLENGES, EXTERNAL CHALLENGES

At one level, characterizing the EU as a system of management is nothing new. Older practical aspirations for European integration have often emphasized the management of intra-European tensions. A primary example is the Franco–German relationship, transformed in a series of postwar acts of reconciliation from militaristic competition to jointly beneficial economic co-management. Conceptually, European integration has been seen as an effort to manage the eroding powers of national states, to manage the creation of an integrated market, and to manage the 'pooling' of national sovereignty.

Yet what all of these different 'management' approaches have in common is a focus on tensions and challenges with largely *intra-European origins*. The European Coal and Steel Community had external implications but mostly managed intra-European tensions. The 1980s move to the Single Market was primarily an intra-European exercise, which third countries deplored as 'Fortress Europe', though the Single Market brought the EC/EU leverage in broader global conversations. More recently, the concept of 'managed globalization', articulated explicitly as the central doctrine of EU trade policy since 1999, suggests that order and control should be restored to the process of globalization by framing it with rules, obeying these rules, and empowering international organizations to make and implement these rules (Abdelal and Meunier, this book). Arguably, the EU is well placed to provide the institutional foundations for this, since economic liberalization has been such a fundamental part of European integration. Europe has conjured and then managed the world's most impressive variant of regionalism (or so goes the intuition); why then would it not attempt to modify some key mechanisms and invent others in order to also manage globalization as well?

We explore how over the past 25 years European policy-makers have tried to manage globalization, both inside and outside Europe, in a variety of policy areas. We suggest that this concept of managed globalization, originally and explicitly developed with respect to trade and finance, has become the underlying driver of a number of major policy initiatives undertaken by the EU in the past decade. Whether the euro, immigration, enlargement, the Neighborhood Policy, or even the Lisbon Process, all these policies have been designed, at least in part, to restore order and control in the face of challenges posed by globalization. To be sure, some of these policy sectors go back almost to the founding of the EC/EU, but only with the rise of the Single Market did the European states find leverage that allowed them to act jointly to shape global structures. Understandably, most existing analyses of these policies have tried to understand their effects inside Europe, but aside from efforts to make Europe 'fit for globalization', we are also interested in efforts to make 'globalization fit for Europe' (Tsoukalis 2010). A common denominator in these efforts is an attempt to supplant 'ad hoc globalization', based primarily on the removal of regulations, with rule-based globalization that seeks to channel, regularize, and sometimes limit certain aspects of competition.

FIVE MECHANISMS

Over the past two decades, the EU has developed several mechanisms to try to manage globalization. Some seek to ensure that globalization happens on European terms, with other countries conforming to Europe's ways and standards.

Other mechanisms ensure that external challenges brought about by globalization have as little negative, disruptive effect upon European citizens as possible. Some mechanisms may be used for both purposes. All five of these mechanisms, depending on the policy area in which they are used, are addressed in the contributions written for this project. The first mechanism, expanding policy scope, addresses solutions that apply, at least initially, only to European actors. Of course, only some of these policies are plausibly connected to the response to globalization pressures, and this project focuses on the euro as a key example of this mechanism. The other four mechanisms presume that the EU members have some set of common preferences they wish to extend to affect the behavior of non-members. The EU often prefers, where it can, to have European regulatory standards used as the foundation for global standards. Obviously, this is not always possible due, not least, to substantial preference heterogeneity on issues of global regulation. In such cases, however, the EU has developed other mechanisms to help Europe manage globalization.

Expanding policy scope

European states use the EU to develop and execute joint policies. Some may be understood as responses to globalization pressures, and these are the subset of interest to this collection. An example is the euro, which grew out of European experiences with the breakdown of Bretton-Woods – the prior regime for managing globalization – and the discontents of the European Monetary System. EMU led to a new framework for unified monetary policy and – to a lesser extent – co-ordinated economic policy among the 12 member states that adopted the euro in 2002.[11] Nicolas Jabko argues that this expansion of EU policy scope was an important way of managing globalization. The creation of an independent European Central Bank (ECB) with the primary objective of fighting inflation is generally cited as evidence of the EU's 'neoliberal' proclivities. Yet EMU may also be described as an example of EU empowerment, since the euro sheltered member states from the constraining pressure of currency fluctuations. Although they have transferred their monetary prerogatives to the ECB, governments have regained some maneuvering room *vis-à-vis* market actors in the conduct of economic policies. Their fiscal policies are now subject to a process of peer evaluation, which enables them to defuse the often much harsher verdict of financial actors. The treaty also provides an embryonic framework for international economic coordination, potentially empowering the EU to assert collective priorities in addition to that of low inflation (Jabko 2010).

Thus, expanding policy scope led to state empowerment that is just as real as the market-friendly policies usually emphasized; but will eurozone member states be content to adopt an attitude of 'benign neglect' *vis-à-vis* their currency, or will they manage EMU more actively and use it as a power resource for global leadership? As Jabko points out, the latter would open a Pandora's box since Europeans are not ready to stand united *vis-à-vis* the rest of the world.

7

Nowhere are such strains more evident than in the regulation of financial markets, as the contribution by Posner and Véron demonstrates. In the decade prior to the recent global economic crisis, EU policy-makers used legislation and co-ordination mechanisms to harmonize financial regulation and shifted many rule-making procedures (though not supervision) to the European level. Yet unlike monetary policy where, according to Jabko, unionization was, in part, a mechanism for managing globalization, Posner and Véron contend that expansion of the EU's policy scope in finance gave international firms more discretion and autonomy. To date, they have found little evidence that European states have developed new EU instruments (or so substantially strengthened old ones) that we could meaningfully speak of managed globalization in the financial arena.

The mixed pattern of both substantial efforts and results in managing globalization (EMU) and of market difficulty in doing so (financial market regulation) encountered in this first mechanism will be repeated in much of this book. For every area where we can point to achievements (e.g., the environment), we can also point to areas in which stated European ambitions to respond to globalization pressures have led to only modest change (e.g. the Lisbon competitiveness agenda) or virtually none at all (e.g., the common energy policy).[12] Where expanding policy scope is successful, however, there is often the possibility that common European solutions can be followed by extending that regulatory influence to larger geographical spheres at a later date. It is to this mechanism that we now turn.

Exercising regulatory influence

A central strategy for managing globalization is for the EU to develop its own regulatory power in a way that decisively shapes global governance. In many liberalized sectors, competition is ensured by regulatory institutions (e.g., agencies, courts, ombudsmen). The EU has become the world's largest regulatory power across a range of sectors, including food, industrial chemicals, and telecommunications (Drezner 2007). The case of the 1995 EU Data Privacy Directive is a telling example. Although the US actively opposed the EU approach, more than 30 countries have emulated EU regulations, including some key markets for the US such as Japan, Canada, and Australia. In the end, the US agreed to abide by EU rules in many cases, and European regulations have thus become the de facto international standard (Bach and Newman 2007). Here, Europe has managed to shape global rules on its own terms. Likewise, Daniel Kelemen's contribution shows that the EU has attempted to spread its environmental standards by leveraging its market power to pressure firms and foreign governments to ratchet up their rules to conform with EU standards (Kelemen 2010).

There are also, however, indications that the EU's internal diversity may at times serve to undermine its ability to exercise regulatory influence. Orfeo Fioretos discusses several areas of global governance in which variations in EU member states' economic systems prevent a common EU position in regulatory matters. For example, in global hedge fund regulation, differences in national financial systems caused European governments to adopt divergent positions on global standards. This made managing globalization through EU-level regulations impossible. Moreover, the EU's internal diversity also prevented a common EU position in the G7 and IMF with the result that the global non-regulation status quo prevailed (Fioretos 2010).

In other areas, Fioretos shows a strikingly different pattern, namely that EU institutional innovations such as mutual recognition, common minimum standards, the open method of co-ordination, and variable geometry 'model' for non-European actors how diverse interests among sovereign states can be overcome while high levels of economic openness, international co-operation, and national discretion in economic management are sustained. Kelemen's contribution complements this by showing how EU policy-makers have sought to manage globalization by spreading EU environmental standards around the world, through support of multilateral environmental agreements and through the EU's normative and market power.

In finance, as noted, post-EMU regulatory harmonization and regional rule-making procedures increased the international clout of EU representatives. Yet unlike in data privacy and the environment, Posner and Véron argue that the EU's international agenda focused primarily on ensuring equal access to foreign markets for European banks and other financial services companies. In fact, rather than promoting a managed approach to financial regulation, the EU's international aims (like the principles underpinning regional financial regulation) did not challenge the dominant normative ad hoc globalization framework, as largely embodied by American and British models. Again, then, the picture is mixed.

Empowering international institutions

A related mechanism for managing globalization is to involve other international institutions. This mechanism is often a complement to expanding policy scope insofar as global rules are often written 'through' international organizations. Abdelal and Meunier argue that as globalization in trade and capital proceeded, the EU sought to write the rules of the game, develop the institutional architecture to monitor those rules, and build the capacity of international organizations to enforce them. This is by no means exclusively an effort to place the EU itself at the center of such deliberations; in fact, the EU has often tried to strengthen organizations such as the Organization for Economic Cooperation and Development (OECD), International Monetary Fund (IMF), and WTO and expand their membership, which has paradoxically contributed to diluting its own influence. This strategy clearly has its risks. In fact, a central paradox is that the same global institutions the EU often seeks to strengthen have come under fierce criticism for not managing globalization but for accelerating it, and therefore the organizations become the target of attacks and lose political legitimacy – a trend for which the WTO may be the best example (Abdelal and Meunier 2010).

A related drawback is that the EU has discovered that empowering international institutions (the WTO in particular) hardly guarantees that the EU will secure its own interests. Alberta Sbragia shows that competitors – such as the US and also China – can use such institutions to restrain the EU just as easily as the EU can use them to advance its own economic interests. Seeing the EU and US as operating interdependently while acting as 'geo-economic competitors', Sbragia explains why European attempts to manage globalization stimulate a dynamic cycle of action and reaction. Put differently, the European countries are not the only ones trying desperately to manage globalization on their terms, and these efforts continually interact with other actors' strategies (Sbragia, this book). This is a point underscored again by Kelemen, who shows how the EU leapfrogged the US in terms of policy leadership on the environment by promoting the insertion of the 'precautionary principle' into multilateral environmental agreements regulating genetically modified organisms (GMOs), climate change, and chemicals but that this sparked off a dynamic process in which the institutional high ground is always contested and never secured.

Enlarging the territorial sphere of EU influence

The EU engages non-members with varying degrees of intensity, with the most intensive engagement saved for states seeking to become full members. Wade Jacoby argues that one part of managing globalization has meant managing both 'threats and opportunities' from Central and Eastern European (CEE) states who sought EU membership (Jacoby 2010). By expanding its territory through enlargement, the EU 'subtracts' new countries from the unadulterated reach of globalization and expands its influence. Of course, all the EU's neighbors acclimate themselves to EU rules, but this is not something the EU leaves to chance or to voluntary actions on the part of its neighbors. Instead, the ten CEE states that joined in 2004 and 2007 were managed in systematic ways (Jacoby 2004). For example, the European Commission developed a thorough 'screening' of more than 30 separate policy domains for each of the prospective CEE members. This involved Commission experts meeting with government officials of each CEE aspirant member and going line by line through the *acquis communautaire*. Jacoby shows that the accession process managed and softened incentives towards competitive deregulation across Europe and helped organize the CEE region as a complementary platform for firms from existing member states. But a critical caveat is that however successful this management has been, the EU has much less leverage over states that are not credible future members.

Sbragia also argues that the EU is trying to bring more territory under the scope of EU-inflected rules through the use of regional trade agreements. Once again, however, such efforts are not guaranteed to succeed, and she argues that actually the US has outflanked the EU on territorial influence and that the EU is now playing a catch-up game. The critical point is that European actors are engaged in intense competition with American and, increasingly, groups of emerging market states to set the rules for global competition. The barriers to European efforts to manage globalization are not only (or perhaps even primarily) the collective action problems and preference differences of the European states but rather the active efforts of other geopolitical actors to set those terms in different ways.

The EU is also exercising influence in international organizations in less direct ways. Fioretos argues in his contribution that the EU is emerging as a common reference point in discussions over how international economic organizations may be reformed to gain legitimacy and broad support (Laidi 2008). Through what he terms its 'model power', Fioretos contends that the EU is contributing to establishing a new global consensus on the appropriate form and role for international economic organizations. The new shared understanding that the EU is instrumental in producing is another self-conscious extension of the EU's doctrine of managed globalization (Lamy 2004, 2006). Specifically, the EU is contributing to a form of global governance that is palatable to its own member states and a growing number of states around the world by exemplifying a model of how economic openness can be reconciled with social progress and sustainability while observing the principles of transparency and subsidiarity.

Redistributing the costs of globalization

Managing globalization means not only building a framework of rules within which exchange may occur, but also redistributing its costs and benefits. These strategies can play a crucial role in sustaining public support for economic openness. In principle, some of these redistribution efforts try to extend social democracy to the global level. Such global redistribution includes using non-reciprocal trade benefits to help the least advanced countries or recent efforts like the EU-initiated 'Aid for Trade' program set up within the WTO to channel development assistance to help member-developing countries adjust to freer trade. Such redistribution may also occur within Europe: the European Globalization Adjustment Fund, started in 2007, is designed to train and relocate about 50,000 workers a year throughout Europe when their jobs are lost to the dynamics of trade. As Brian Burgoon stresses in his contribution, however, the development of many EU redistributive efforts are modest and constrained (perhaps more than other mechanisms of managed globalization) by national-level policies. They can also fall victim to the development of other mechanisms of management. For instance, EU-level adjustment funds are constrained by opposition to initiatives that might displace national welfare states and also perhaps by the way EU efforts to introduce WTO regulation of labor standards drain off political support for redistribution (Burgoon 2010).

11

Again, these redistributive tensions have long pedigrees, having been prominent in older attempts at managed globalization. For example, before the euro
was created, the main question was who would bear the cost of adjustment
within the EMS in case of economic shocks. Jabko shows that with the end
of the Bretton-Woods system and the rising tide of capital movements as
early as the 1970s, the question of exchange rate realignments was increasingly
forced by market developments and speculation. Weak-currency governments
in France or Italy often complained that they bore a disproportionate share of
the adjustment burden in comparison with Germany, whose currency provided
the 'anchor' of the European Monetary System (EMS). Although German officials disputed that claim, there is no question that these countries' currencies
were primary targets for currency speculators and that they were often forced
to change their policies in order to reassure both their partners and market
actors. Meanwhile, Germany risked currency appreciation, which in turn hurt
its export competitiveness. By moving to the euro, the weak-currency countries
gained complete immunity to internal currency speculation – simply because
markets for national currencies no longer exist. Because the ECB was designed
to pursue a monetary policy for the eurozone as a whole, it no longer bore an
asymmetric burden of adjustment. As for strong-currency countries, the euro
eliminated the risk of competitive devaluations on the part of their main
trading partners. With the Stability and Growth Pact, strong-currency countries
also gained an assurance against their partners' potentially inflationary policies.

The difficulty of compensating for the costs of globalization means that
supranational solutions must compete against national ones. For example,
though the redistributive effects of financial regulation are notoriously difficult
to pinpoint, Posner and Véron suggest that the new EU financial regime and
increased transatlantic compatibility appear to have benefited the City of
London and multinational European and American financial services companies. Meanwhile, the main losers have been local financial players that formerly
benefited from monopoly or oligopoly positions and failed to find a successful
position in a newly integrated market, such as most of Germany's *Landesbanken*.
Tensions abound and form formidable barriers to supranational regulation.
Meanwhile, according to Jabko, the issue of sharing sovereignty is also the
major hurdle for the euro to work as a real managerial instrument. In addition,
in the case of EMU, there is also a risk of re-nationalization and of national-
instead of EU-level level management for fiscal policy.

Such incomplete forms of management seem set to persist with the July 2009
decision of the German Constitutional Court, which, while accepting the
Lisbon Treaty, explicitly noted that no further delegation of German sovereignty in the fiscal policy realm would be allowable. This enormously complicates ambitious programs for greater EU management of globalization
contained in Cohen-Tanugi (2009), who calls for augmenting the Lisbon
Agenda and existing common policies (internal market, trade, Common
Agricultural Policy (CAP) and economic and monetary Union (EMU) with a
set of new common policies, especially in energy, immigration, development,

financial regulation, industrial standards, and monitoring sensitive inward investment.

MANAGED GLOBALIZATION'S DUAL LOGIC

Managing globalization entails a dual and often contradictory logic. On the one hand, many players seek to define the rules of globalization, specifying more clearly what is allowed and when. On the other hand, they would also like to co-ordinate their responses on what practices are out of bounds. As a political matter, European leaders would no doubt love to be praised both for how they let certain things in and also for how they keep other things out. In practice, however, it is also possible to face voters' wrath on both counts. Thus, the EU may resemble a 'Trojan Horse' because it has facilitated the penetration of globalization into Europe, notably by constructing the European single market and opening up protected economies to substantial competition (Jabko 2006). As a result, critics of globalization are also often critics of European integration. Yet, as noted, the EU also appears as the best bulwark against globalization, since its scale makes it more effective and credible in the face of competitive practices and products that Europeans collectively deem illegitimate.

Under what conditions does Europe appear as facilitator or even accelerator of globalization, and when does it appear more as a barrier to globalization? This question can be surprisingly tricky. A substantial tradition in international political economy would lead us to expect that where the key competition is intra-European, the strongest players will likely want the fewest global restrictions, and the weakest will want the strongest constraints (e.g., Rogowski 1989). Other recent work suggests, however, that rather than the strong setting the regulatory agenda, it is the weakest actors who are most willing to expend political capital to erect barriers to more market integration (Drezner 2007). So where competition is with extra-European players, all European players in a given sector may want to co-ordinate external barriers (agriculture is an obvious example).[13] But whatever their differences, both of these intuitions essentially posit one major form of liberalization, and the disagreement seems to be more over whether the details are determined by the strong or by the weak. In this collection we are injecting a new level of complexity by positing that there is not simply one kind of liberalization on offer but rather a competition of different blueprints for globalization. By extension, the acquiescence of various actors is conditional upon the *kind of liberalization* on offer.

Obviously, the kind of liberalization on offer varies across a number of dimensions explored by our contributors. For one thing, variation in levels of managed globalization is likely affected by the amount of power delegated to the EU. Yet there are few easy equations here. For example, note that the dominant model explains variation in delegation to the supranational level by reference to a combination of homogeneous member state preferences, economies of scale in policy-making, high externalities, and low transaction costs (Sapir 2007). By this logic, trade policy – an area where member states have delegated substantially to the EU – might be held a promising location for evidence of managed globalization while policy areas that remain deeply tied to member state prerogatives – such as taxes or immigration – might be thought unlikely cases to find evidence of managed globalization. Yet the contributions by Abdelal and Meunier and by Sbragia both find that the EU's oldest and arguably strongest area of joint activity – trade negotiations – is not its most successful arena for managing globalization. Meanwhile, Kelemen shows that one of the EU's most effective areas for managing globalization – asserting its preferences on environmental policy – is an area where its leadership has only recently come to the fore and where delegation to the EU remains moderate.

Moreover, as noted earlier, managed globalization is generally the project not merely of EU officials but of powerful member state governments. This suggests that evidence of managed globalization may be found even in policy areas where, for reasons developed elsewhere in the literature, states have delegated relatively little authority to the EU. Indeed, some scholars locate the management impulse squarely inside specific national states. For example, Abdelal and Meunier cast managed globalization in trade and finance as a largely French idea. They show that the doctrine of managed globalization was developed mostly by French socialists – those policy-makers who had turned France towards the market, Europe, and the world in the 1980s. The disorganized nature of ad hoc globalization was particularly anathema to the French belief that a centralized, *dirigiste* bureaucracy could manage the economy.

OPEN QUESTIONS

This book aims to start a conversation, not finish one. By posing managing globalization as an empirical challenge rather than as a mere rhetorical tool, we hope to spur on others to take up these issues. A number of areas not covered in this collection are obviously ripe for investigation using either the same five mechanisms we have emphasized or indeed by stressing those we have not broached. Obvious examples include agriculture, competition, energy policy, global spillovers from the Lisbon process, research and development policies, and many more. As other scholars take up research in these areas, we are particularly interested in their answers to a number of questions, some of which are classic and some relatively new:

- When does Europe's internal diversity in matters of political economy lead to regulatory impasses that cause the EU to 'underprovide' leadership at the global level? (e.g. paralysis at home leads to quiescence abroad).
- When does the fact that the EU is home to all of the varieties of capitalism lead, on the contrary, to common rules that are easier to broker at the international level? (e.g. diversity at home leads to leadership abroad).
- Has Europe's historical over-representation in the major Bretton-Woods International Financial Institutions (IFIs) damaged its incentives to coordinate at the international level?

- How do the sectoral parts shape the economic whole? For example, how can the EU really manage globalization, which requires liberalization, as long as it is essentially protectionist in important areas such as agricultural policy?
- Will the emerging set of overlapping jurisdictions at the international level start to work against the EU as 'forum shopping' allows strong players like the US to submit only to the fora that they find congenial?
- How do different mechanisms for managing globalization affect one another – perhaps mutually reinforcing or perhaps undermining one another?

Many of these questions return us to the dual logic outlined above in which all efforts to manage globalization are fraught with the risk that the efforts will bring more blame than acclamation. To a certain extent, European leaders face the same dilemma as all politicians. Except, of course, that they don't. Most national politicians outside Europe face a choice between confronting incentives for liberalization using exclusively national tools or trying instead to augment national tools by working through international organizations. Only in Europe is there also a third option: a regional level of policy-making with real potential and capacity in the here and now.

The task for European political leaders is to reconcile this dual logic of managed globalization – that they can act jointly only at the risk of incurring blame in the eyes of European citizens – while not losing their own political legitimacy. Our contributors provide a foundation for understanding whether the EU can indeed protect its model(s) from the negative effects of globalization, while asserting this model in the wider world. There are plenty of familiar reasons to be pessimistic. Major recent statements about the EU as a regulator of global markets point to substantial gaps in its capacity to shape global rules (Sapir 2007; Tsoukalis 2010). Others are cautiously positive, however, pointing to the EU's influence over global norms as essentially an unintended by-product of initially reactive and incoherent strategies that grew in stature in the face of American withdrawal from prior domains of global leadership (Laidi 2008). Others are even more optimistic still, especially when they begin from the substantial power conferred upon Europe through the sheer size of its market (Drezner 2007). But since there are no good reasons to believe that market size alone can endow Europe with the capacity to manage globalization, the task is to understand the variety of ways in which the EU can lead – or fail to lead – in turning its local hegemony into some variant of global leadership.

After all, what descriptions of current EU practice related to globalization would be alternatives to managed globalization? Broadly, there are only two such alternatives – one that sees no globalization and the other that sees no management. The first alternative is that globalization is not happening – to use a category already in the literature, that it is 'feeble' (Guillén 2001; Hirschman 1982). By this reading, adding the modifier 'managed' is super-fluous because the basic phenomenon of globalization is simply overhyped (Hirst and Thompson 1996). By contrast, the contributions here give ample

15

warrant for the argument that globalization is a real challenge to European models of capitalism.

The second alternative is to acknowledge the power of globalization per se (and its effects on Europe) but to deny that there is anything coherent enough about EU policies to deserve the term 'management'. Most accounts that stress one of the variants of 'multi-speed Europe' implicitly suggest that the EU is now such a sprawling entity that few coherent external policies are still possible. This family of scholarship has received a shot in the arm both from the difficulties of the Constitutional and Lisbon treaties – intended in part to bring more coherence to EU decision-making – and indeed from three rounds of enlargement during the period in question. Can only a small Europe actively manage its members' response to their collective environment? Collectively, the contributions gathered here answer 'no' to this question and try to show what European states and the EU, with all their limitations, are now doing.

CONCLUSION

Europe is trying to manage globalization, and this introduction has detailed five ways in which EU efforts to manage globalization go beyond the undeniable rhetorical uses to which the term lends itself. First, management involves expanding policy scope by developing new instruments for use in Europe. Second, management entails an effort to set regulatory standards in the international economy, including outside of Europe. Third, management includes an effort to empower international organizations. Fourth, it involves various strategies for enlarging the territorial sphere of EU influence. Finally, management can entail efforts to redistribute the costs of globalization. Examples of each mechanism are noted above and fleshed out in detail in the individual contributions.

But every piece of this agenda also makes the EU vulnerable as well. For example, when the EU loses trade cases, this tends to erode the legitimacy of efforts to promote further institutionalization of WTO rules. EU efforts to bring more states into international trade organizations also tends to weaken its voice inside those organizations as some new members have preferences uncongenial to EU interests. Its commitment to multilateral approaches left the EU with a large deficit to overcome when the US moved aggressively towards more bilateral trade agreements while the EU long kept a moratorium on such deals. The enlargement tool has few places left where it can plausibly be deployed, and the EU's redistribution of costs to its own material detriment has not (yet) really bought it new allies in multilateral forums.

The final paradox facing European efforts to manage globalization is that the same global institutions the EU often seeks to strengthen have come under fierce criticism from Europeans for failing to correctly manage globalization and even for accelerating it in some cases. All of these tensions are sobering as the EU now faces a financial crisis that poses a stiff challenge to all capitalist economies. For the five mechanisms we identify are hardly exclusively European tools. Not only is the US seeking to put globalization on terms congenial to its interests, but the Chinese are trying to do this as well. If the crisis that began in 2008 was a failure of ad hoc globalization, that crisis also represented the limits of the European attempt to organize the world economy without the participation of the most important borrower and spender in the world, namely the US, and perhaps the most influential exporter and saver, namely China. The EU cannot rig the game of globalization, but it can try to provide predictability, oversight, and regularity with rules that accommodate European interests.

ACKNOWLEDGEMENTS

We thank the participants of the Princeton and Park City workshops and seminars at the University of Hamburg, IBEI Barcelona, BYU, EUSA, IPSA, and Keio University, and two meetings of the Council of European Studies. We thank in particular Carles Boix, Erik Jones, Paulette Kurzer, Kathleen McNamara, Kendall Stiles and Hubert Zimmermann, as well as our contributors, for their valuable comments. For funding, we thank the Council for European Studies, the EU Program and the Niehaus Center for Globalization and Governance at Princeton, and the David M. Kennedy Center, Center for the Study of Europe, and FHSS College at BYU.

NOTES

1 http://www.delalb.ec.europa.eu/en/romano_prodi_president_of_the_european_commission_signing_the_treaty_of_accession_athens
2 http://www.eurunion.org/news/speeches/2007/070404jb.htm
3 http://www.ilo.org/public/english/wcsdg/docs/report.pdf
4 http://www.hm-treasury.gov.uk/newsroom_and_speeches/press/2005/press_111_05.cfm
5 http://www.globalisierung-gestalten.de/merkel-redet-klartext/
6 http://europa.eu/rapid/pressReleasesAction.do?reference=SPEECH/08/387&format=HTML&aged=0&language=EN&guiLanguage=en
7 http://www.redaccionmedica.com/ ∼ redaccion/pastor_foro_nueva_economia.doc
8 http://www.psoe.es/ambito/europa/news/index.do?action=View&id=66999
9 http://www.harrisinteractive.com/harris_poll/index.asp?PID=791

10 There is a growing literature as well on Asian efforts to manage globalization, but this tends to take place at the nation-state level (Alon *et al.* 2009).
11 More recently, Slovenia, Malta, Cyprus, and Slovakia have also joined since 2007.
12 Explaining these differences is an important task for another paper. The state of the art is the work combining state preference heterogeneity and policy delegation complexity in Sapir (2007).
13 Obviously, other European actors may want to give up restrictive agricultural policies in order to win better bargains in their sectors of interest.

REFERENCES

Abdelal, R. and Meunier, S. (2010) 'Managed globalization: doctrine, practice and promise', *Journal of European Public Policy* 17(3): 350–67.
Alon, I., Chang, J., Fetshcerin, M., Lattemann, C. and McIntyre, J. (2009) *China Rules: Globalization and Political Transformation*, London: Palgrave Macmillan.
Bach, D. and Newman, A. (2007) 'The European regulatory state and global public policy', *Journal of European Public Policy* 14(6): 827–46.
Burgoon, B. (2010) 'Betwixt and between? The European Union's redistributive management of globalization', *Journal of European Public Policy* 17(3): 433–48.
Cohen-Tanugi, L. (2009) *Beyond Lisbon: A European Strategy for Globalisation*, Brussels: PIE Peter Lang.
Cooper, A., Hughes, C. and De Lombaerde, P. (2007) *Regionalization and Global Governance: The Taming of Globalization?*, London: Routledge.
Drezner, D. (2007) *All Politics is Global: Explaining International Regulatory Regimes*, Princeton, NJ: Princeton University Press.
European Opinion Research Group (Eurobarometer) (2004) *Eurobarometer 61: Globalisation*.
Fioretos, O. (2010) 'Europe and the new global economic order: internal diversity as liability and asset in managing globalization', *Journal of European Public Policy* 17(3): 383–99.
Friedman, T. (2000) *The Lexus and the Olive Tree: Understanding Globalization*, New York: Farrar, Strauss & Giroux.
Friedman, T. (2007) *The World is Flat: A Brief history of the Twenty-first Century*, New York: Picador.
Guillén, M. (2001) 'Is globalization civilizing, destructive, or feeble? A critique of five key debates in the sociological literature', *Annual Review of Sociology* 27: 235–60.
Hay, C. (2007) *Why We Hate Politics*, Cambridge: Polity Press.
Hirschman, A. (1982) 'Rival interpretations of market society: civilizing, destructive, or feeble?', *Journal of Economic Literature* 20: 1463–84.
Hirst, P. and Thompson, G. (1996) *Globalization in Question*, London: Polity Press.
Jabko, N. (2006) *Playing the Market: A Political Strategy for Uniting Europe, 1985– 2005*, Ithaca, NY: Cornell University Press.
Jabko, N. (2010) 'The hidden face of the euro', *Journal of European Public Policy* 17(3): 318–34.
Jacoby, W. (2004) *The Enlargement of the European Union and NATO: Ordering from the Menu in Central Europe*, Ithaca, NY: Cornell University Press.
Jacoby, W. (2010) 'Managing globalization by managing Central and Eastern Europe: the EU's backyard as threat and opportunity', *Journal of European Public Policy* 17(3): 416–32.
Jacoby, W. and Meunier, S. (2009) 'Europe and globalization', in M. Egan, N. Nugent and W. Paterson (eds), *Studying the European Union: Current and Future Agendas*, London: Palgrave-Macmillan.

Keleman, R.D. (2010) 'Globalizing European Union environmental policy', *Journal of European Public Policy* 17(3): 335–49.

Laidi, Z. (2008) 'The normative empire: the unintended consequences of European power', *Garnet Policy Brief No. 6.*

Lamy, P. (2004) 'Europe and the future of economic governance', *Journal of Common Market Studies* 42(1): 5–21.

Lamy, P. (2006) 'Humanising Globalization', Santiago, Chile, Speech delivered on 30 January.

Monti, M. (2009) 'How to save the market economy in Europe', *Financial Times,* 6 April.

Posner, E. and Véron, N. (2010) 'The EU and financial regulation: power without purpose?' *Journal of European Public Policy* 17(3): 400–15.

Rogowski, R. (1989) *Commerce and Coalitions: How Trade Affects Domestic Political Alignments,* Princeton, NJ: Princeton University Press.

Sapir, A. (2007) *The Fragmented Power: Europe and the Global Economy,* Brussels: Bruegel.

Sbragia, A. (2010) 'The EU, the US, and trade policy: competitive interdependence in the management of globalization', *Journal of European Public Policy* 17(3): 368–82.

Tsoukalis, L. (2010) 'The EU in a world in transition: fit for what purpose?', Policy Network.

The hidden face of the euro

Nicolas Jabko

ABSTRACT   Europe's economic and monetary union is often depicted as a market-conforming institutional order. The creation of an inflation-fighting independent European Central Bank and the obligation of member governments to maintain fiscal discipline are widely cited as evidence of the European desire to maintain stability and thus placate financial markets. But the euro also has a more hidden face, which is much less liberal and more decidedly managerial. The single currency is itself the boldest expression of a nascent federal power at the European level. It represents a far-reaching delegation of competence from the member states to the institutions of the European Union. It has also enabled member states not only to create a framework for multilateral fiscal discipline – the Stability and Growth Pact – but also to collectively regain some clout *vis-à-vis* market actors. The question for the future is whether EU and national policy-makers will be able and willing to pursue collective priorities beyond monetary stability and the rules of the Stability Pact.

Like the ancient god Janus, the euro has two faces – an overt, market-conforming face; and a more hidden face, which is much less liberal and more decidedly managerial. In public debates and scholarly analyses, the overtly liberal face of the euro has attracted the most attention so far. The creation of an inflation-fighting independent European Central Bank (ECB) and the obligation of member governments to maintain fiscal discipline under the Stability and Growth Pact (SGP) are often cited as evidence of the European desire to maintain stability and thus placate financial markets. In scholarly analyses as well, Europe's economic and monetary union (EMU) is often characterized as a rational response to global economic forces (Eichengreen and Frieden 1998; Frieden 1991; Gros and Thygesen 1992; Jones 2002; Moravcsik 1998) or as the apotheosis of an orthodox consensus in favor of anti-inflationary policies (Marcussen 1999; McNamara 1998; Moss and Michie 2000; Sandholtz 1993; Verdun 1999). There is no question that such portrayals do capture one side of reality, namely the market-conforming face of the euro. The euro can appear, in this sense, as a response to rapid innovations in finance and telecommunications that made governmental controls on cross-border capital movements obsolete and that increased the potential for currency rises. In addition, the statute of the ECB, like the design of Europe's economic and monetary union more generally, certainly institutionalized German-style anti-inflationary policies.

Yet the dominant focus on the market-conforming face of the euro tends to obscure another more managerial set of motivations behind Europe's move to a single currency, which remain relevant today. As I will argue, many of the policy-makers who pursued Europe's economic and monetary union saw the euro as a way to regain some political control – what they called 'sovereignty' – in a world of mobile capital and hegemonic financial markets. Even though they did not openly contest the power of markets, they saw the euro as a way for Europe to shape, rather than merely conform to, globalization. Seen from this managerial perspective, the euro is the boldest expression of a nascent federal power at the EU level. Monetary policy powers in the eurozone are now fully transferred to the European System of Central Banks, with the ECB at its core. Although the SGP is often criticized as biased in favor of fiscal conservatism, it also represents an attempt to proactively co-ordinate economic policies while essentially respecting member states' national prerogatives over fiscal policy. In comparison to the pre-EMU situation of market-enforced fiscal discipline, EU and national policy-makers have thus regained clout *vis-à-vis* market actors. The open question for the future is whether this hidden managerial face of the euro will become more visible, or even overshadow the overtly liberal face of the euro. This is the crux of contemporary debates about the economic governance of the eurozone, which have been reignited by the advent of global economic trouble.

THE JANUS-FACED EURO

By highlighting the hidden face of the euro, this contribution aims to redress an imbalance of scholarly attention. It starts from the premise that contemporary debates about the economic governance of EMU cannot be understood without consideration of the Janus-faced nature of the euro – and, more generally, of the European Union – as it emerged from the 1980s and the 1990s (Jabko 2006). Although the euro is widely seen as a manifestation of conservative monetary and fiscal policies, the quest for a single currency was also fuelled by diametrically opposite motivations. Some exhaustive political analyses of EMU – both in the constructivist and the rationalist vein – recognize the wide variety of motivations behind the euro (Dyson and Featherstone 1999; Jones 2002). But even they tend to give much more emphasis to the market-conforming side of EMU – its significance as the 'triumph of technocratic elitism' (Dyson and Featherstone 1999: 801), or the 'central' importance of Germany's preference for 'fiscal rectitude above other concerns such as growth and unemployment'(Jones 2002: 144). In the end, therefore, the political science scholarship on EMU appears to be dominated by a rather one-sided conventional wisdom, according to which 'the creation of the euro was the natural last step to be taken by European countries on the historical path

21

toward powerful international financial markets, the decline of capital controls, and the demise of one-country Keynesian policies' (Boix 2000: 73).

Why has the managerial face of the euro attracted less attention than its market-conforming face? The answer I will offer here is that the managerial face of the euro was generally *hidden* from view. The main actors of monetary unification all paid respect to German-style economic stability and rarely dwelled on their differences. Only careful observers of monetary debates were aware that the apparent convergence of views between German and French leaders remained superficial. Even the staunchest (French) supporters of sovereignty did not often talk about their real motivations, preferring to offer 'globalization' and 'the Single Market' as central justifications for the single currency – just like the proponents of orthodoxy. There were good political reasons for supporters of EMU to play down their political differences. In the face of adversity, they needed to close ranks. French leaders needed Germany on board, and they could not afford to antagonize the United States; therefore, it would have been especially impolitic for them to talk openly about the euro as an antidote against what they perceived as the excessive power of the Bundesbank and of the US dollar. German leaders were not duped, of course; but they needed to reassure their worried citizens that the euro would be run as a German-style currency and that stability would trump everything else. In the eyes of many observers, EMU thus came to be seen as the pinnacle of orthodoxy – what French commentators of both Left and Right vilified as *'la pensée unique'*.

In contrast to this view, I argue that sovereignty motivations played a central albeit underappreciated role in the birth of the euro, and that sovereignty concerns continue to play an important role today. The fact that actors invoked 'the market' as a reason for monetary unification does not itself make the euro a liberal currency. Many actors, especially in weak-currency countries and on the Left, viewed the market with resignation. They worried increasingly that state autonomy was being threatened by capital mobility, currency crises, and German power. Typically, these actors were searching for new ways of asserting a measure of political control in an age of globalization (Jacoby and Meunier, this issue). They came to favor monetary union when they became convinced that market globalization altered the meaning of sovereignty and that the establishment of an economic and monetary union was the best way to reinvigorate sovereignty. Of course, I am not saying that this was the whole story, nor even that these sovereignty-conscious actors prevailed. Another group of actors, especially large in strong-currency countries and among fiscal conservatives, saw the market as a salutary source of financial discipline. These actors lobbied for an inflation-focused independent central bank and for strict fiscal rules in order to clip the wings of undisciplined governments. These actors were obviously influential in the making of the euro. Yet to say that their more orthodox worldview prevailed is to ignore the sovereignty motivations behind the euro and their long-term effects on the legal-institutional structure and the macro-economic governance of Europe's EMU.

Orthodoxy and sovereignty are best conceived as two extreme poles in a continuum of motivations for the euro. Nowadays, few actors could actually be identified as 'pure' defenders of sovereignty (i.e., political control over markets), or 'pure' adepts of orthodoxy (i.e., a policy agenda aimed chiefly at fighting inflation). In today's increasingly volatile markets, old-style *dirigisme* has practically disappeared; few informed actors think that it is possible to successfully govern the economy without an acute concern for monetary stability. Likewise, strict monetarism has become a minority position; this has become even more obvious with the financial crisis, as central bankers have rushed to supply enormous amounts of liquidity. Since the 1970s, most actors have thus clearly moved away from the two extremes of 'pure' orthodoxy and 'pure' managerialism – which is an important reason why the supporters of EMU were able to fudge their differences and to rally behind the banner of 'the market'. Yet differences of view were and are important. It still matters enormously where exactly the cursor is set between the two extreme poles of the continuum. Where actors want to set the cursor largely depends, in turn, on national and partisan views on the market and on the desirable degree of political control over market developments. Since there was no agreement on a particular solution among the main advocates of the euro, the institutional design of Europe's economic and monetary union does not fundamentally resolve this question. This is why EMU governance has remained an object of political contest between two rather different and contradictory orientations.

Not very surprisingly perhaps, the tug of war intensified between the two sides when a global financial and economic crisis erupted in 2008. The main question was the extent to which Europe should be daring in its policy response to global economic problems, now that eurozone member states shared the same currency. The orthodox response was that European member governments and central bankers should react coolly. They should let automatic stabilizers do their work and focus on rationalizing their economic structures while waiting for the return of better times, rather than let public deficits balloon in a short-sighted attempt to substitute for America's past spending frenzy. That response was especially influential among German politicians and in central banking circles. Other actors advocated more assertive responses, however. They saw the crisis as an opportunity for Europe to assert itself in managing globalization. French policy-makers, in particular, saw the eurozone as a potential platform for policy initiatives aimed at shaping market developments. As we will see, the terms of this debates have somewhat evolved – but the fundamental issue has remained unresolved.

SOVEREIGNTY CONCERNS BEHIND THE EURO

The euro was born at a time when many state actors were worried by the increasing fluidity of financial markets. Advocates of monetary union progressively gained the upper hand when they managed to diffuse the paradoxical idea that national sovereignty could best be preserved by transferring it to the European level. The euro was thus increasingly perceived as an improvement over a de facto situation in which most member states no longer controlled their own monetary policies.

Origins of the euro: the centrality of sovereignty concerns

The story of the euro officially began in January 1988, when French Finance Minister Edouard Balladur issued a memorandum calling for a 'common currency'. Both Italian Finance Minister Giuliano Amato and German Foreign Minister Hans-Dietrich Genscher quickly responded positively. Why did monetary union suddenly become so attractive in the eyes of these European political leaders? Strangely, many accounts of the recent EMU process imply that the only real puzzle is why Germany would willingly give up its deutschmark – perhaps because German officials often portrayed monetary union as a pure act of Europeanist generosity. Although the German Chancellor's steadfast personal commitment to the EMU process certainly played an important role, his conceptualization of German national interest was not new. Until the fall of the Berlin wall, European integration was a foremost foreign policy priority, since Germany wanted to regain full sovereignty and to upgrade from its 'semi-sovereign' status (Katzenstein 1987). Yet until the 1980s, Germany's sovereignty-related interest in European integration, including monetary integration, had never been sufficient to bring about EMU.

In order to understand the salience of sovereignty concerns in the making of the euro, it is useful to ponder not only Germany's but also France's (or Italy's) strong push for monetary union. It is often forgotten that, up until the 1980s, the biggest hurdle to monetary unification was not Germany but France (Tsoukalis 1977). Ever since France had turned to de Gaulle in 1958, there had been considerable domestic political opposition and a lack of clear governmental commitment in the face of a perceived dilution of sovereignty (Hoffmann 1966). According to Tsoukalis's study of the first attempt to create an EMU in the 1970s: 'From the French point of view, monetary integration used to be desirable only as a means of promoting EEC unity in external relations. In this respect, French politicians were torn between the objective of having a common external monetary policy and their fear of loss of national sovereignty' (Tsoukalis 1977: 80). By the 1980s, this state of affairs had changed so radically that most analysts tend to take for granted the existence of a French national interest in moving towards EMU.

France's sovereignty-related interest in monetary union must be understood in light of the early 1980s currency crises and the important political decision, made by Mitterrand in March 1983, to remain in the European Monetary System (EMS) of pegged exchange rates. On the one hand, France could have decided after this key decision to shed any ambition of national monetary autonomy. There was a coherent economic case in favor of 'tying one's hands' to the German currency 'anchor' (Giavazzi and Pagano 1988). In addition, many French policy-makers, especially in the Ministry of Finance and the Bank of France, did become convinced of the virtues of *franc fort* (the strong franc) pegged to the deutschmark. On the other hand, French officials never came to terms with the consequences of Mitterrand's EMS choice, which was accepting Germany's superior position within the monetary system. The 'asymmetry' of the EMS was not primarily an economic problem.[1] The EMS did not require institutional symmetry in order to function well. The heart of the matter is that French and Italian political leaders increasingly resented Germany's dominance of the system.

The politics of sovereignty was thus a key ingredient in the making of the euro. The Bundesbank had become 'the bank that ruled Europe' (Marsh 1992) – and this was unacceptable to French politicians, for electoral as well as historical reasons. Since the late 1970s, French governments had consistently tried to prevent the transformation of the EMS into a de facto deutschmark zone (Ludlow 1982: 196–205). Yet this policy had failed, and the Bank of France was increasingly forced to follow the leadership of the Bundesbank. In that context, many French elites were increasingly seduced by the notion that an EMU would reinvigorate, rather than dilute, French sovereignty. As national monetary policies were de facto aligned with Germany's, Prime Minister Thatcher's fierce critique of EMU in the name of sovereignty was quite atypical. The anti-EMU position never took hold in the political establishments of those member states that were strongly committed to the EMS (except, of course, Germany).

Adding fuel to the fire: capital liberalization and the fall of the Berlin wall

Although the French and Italian governments wanted to recover some of their lost sovereignty, this very prospect could easily alienate traditional German sympathies to the cause of European economic integration. Germany had to be reassured that 'strengthening the EMS' was not a thinly veiled way of shifting the burden of adjustment on to strong-currency countries. This is where the European Commission played an important role by advocating a transition to EMU in parallel with capital liberalization and by taking active steps to liberalize capital movements as early as 1986 (Abdelal 2007; Jabko 1999). German officials had made it clear that they would be prepared to consider any further strengthening of the EMS only if other countries liberalized capital movements and submitted their economic policies to the test of 'market discipline' (Bakker 1996). By standing behind the German–Dutch demand to liberalize capital movements, Commission officials were not only balancing their support of France's demand for a more 'symmetric' EMS; they were effectively countering both the *dirigiste* nostalgia of French politicians and the German apprehensions regarding their partners' 'inflationary' temptations.

At the same time, capital liberalization fuelled the sovereignty-based momentum towards EMS reform. The removal of capital controls massively reinforced an already strong French desire to somehow compensate for a perceived loss of sovereignty *vis-à-vis* market actors and the German central bank. In practice, capital liberalization meant that France had no protection at all against currency speculators, which made its monetary policy autonomy appear more illusory than ever. In turn, the removal of controls made it increasingly hard for Germany to resist its partners' pressures in favor of EMS reform. If German officials had been ready to for go the EMS, they would have been able to ignore these pressures. But the German government valued the EMS as a haven of relative stability in a highly volatile international monetary environment and in the context of recurring conflicts between German and US priorities (Henning 1998). The growing perception of the EMS as the embodiment of German monetary hegemony was a genuine cause for concern, since it carried the threat that other member states would eventually defect from the EMS.[2] If the EMS collapsed, the German mark might have become, as in the 1970s, the object of massive speculation, with potentially negative consequences for German competitiveness. Thus, German government officials believed they had a lot at stake in the preservation of the EMS in some form.

Of course, the sovereignty concerns behind EMS reform did not *directly* lead to the creation of the euro. In the 1990s, more orthodox concerns clearly took precedence, as it became necessary to lock in the support of central bankers, financiers, and potentially reluctant governments (especially Germany). For instance, the Delors committee of central bankers that convened in 1988 to 1989 functioned as a sort of 'epistemic community' (Verdun 1999) and did not really attempt to address member governments' sovereignty concerns. Even so, sovereignty concerns were never far from the surface. The committee's meetings did not take place in a political vacuum. In consenting to monetary union on their terms, Germany's central bankers apparently underestimated the powerful logic of France's or Italy's desire for sovereignty and their unwillingness to live under the current conditions.[3]

Moreover, Germany's reunification in 1990 only reinforced the widespread perception that German hegemony was a risk and that a solution must be found to prevent a major imbalance of power at the heart of Europe. This was again barely discussed at Maastricht, but it was on everyone's mind. In the ensuing context of increasing economic hardship and political turbulence, the priority was to reassure market actors that the euro would indeed be implemented according to plan. Political leaders thus chose to emphasize their respect for the Treaty's orthodox convergence criteria, rather than dwell on their disagreements. Yet the fact that member states were willing to pay the price of a prolonged recession in order to stay the course highlights the intensity of the sovereignty motivations behind the euro.

At a fundamental level, the coming of the euro did *not* herald a pan-European conversion to the anti-inflationary benefits of the 'German model' of monetary policy. Of course, many French policy-makers increasingly saw currency stability as a way to avoid the inflationary spiral of easy-money policies. There was an especially noticeable shift among financial officials in the direction of that model (McNamara 1998; Verdun 1999). Yet anti-inflationary policies remained far from consensual, and it is not clear whether politicians – who in the end made all the important decisions – really changed their policy paradigms.[4] As far as they were concerned, French government officials never wanted inflationary policies. The periodic emergence of inflation was an unintended consequence of the government's reliance on expansionary policies in order to defuse political conflicts about the public allocation of resources (Shonfield 1969: 133). In the 1980s, successive French governments endorsed 'competitive disinflation' not because they viewed monetary stability as desirable in itself, but because they believed that it could translate into higher competitiveness and growth.[5] Thus, there is little evidence that French politicians' strong preference for growth and employment, even at the risk of (moderate) inflation, has been fundamentally changed. Today, they constantly repeat that the euro should be at the service of growth and employment. If such managerial motivations have always been present, then it is an exaggeration to portray the euro as a product of economic orthodoxy.

THE NEW FRONTIER OF SOVEREIGNTY

Although the governance model of the eurozone today can certainly not be characterized as unorthodox, the euro does live up to many expectations of actors who pushed for its creation out of a concern for sovereignty. It serves to protect member states from potentially destabilizing capital movements in the form of currency speculation. By establishing a sphere of exchange rate stability with their main trading partners, it buffers eurozone member states' economic policies from the judgement of market actors – thus giving them greater control of their destiny, which is another way of saying that it reaffirms their sovereignty. Will the Europeans now be content and pursue market-conforming policies in the context of the global economy, or will they try to expand the frontier of sovereignty? While this question cannot be answered in any definite manner, it is possible to assess the institutional legacies of the monetary unification process and the first decade of experience with the euro in the context of global markets.

The contradictory legacies of the monetary union process

We have seen that sovereignty concerns created and sustained a strong demand for EMU, but it would be obviously wrong to deny the importance of 'sound money' policies in the eurozone. Although the pursuit of sovereignty was an important motivation for state actors in the 1980s, the anti-inflationary and fiscally conservative orientation of Europe's march towards the euro soon overshadowed these original motivations. France and Italy wanted the euro for sovereignty-related reasons, but Germany agreed to move in that direction only under the condition that EMU would be run in a German-style fashion. For most of the 1990s, then, the countries that were to qualify for eurozone membership went through a major process of deficit and debt consolidation that continued beyond the starting date of the euro. As a result, Europe's EMU today is often equated with an orthodox economic policy agenda centered on the fight against inflation and fiscal deficits. The question is whether this a fair characterization, and whether sovereignty concerns have indeed vanished from the underlying governance model of the euro.

On the one hand, the turn towards orthodoxy in the 1990s has undeniably led to the euro's distinctively market-conforming policy orientation. The orthodox dimension of the euro is certainly the most obvious legacy of the politics that led to its creation. First, the ECB is an inflation fighter. Under the terms of the Treaty, it can pursue other economic objectives, but only 'without prejudice' to its primary objective of price stability. Although the ECB is certainly not oblivious to growth considerations and has swiftly reacted against the risks of financial collapse in 2007 to 2008, many observers still believe that its mandate creates a bias in favor of a cautious rather than an activist interest rate policy. Second, the ECB's independence is very extensive. In addition to steering interest rates independently, it also sets its own targets (or 'reference values') without negotiation with the member states – unlike the Bank of England or the US Federal Reserve, for example. Third and perhaps most intriguing, the member states of the eurozone have adopted the SGP, a legally constraining set of deficit- and debt-consolidation rules. If they do not keep their public deficits under 3 per cent of GDP, they are legally subject to a financial sanction mechanism, unless they are able to make the case that they are facing 'exceptional circumstances'. Even though the Pact's sanctions are difficult – perhaps even impossible – to implement, their mere legal exist-ence constitutes an avenue for peer pressure, a source of political capital for member states that abide by the rules, and a scarlet letter for those that do not.

On the other hand, the sovereignty motivations that created the momentum towards the euro also left a clear legacy. Not only did sovereignty concerns limit the emergence of a widely shared orthodox outlook at the EU level, but they also contributed to a considerable empowerment of the EU (writ large). This is a legacy that observers often overlook or take for granted, but it is no less real and tangible than the legacy of orthodoxy. First, the Bundesbank is no longer the 'bank that rules Europe'. A supranational ECB means that a Dutch or a French citizen can aspire to become the most powerful central banker in Europe, and even more importantly that central bankers take into consideration the welfare of the entire eurozone when making their decisions. Second, the euro is both a vivid symbol of European unity and a shield against currency crises. Eurozone member states are no longer at the mercy of currency specu-lation, and they no longer have to pay a currency risk premium for conducting policies that do not meet the expectations of international financiers. Third, fiscal policy has been successfully reasserted as a national prerogative. Of course, individual member states are subject to peer pressures for the way in which they manage their budgets, especially within the framework of the SGP, but this peer pressure is likely to remain gentle, given that governments are generally reluctant to pillory each other. Compared with the scrutiny that governments had to endure in the EMS under the threat of currency crises, this is a much more comfortable situation.

This remarkable duality of EMU raises an important question. In the long run, which of the orientations – market-conforming or market-shaping – will receive more attention from policy-makers? A rather hands-off attitude towards markets is powerful not only because it corresponds to the preferences of many actors in the eurozone, but also because it is the path of least resistance. It is always more difficult to articulate and assert collective priorities than to adjust to global market forces at the margin. Thus, it is not clear that the managerial orientation will prevail. Yet governments' desire for maneuvering room is deep – especially in hard times. In the past few years and with increasing urgency, eurozone states have been groping for new managerial instruments to deal with the consequences of globalization, both among themselves and vis-à-vis the outside world.

How the EU manages globalization internally

From an internal EU perspective, the critical question that Europeans have increasingly had to address is whether economic co-ordination must go beyond the market-conforming dimension of the SGP. In the eyes of its most hawkish supporters, the SGP was introduced in 1997 as a constraining punishment procedure against fiscally deviant member states (Heipertz and Verdun 2004). Yet the Pact was not enforced against Germany and France in 2003, despite their egregious failure to comply with the 3 per cent limit. After Germany breached the pact that it had fought so hard to impose, the orthodox orientation of the EU's economic policies was seriously in question. In July 2004, the European Court of Justice ruled that the Council is not forced to take punitive action, yet had acted illegally by suspending the excessive deficit procedure against France and Germany. The Pact was reformed in March 2005 in order to clarify the legal situation and to more explicitly allow for cyclical deficits, even though the obligation of fiscal discipline remained the cornerstone of the Pact. When the financial and economic crisis hit the eurozone in the fall of 2008, however, the departure from orthodoxy was even more dramatic and less contested. On 12 October 2008, the leaders of the eurozone decided on an 'action plan' in order to prevent the collapse of the European banking system. A few weeks later, they decided to suspend the application of the Pact and rushed to come up with economic stimulus packages.

The interesting novelty of the 2008 crisis is that the criticism was not at all directed against the lax policies of deficit spenders – as had been the case even during the Pact's reform debate in 2003 to 2005. This time, fiscally virtuous member states were under pressure to act, as they stood accused of inertia. On 12 December 2008, European leaders announced a €200 billion European Economic Recovery Plan (equivalent to 1.5 per cent of EU GDP) and agreed that 'Europe will act in a united, strong, rapid and decisive manner to avoid a recessionary spiral and sustain economic activity and employment'.[6] Even

German Chancellor Angela Merkel, who initially seemed reluctant to engage in deficit spending, finally came up with her own stimulus package in January 2009. Although the Commission and the ECB were quick to point out that stimulus measures should be temporary and that fiscal consolidation should remain the long-term goal, the mood had clearly changed in the eurozone. In comparison to the 1990s, EU officials seemed more willing to admit that the consolidation of fiscal deficits might be put on the backburner for member states faced with serious economic adversity. Of course, the promoters of strict orthodoxy continued to stress the need for fiscal discipline and the treaty prohibition over bailing out profligate member states. Yet an increasingly vocal group of actors now stressed the need for a pragmatic rather than a legalistic approach, as well as the member states' collective right to circumvent the prohibition over bailouts in the face of 'exceptional circumstances'.

It is too early to say whether this new state of affairs will provoke a permanent reinforcement of economic co-ordination beyond the current crisis situation. What has become clear is that EMU governance does not always have to lean in the direction of orthodoxy. Although treaty articles about the 'co-ordination of economic policies' (Articles 102 and 103, now Articles 120 and 121 since the Lisbon Treaty came into force in December 2009) are extremely vague in comparison with monetary policy provisions, Maastricht does contain a few guideposts for the future. A modest form of economic co-ordination now takes place at the level of the Eurogroup, a German concession to the French demand of an 'economic government' at the EU level. The Eurogroup has so far remained an informal body, which means that it adopts common positions only if a consensus is reached among its members. Formal voting rules and decision-making power are still in the hands of the Economic and Financial Affairs Council (EcoFin), which is made up of the Economics and Finance Ministers of the member states. With the Lisbon Treaty, the member states have nonetheless agreed to adopt a new 'Protocol on the Euro Group', declaring their intention to 'develop ever closer co-ordination of economic policies within the euro area'. Even before the Lisbon Treaty was ratified, the Eurogroup has been endowed with a stable chairmanship of two and a half years (position held since 2004 by Luxembourg Prime Minister Jean-Claude Juncker. When his peers re-elected him for a new mandate in January 2010, Juncker pledged to strengthen the economic governance of the eurozone).

The further development of economic co-ordination is not a foregone conclusion, however. The Treaty was designed to ensure both the prevalence of orthodoxy in the centralized conduct of monetary policy and the benefits of autonomy for member states' fiscal policy. Since they no longer control monetary policy, member governments have become increasingly jealous of their *national* sovereignty in the area of fiscal policy. The Eurogroup's maneuvering room therefore remains limited. It is certainly a far cry from the French dream of an 'economic government' – an ideal that France itself is not in a good position to defend, given its insistence on autonomous economic policies and its poor record of co-ordinating with other member states in the process of fiscal consolidation under the SGP (Howarth 2007). All governments – especially France – are clearly tempted to maximize their individual autonomy rather than participate in binding co-ordination. Even the October 2008 European Action Plan to prevent financial collapse and the December 2008 Economic Recovery Plan are better described as additions of national action plans than as truly European plans. Since the member governments remain in control of fiscal policy, the evolution of economic policy co-ordination will therefore hinge on domestic situations as well as on the political will of national actors when they come to the European Union's negotiating table.

How the eurozone manages globalization externally

The question of how the eurozone relates to the outside world also highlights the tensions between the orthodox vision of a market-conforming euro and a more managerial approach to globalization. Throughout the 1990s, advocates of the euro avoided this question, since it was potentially a source of conflict not only among member states but also with the US. After the transition to the euro in 1999 to 2002, the question could no longer be avoided, but so far, central bankers have given a conservative answer. The ECB manages the euro primarily in view of internal considerations, with relatively little regard for its exchange rate *vis-à-vis* other currencies and its international role more generally. The official line is that the ECB 'does not pursue the internationalisation of the euro as a policy goal and neither fosters nor discourages its use by non-residents of the euro area'.[7] For the same reason, the ECB generally adopts a hands-off attitude towards the exchange rate of the euro. This de facto policy of benign neglect on the external value of their currency is similar to the US approach to the dollar's exchange rate since the 1970s (Destler and Henning 1989). Club members can quietly enjoy the safety and credibility of an internationally recognized currency. Since they do not really need to adjust to any currency other than their own, they can preserve a large degree of policy autonomy. The countries that choose to peg their currencies to the euro, on the other hand, must adjust their economic policies accordingly.

This focus on eurozone interests and benign neglect of non-eurozone countries may well become entrenched as a way for the eurozone to manage its insertion into the global economy. It is probably the most realistic in view of the complex institutional balance of the EU (Fioretos, this issue). Furthermore, the EU's difficulty in speaking with one voice on the issue of exchange rates illustrates how difficult it may be to do more (McNamara and Meunier 2002). In theory, the eurozone is capable of conducting an exchange rate policy. Article 219 of the Treaty on the Functioning of the European Union states that the Council 'may formulate general orientations for exchange-rate policy in relation to these currencies'. Yet there are problems with this prospect. First, any exchange rate orientations for the euro would be relative to other currencies, and may therefore lead to conflicts with Europe's partners, especially the US. Second, an exchange rate objective is credible only if monetary policy decisions take it into account. As it happens, Article 219 also stipulates that 'These general orientations shall be without prejudice to the primary objective of the ESCB to maintain price stability'. In practice, this means that central bankers are always able to contest an exchange rate orientation based on the objective of price stability. Not very surprisingly, the Euro group has thus never defined an exchange rate orientation.

The second possible path for the Europeans would be to rely on the unity of the eurozone in order to assert global leadership. This scenario corresponds to the dream of Jean Monnet and others, who saw in Europe's integration a step towards collective responsibility and the return of Europe as a leading player on the world stage. In the immediate postwar period, the US dollar alone exercised international economic leadership (Kindleberger 1973; Ruggie 1982). Now that the Americans have retreated from this ambition (since the end of the Bretton-Woods system), there may be room for the Europeans to move in and share global monetary responsibilities with the US, but we are still far from such a situation. According to Cohen (2003), the possibility of active management is impeded by the 'anti-growth bias' of EMU, as well as by its complex decision-making structure: 'In place of decisive management, market agents see fragmented decision-making and a potential for chronic bickering' (Cohen 2003: 591). For this very reason and also owing to their long-standing deference to US leadership, the Europeans have made few attempts to assert their leadership. In this respect, the difference with the US is striking (Henning and Meunier 2005). Following the Asian financial crisis of 1997 to 1998 and after 9/11, the US – not Europe – came to the rescue of the global economy. In both cases, the Federal Reserve aggressively lowered its interest rates. This was a high-risk strategy that sent America's external deficits soaring and may have sown the seeds of the 2008 recession. Yet, in the short run, it averted the risk of a global recession, and the US economy played the role of a growth engine for the global economy. Meanwhile, the Europeans took refuge in their zone of stability and rarely adopted a leadership role in helping defuse financial crises in emerging economies.

The question for the future is whether Europe's inward-looking and rather stand-offish attitude is temporary or permanent. In the current climate of financial and economic crisis, the Europeans may take advantage of the opportunity of a battered American leadership to assert new claims to manage globalization. France and Germany pushed hard for President Bush to summon a G-20 summit in November 2008, which led to a declaration calling for important 'needed reforms in the world's financial systems'.[8] In the run-up to the G-20 summit in April 2009, they led the campaign in favor of international financial regulation against a rather cautious Obama Administration, obtaining a remarkable victory against tax havens. In this case, the French and German governments co-operated quite effectively on a joint demand to strengthen the international regulation of financial markets. Furthermore, this is an area where the two leading countries of the eurozone clearly stood on higher moral ground, since they did not go nearly as far as the US or Britain in the direction of deregulated financial markets.

Yet it is not clear how far the Europeans will be willing and able to push their advantage much further. Serious differences have emerged in national responses to the economic recession, thus calling into question the European capacity to co-ordinate – let alone exert global leadership (Posner and Véron 2010). At 1.5 per cent of GDP, the European Economic Recovery Plan of December 2008 remained paltry in comparison to President Obama's stimulus package. The façade of unity quickly fell apart in 2009, as member states introduced anti-recession measures that were not genuinely co-ordinated in magnitude or nature. That France and Germany co-operated on financial market regulation hardly makes up for their inability to co-ordinate fiscal policy. Leadership thus remains a serious challenge for a EU whose political unity is not firmly established. There is room today for a Europe that would take up global responsibilities – in part because the US position is made more fragile by the sheer size of its deficits, and because the eurozone is comparatively resilient. Yet there is still little appetite for leadership in Europe, and there are many good reasons for individual member states to keep their economic policy co-ordination to a minimum. So far, therefore, the Europeans are not playing in the same league as the US, despite the economic weight of the eurozone and the short-comings of US leadership.

CONCLUSION

The governance of the euro today highlights both the accomplishments and the limits of the EU as a way to manage globalization. These must be understood in historical perspective. From the outset, the euro has embodied a fragile political balance between two broad and very different approaches to market globalization – an orthodox approach, according to which the euro must be run above all in a prudent way so as to stabilize the inflationary expectations of market actors; and a managerial approach, according to which new room must be found for the exercise of sovereignty in the face of powerful global market forces. During the gestation of the euro in the 1990s, the orthodox face was more visible, and the managerial face was hidden, since the advocates of the euro wanted to keep Germany on board and convince market actors that monetary union was a realistic prospect. Yet EMU's institutional design was profoundly influenced by both approaches. An independent and inflation-averse central bank is now in charge of monetary policy for the eurozone, but it has proved its capacity to adopt unconventional and potentially risky measures to prevent financial collapse in 2007 to 2008. In addition, although European governments are bound by the rules of the SGP, they have also gained considerable freedom in comparison to a pre-EMU situation in which they were under the ever-present threat of currency speculation.

The question of what to do with this new freedom has become more pressing. Thanks to the euro, the Europeans have created a zone of currency stability and considerably reduced their exposure to the destabilizing effects of globalization, but they have not yet really figured out how to use this new-found resilience as a resource for global leadership. Part of the difficulty of doing so is that the

Europeans may find themselves competing with other countries that have leading international currencies, especially the US. As eurozone member states have become aware of this problem, they have tried to improve the representation of the eurozone on the international stage. But this also opens a Pandora's box, since it is not clear that the Europeans are yet ready to stand united *vis-à-vis* the rest of the world in the face of centrifugal forces. History sometimes repeats itself. As in the 1970s, the Europeans may find it too difficult to achieve a robust co-ordination of their economic policies and to exert a powerful voice in shaping the new rules of the global economy. The main difference with the 1970s is that the euro and its institutional framework are now available as potential levers for collective action. If European leaders find ways to agree among themselves on how to make use of this new resilience, history may not forever repeat itself.

ACKNOWLEDGEMENT

The author thanks Scott Cooper and two anonymous referees for comments on an earlier draft of this article.

NOTES

1 Against McNamara's (1998) thesis of a Europe-wide conversion to monetarism, Moravcsik (1998) argues that France pursued EMU because the burden of adjustment within the EMS was too costly. Yet this overlooks the benefits of 'tying one's hand', which could counterbalance these costs, and the contradiction between the French choice of '*franc fort*' and the resentment against German dominance through its anchor currency. France's membership in the EMS was costly, of course, but it brought important economic benefits as well. What is striking is that French political leaders seem prepared to do away with the EMS altogether. See Edouard Balladur (1987), 'EMS: advance or face retreat', *Financial Times*, 17 June.
2 For example, French Prime Minister Jacques Chirac declared that unless the EMS were strengthened, 'it would be better to abolish it'. See 'M. Chirac annonce qu'il prendra des initiatives dans le domaine monétaire,' *Le Monde*, 9 January 1988.
3 David Marsh (1992: 215) gives the following overall appraisal of the Bundesbank's attitude towards EMU: 'Up until the last moment, the Bundesbank did not realize that, to release themselves from the grip of the deutschmark, the French and the Italians were ready to promise almost anything'.
4 Nor, in fact, does the German model reflect an unquestioned consensus even among German politicians. According to Katzenstein (1987: 97), 'The Bundesbank's pursuit of monetary stability has been the most constant element in West Germany's economic policy to the chagrin of the Christian Democrats and the Social Democrats alike'.
5 An assessment by two French economists of France's deflationary policy of the 1980s and 1990s suggests that the 'implicit framework [of policy-makers] was a neo-Keynesian model under fixed exchange rates, in which disinflation automatically

translates into real exchange rate depreciation, gains in market shares, and growth'. See de Boissieu and Pisanni-Ferry (1998).

6 Conclusions of the Presidency of the European Council meeting, Brussels, 12 December 2008, p. 4.

7 ECB, *Monthly Bulletin*, Tenth Anniversary of the ECB Special Edition (June 2008): 96.

8 Declaration of the Summit on Financial Markets and the World Economy, Washington, 15 November 2008.

REFERENCES

Abdelal, R. (2007) *Capital Rules: The Construction of Global Finance*, Cambridge, MA: Harvard University Press.

Bakker, A. (1996) *The Liberalization of Capital Movements in Europe*, Dordrecht: Kluwer Academic.

Balladur, E. (1987) 'EMS: advance or face retreat', *Financial Times*, 17 June.

Boix, C. (2000) 'Partisan governments, the international economy, and macroeconomic policies in advanced nations, 1960–1993', *World Politics* 53(1): 38–73.

Cohen, B. (2003) 'Global currency rivalry: can the euro ever challenge the dollar?', *Journal of Common Market Studies* 41(4): 575–95.

de Boissieu, C. and Pisanni-Ferry, J. (1998) 'The political economy of French economic policy in the perspective of EMU', in B. Eichengreen and J. Frieden (eds) *Forging an Integrated Europe*, Ann Arbor, MI: University of Michigan Press, pp. 66–7.

Destler, I. and Henning, C. (1989) *Dollar Politics: Exchange Rate Policymaking in the United States, Institute for International Economics*, Washington, DC: Institute for International Economics.

Dyson, K. and Featherstone, K. (1999) *The Road to Maastricht: Negotiating Economic and Monetary Union*, Oxford: Oxford University Press.

Eichengreen, B. and Frieden, J. (eds) (1998) *Forging an Integrated Europe*, Ann Arbor, MI: University of Michigan Press.

Fioretos, O. (2010) 'Europe and the new global economic order: internal diversity as liability and asset in managing globalization', *Journal of European Public Policy* 17(3): 383–99.

Frieden, J. (1991) 'Invested interests: the politics of national economic policies in a world of global finance', *International Organization* 45(4): 425–51.

Giavazzi, F. and Pagano, M. (1988) 'The advantage of tying one's hands – EMS discipline and central bank credibility', *European Economic Review* 32(5): 1055–75.

Gros, D. and Thygesen, N. (1992) *European Monetary Integration*, London: Longman.

Heipertz, M. and Verdun, A. (2004) 'The dog that would never bite? What we can learn from the origins of the stability and growth pact', *Journal of European Public Policy* 11(5): 765–80.

Henning, C. (1998) 'Systemic conflict and regional monetary integration: the case of Europe', *International Organization* 52(3): 537–74.

Henning, C. and Meunier, S. (2005) 'United against the United States? The EU's role in global trade and finance', in N. Jabko and C. Parsons (eds), *With US or Against US? European Trends in American Perspective*, Oxford: Oxford University Press.

Hoffmann, S. (1966) 'Obstinate or obsolete? The fate of the nation-state and the case of western Europe', *Daedalus* 95(3): 862–915.

Howarth, D. (2007) 'Making and breaking the rules: French policy on EU "gouvernement economique"', *Journal of European Public Policy* 14(7): 1061–78.

Jabko, N. (1999) 'In the name of the market: how the European Commission paved the way for monetary union', *Journal of European Public Policy* 6(3): 475–95.

Jabko, N. (2006) *Playing the Market: A Political Strategy for Uniting Europe, 1985– 2005*, Ithaca, NY: Cornell University Press.

Jacoby, W. and Meunier, S. (2010) 'Europe and the management of globalization', *Journal of European Public Policy* 17(3): 299–316.

Jones, E. (2002) *The Politics of Economic and Monetary Union: Integration and Idiosyncrasy*, Lanham, MD: Rowman & Littlefield.

Katzenstein, P. (1987) *Policy and Politics in West Germany: The Growth of a Semisovereign State*, Philadelphia, PA: Temple University Press.

Kindleberger, C. (1973) *The World in Depression, 1929–1939*, Berkeley, CA: University of California Press.

Ludlow, P. (1982) *The Making of the European Monetary System*, London: Butterworth.

Marcussen, M. (1999) 'The dynamics of EMU ideas', *Cooperation and Conflict* 34(4): 383–411.

Marsh, D. (1992) *The Bundesbank: The Bank That Rules Europe*, London: William Heinemann.

McNamara, K. (1998) *The Currency of Ideas*, Ithaca, NY: Cornell University Press.

McNamara, K. and Meunier, S. (2002) 'Between national sovereignty and international power: what external voice for the euro?', *International Affairs* 78(4): 849–68.

Moravcsik, A. (1998) *The Choice for Europe: Social Purpose and State Power from Messina to Maastricht*, Ithaca, NY: Cornell University Press.

Moss, B. and Michie, J. (eds) (2000) *The Single European Currency in National Perspective: A Community in Crisis?*, London: Macmillan.

Posner, E. and Véron, N. (2010) 'The EU and financial regulation: power without purpose?', *Journal of European Public Policy* 17(3): 398–413.

Ruggie, J. (1982) 'International regimes, transactions, and change – embedded liberalism in the post-war economic order', *International Organization* 36(2): 379–415.

Sandholtz, W. (1993) 'Choosing union: monetary politics and Maastricht', *International Organization* 47(1): 1–39.

Shonfield, A. (1969) *Modern Capitalism: The Changing Balance of Public and Private Power*, Oxford: Oxford University Press.

Tsoukalis, L. (1977) *The Politics and Economics of European Monetary Integration*, London: George Allen & Unwin.

Verdun, A. (1999) 'The role of the Delors committee in the creation of EMU: an epistemic community?', *Journal of European Public Policy* 6(2): 308–28.

Globalizing European Union environmental policy

R. Daniel Kelemen

ABSTRACT   This contribution explores the European Union's (EU) efforts to 'globalize' EU environmental regulation. EU leadership on global environmental governance emerged as a result of the combined effects of domestic politics and international regulatory competition. The growing power of environmental interests in Europe from the late 1980s, coupled with dynamics of EU policy-making, led the EU to commit to ambitious environmental policies. Given this commitment, it was in the EU's international competitive interests to support international agreements that would pressure other jurisdictions to adopt similar environmental regulations. Promoting treaties that spread EU environmental norms internationally also served to legitimize EU rules and to shield them from legal challenges before world trade bodies.

During the past two decades the European Union (EU) has emerged as the global leader in international environmental politics. On issues ranging from climate change, to biodiversity, to trade in toxic wastes, to the regulation of persistent organic pollutants, the EU has taken on a leadership role in promoting multilateral environmental agreements (MEAs). The EU has also led efforts to 'green' international trade institutions, such as the World Trade Organization (WTO).

Neither the EU itself nor its member states have always been leaders on international environmental policy. When environmental issues emerged on the international scene in the early 1970s, the US took on a leadership role in preparation for the 1972 United Nations (UN) Conference on the Human Environment, and championed treaties such as the 1973 Convention on International Trade in Endangered Species (CITES). The US demonstrated leadership again in the mid-1980s, acting as the driving force behind the 1987 Montreal Protocol on Ozone Depleting Substances. The precursor to the EU, the European Economic Community (EEC), was not a significant actor in international environmental policy at the time. The member states of the EEC eventually went along with the international treaties created in this period, but in a number of cases, such as the 1979 Convention on Transboundary Air Pollution and the Montreal Protocol, many did so only reluctantly.

In the past two decades, however, the EU has emerged as the undisputed leader in international environmental politics. EU leadership is not simply the result of laggard behavior by the US or other states. Certainly, the US shift from global environmental leader in the 1970s and 1980s to laggard and obstructionist in the 1990s and 2000s opened up an opportunity for the EU to assert leadership (Sbragia and Damro 1999; Kelemen and Vogel forthcoming), but the retreat of the US did not force the EU to take on the active leadership role that it has.

Why has the EU taken on this leadership role in international environmental politics? EU leadership in international environmental politics is best explained by a model of 'regulatory politics' (DeSombre 2000; Falkner 2007; Kelemen and Vogel forthcoming; Raustiala 1997) that combines the effects of domestic politics and international regulatory competition. Domestic political forces – and by 'domestic' I mean political forces within Europe both at the national level and the EU level – have led EU member states and the EU itself to be committed to stringent environmental policies. Given the EU's commitment to high standards and the exposure of European firms to international competition, it is in the competitive interests of the EU to support international agreements that will pressure other states to adopt similarly costly regulations. Moreover, the passage of international environmental agreements can legitimize existing EU rules and thus shield the EU from legal challenges before world trade bodies.

EU leadership in international environmental politics provides striking examples of two of the strategies that Jacoby and Meunier (2010) highlight as central to the EU's efforts to manage globalization: exercising regulatory influence and empowering international institutions. Globalization generates, or at least is commonly perceived as generating, two primary threats to environmental policy in Europe. First, trade liberalization, it is argued, will pressure EU member states to 'race-to-the-bottom', lowering their standards towards the lowest common denominator in order to maintain competitiveness. The second perceived threat stems from the international institutions charged with promoting economic liberalization, above all the WTO. The logic here is that where EU member states resist race-to-the-bottom pressures and maintain stringent environmental standards, these may be struck down by the WTO as illegal non-tariff barriers to trade. Whether these threats are real or imagined, they have triggered a reaction from European policy-makers. Policy-makers have not treated these globalization pressures as inexorable forces that will determine their policies. Rather, they have sought to manage globalization by spreading EU environmental standards around the world, through support of MEAs and through the EU's normative and market power.

The remainder of this article is divided into three sections. The first details my 'regulatory politics' explanation for EU environmental leadership and discusses alternative explanations. The second provides empirical support for the regulatory politics explanation, offering a brief account of the domestic political developments that have led to strong demand for strict environmental policies and shows how these demands, coupled with concerns over regulatory competition, stimulated EU leadership on genetically modified organisms (GMOs), climate change and the 'greening' of the world trade regime. The third section concludes.

EXPLAINING EU GLOBAL ENVIRONMENTAL LEADERSHIP

Some environmental issues, such as climate change, are inherently global, and addressing them will require international co-operation. Therefore, any state committed to solving these issues will be inclined to support co-operative, international efforts designed to address them. However, we cannot explain the intensity and scope of EU global environmental leadership solely on functional grounds. Global problems may require co-operative solutions, but this does not tell us why the EU has been the chief *demandeur* of every major international environmental agreement since the early 1990s. Nor can functional considerations alone explain EU efforts to 'green' international trade rules and to spread some of its regulatory practices – such as the 'precautionary principle'.

Moving beyond purely functionalist explanations, there is an established literature in political science and sociology examining sources of state support for MEAs. However, the leading arguments in this literature do not offer adequate explanations for the emergence of EU leadership. One line of argument suggests that increases in wealth encourage the spread of post-materialist values that inspire greater public support for environmental protection. As this support is channeled through the political process, it translates into a greater propensity of states to sign and ratify international environmental treaties. A variety of large-N studies do demonstrate positive correlations between wealth and post-materialist values and the ratification of MEAs (Recchia 2002; Roberts *et al.* 2004; Scruggs 2003: 83–106). However, arguments based on these factors are designed to predict a state's propensity to sign environmental treaties, not their willingness to play a leadership role. If one stretches these explanations in an effort to explain leadership, they would seem to suggest that the US – not the EU – should have remained the environmental leader in the 1990s. Trends in economic growth and post-materialist values in the 1980s and 1990s – when the US made greater gains in both areas than the EU – would not lead one to expect that the EU would assume the mantle of global environmental leadership in the 1990s (Scruggs 2003: 106; Kelemen and Vogel 2010).

Scholars working in the social constructivist tradition have argued that a state's support for international environmental treaties is not determined by domestic interests, but rather is 'constructed' by a 'world environmental regime' (Meyer *et al.* 1997) that informs and structures national preferences. States internalize a form of peer pressure, and seek to 'enact' behaviors expected of modern states, including the ratification of environmental treaties (Frank 1999: 527–9). These scholars argue that those states most deeply embedded in world society tend to ratify more environmental treaties (Frank 1999: 534). Whatever the merits of this perspective, it cannot by itself explain EU leadership, because a host of other advanced industrialized democracies such as Japan, the US, Australia and Canada are embedded in world society to a similar degree as the EU, but none of them has asserted a role of global environmental leader on a par with the EU.

The literature on EU foreign policy offers a more plausible set of arguments. This literature suggests that the EU has asserted leadership on questions of global environmental governance in an effort to carve out an identity and a profile for itself as a 'normative' or 'civilian' power on the world stage. Since the 1970s, scholars have argued that in light of the EU's limited military capacity and the intractable divisions between member states on security issues, the EU has focused on asserting itself as a 'civilian power' in areas such as trade and human rights where it did have some capacity to act (Duchêne 1972; Hettne and Söderbaum 2005; Zielonka 1998). Similarly, Manners (2002) has argued that the EU is distinguishing itself as a 'normative power' on the international stage, in that it acts to diffuse a series of norms around the world, such as democracy, human rights and sustainable development. Others have applied this perspective to explain EU leadership on global environmental governance (Scheipers and Sicurelli 2007; Vogler and Stephan 2007).

It is clear that the EU has tried to develop a profile as a civilian or normative power on the world stage, promoting multilateral measures designed to safeguard a variety of norms – including environmental norms (Farrell 2007; Hettne and Söderbaum 2005; Vogler and Stephan 2007). Between the 1970s and 1990s, a series of Treaty amendments, directives and ECJ decisions gave the EU the power to act on behalf of its member states in international environmental negotiations, making it possible for the EU to play a global leadership role. The EU quickly put this power to use, staking out a leadership role at the 1992 Rio Summit, and since then the EU has consistently championed MEAs (Vogler and Stephan 2007: 394–6). Commission President Romano Prodi summarized these ambitions, explaining, 'We must aim to become a global civil power at the service of sustainable global development' (2000: 3).

This literature suggests a variety of reasons why the EU has made such a priority of spreading its environmental norms. Manners argues that the EU promotes norms such as sustainable development in order to legitimate itself with skeptical EU citizens (2002: 244). Scheipers and Sicurelli (2007) suggest that the EU has focused on environmental issues such as climate change in order to develop its identity in contrast to 'the other' of the US. Vogler and Stephan (2007) suggest that the EU's general commitment to multilateralism has been central in explaining its consistent support for MEAs. While the precise causal arguments vary, it does seem likely that the EU's desire to establish an identity and a reputation as a 'normative power' encouraged EU leadership on global environmental issues.

However, these arguments are notably silent on the question of whether, and if so how, global environmental leadership may have served the material interests of the EU. Were these normative commitments necessary or sufficient conditions for the emergence of EU leadership? Would normative commitments alone have led the EU to take on a leadership role if doing so would have damaged the economic interests of the EU? By contrast, is it possible that economic interests provided the primary motivation for the EU taking on a leadership role, while normative commitments played a secondary, complementary role?

I offer a political economy-based explanation for the emergence of EU leadership in international environmental politics. While acknowledging that normative commitments and the desire to develop a reputation as a civilian power played an important complementary role, I argue that the interaction of developments in domestic politics and international regulatory competition provides a more powerful explanation for the emergence of EU environmental leadership.

The regulatory politics perspective (Kelemen and Vogel 2010) fuses domestic politics with international regulatory competition. The ultimate source of a polity's position on international environmental issues can be traced to the strength of environmental constituencies within the political system. The stronger the domestic political influence of environmentalists, the more stringent domestic standards are likely to be and the stronger the political commitment to maintaining those standards in the face of globalization pressures is likely to be. The existence of these strict and entrenched domestic standards, in turn, makes it more likely that domestic producers will support international treaties that impose similar standards on foreign competitors. Where industry sees that, due to the influence of environmental interests, it will be forced to bear the costs of strict environmental regulations, then it will support (or at least not oppose) efforts to spread those standards to other jurisdictions – sometimes joining them in 'Baptist–Bootlegger coalitions' (DeSombre 2000; Vogel 1995; Young 2003). As we will see in the following section, this perspective fits well with the empirical record in the EU, explaining both the general shift towards a leadership position from the early 1990s and the specific positions taken by the EU on a number of important international environmental issues. Instead of allowing globalization pressures to dictate the terms of its environmental policy, the EU has deployed strategies designed to spread its standards to other jurisdictions.

THE POLITICAL ECONOMY OF EU GLOBAL ENVIRONMENTAL LEADERSHIP

The roots of the EU's transformation into the global leader in international environmental politics can be traced to major shifts in domestic environmental politics in Europe beginning in the 1980s. Mass environmental movements had emerged across Western Europe in the 1970s, and governments had responded by establishing new pollution control laws. However, environmentalists in Europe never achieved the prominence or power of their US counterparts, and national environmental laws adopted in Europe during this period were generally less stringent than those established in the US (Vogel 2003). The salience of environmental issues – and the political influence of pro-environment forces – declined in the late 1970s in the wake of the oil shocks. However, in the

1980s, a series of highly publicized environmental calamities, including the 'forest death' (*Waldsterben*) caused by acid rain in the early 1980s, the 1986 Chernobyl nuclear disaster and the discovery of the 'hole' in the Ozone layer in the mid-1980s, all heightened the political salience of environmental issues across Europe. These issues, along with scandals concerning cross-border toxic waste shipments in Europe (Kelemen 2004: 32), also underlined the increasingly transboundary implications of environmental issues. By the late 1980s, Eurobarometer surveys found environmental problems to be one of the chief political concerns in all member states (Hofrichter and Reif 1990). Governments in a number of member states responded to this public concern by supporting strict new domestic standards and enhanced their commitments to international environmental co-operation.

The sensitivity of national governments to these shifts in public opinion was heightened by the emergence of Green parties. Given the opportunities for the emergence of small parties provided by most European electoral systems (particularly those that use proportional representation), environmental activists in Europe became involved in electoral politics in the 1980s. First in Germany in 1983, and later in a number of countries including Sweden, France and Belgium, significant Green parties raised the profile of environmental issues in national political debates (Mair 2001). By the end of the 1990s, Green parties were represented in 11 of 15 national parliaments in the EU and in the European Parliament (EP) (Vogel 2003). These parties moved increasingly from the fringe to the mainstream of party politics during the 1990s and entered national coalition governments along with social democrats in some member states, most prominently Germany.

The power of environmentalists at the national level was magnified by the dynamics of environmental policy-making at the EU level. First, the European Commission and the European Parliament (EP) had strong incentives to see the EU take on a powerful role in environmental policy and to adopt strict standards. National environmental regulations adopted in the 1970s and 1980s threatened to create non-tariff barriers that would impede trade and undermine the progress the EU had made towards completing the internal market. With many on the political Left arguing at the time that the EU merely served the interests of international business, attacking national environmental standards as non-tariff barriers would have been politically disastrous for the EU. Instead, the EU sought to protect the single market by harmonizing environmental standards at high levels of protection.

This approach appealed to the Commission and the EP because they saw that championing a strong environmental policy would increase the EU's popularity and legitimacy in the eyes of European citizens, demonstrating that the EU did not simply serve business interests but public interests as well. In particular, the EP, whose policy-making power was extended dramatically in the late 1990s, strengthened, and became a champion of environmental protection (Pollack 1997). The Commission and Parliament found strong supporters among the greenest member states (the Netherlands, Denmark and, above all,

Germany), who viewed the EU as a forum through which they could export their strict standards to laggard member states (Kelemen 2004; Vogel 2003). ECJ jurisprudence from 1991 onward and Treaty revisions made at Maastricht shifted the decision-making rule for environmental measures from unanimity to qualified majority voting, helping the powerful Green states to overcome opposition from laggards (Kelemen 2004: 28–31). Following the accession of Sweden, Austria and Finland in 1995, the bloc of pro-environment states grew even stronger. Finally, the fact that environment ministers representing their states in the EU's Council of Ministers deliberate amongst themselves – insulated from the critical eyes of ministers of economics and industry – has emboldened them to agree on more ambitious policies (Sbragia 2000).

The combination of the domestic political power of environmentalists and the dynamics of EU policy-making explains why the EU and its member states pursued increasingly stringent and ambitious environmental policies in the 1990s. The policy victories won by environmentalists in Europe unleashed a regulatory competition dynamic. Faced with stringent environmental standards within the EU, European firms and member state governments had strong incentives to see EU standards spread internationally, so that foreign competitors would have to meet similar regulatory burdens. Meanwhile, the EU's capacity to act in a coherent fashion to spread its standards internationally was increasing. This capacity developed gradually, through the extension of the EU's environmental competence and its role in external policies, and through the increasing recognition afforded to the EU in international fora (Jupille and Caporaso 1998; Sbragia and Hildebrand 2000: 217-18; Vogler and Stephan 2007).

These developments culminated in the run-up to the 1992 UN Conference on Environment and Development in Rio where the EU was allowed to join as an equal participant, and Commission President Jacques Delors was given a status equivalent to head of state (Sbragia and Damro 1999; Vogler and Stephan 2007).

So, by the early 1990s, the EU had strong incentives to try to export its environmental standards and an increasing capacity to do so. The EU deployed the strategies of 'exercising regulatory influence' and 'empowering international institutions' to manage globalization and to spread its environmental standards to other jurisdictions. Developments in the fields of GMO regulation, the fight against climate change and in the broader question of 'greening' the world trade regime illustrate these dynamics.

GMOs

In the 1990s, in response to mounting health, consumer safety and environmental concerns in Europe, the EU established the most stringent regulatory regime for the authorization and labeling of GMOs in the world (Bernauer 2003; Pollack and Shaffer 2005). The EU adopted its first common legislation on GMOs in 1990 (Directive 90/220/EEC). Although public opinion on

GMOs and initial policy reactions varied greatly among EU member states (Kurzer and Cooper 2007), states hostile to GMOs were able to dominate at the EU level and to force a de facto moratorium on new GM products in Europe from 1998. The EU introduced new common rules governing the experimental release, marketing, labeling and tracing of GMOs between 2001 and 2003 (Directive 2001/18/EC, Regulation 1830/2003/EC and Regulation 1829/2003/EC). The EU's approach to the regulation of GMOs was guided by 'the precautionary principle' – the principle that policy-makers should act to restrict products that pose potential risks, even where scientific uncertainty makes it impossible to assess the risk conclusively.

From the outset, the EU's regulatory regime for GMOs was confronted with globalization pressures in the form of potential legal attacks before the WTO. The US, which took a far more lax approach to GMO regulation and was home to major producers and exporters of GMOs, viewed EU GMO regulations as an unjustified trade barrier (Bernauer 2003; Vogel 2003; Young 2003). When the EU tightened its restrictions on GMOs in 1998, the US threatened to take legal action before the WTO.

As popular backlash against 'Frankenstein foods' mounted in some member states, any possibility of resolving the dispute simply through opening the European market to GMOs became a political non-starter – even though this would have been the preferred solution of many in the European Commission (Young 2003). The EU responded by leading a drive to 'internationalize' its approach to GMO regulation through a protocol to the 1992 Convention on Biodiversity. The EU succeeded in spearheading the creation of the Cartagena Protocol on Biosafety in 2000 (Depledge 2000). The Cartagena Protocol adopted the EU's precautionary principle as a potential justification for trade restrictions on genetically modified seeds and crops: in other words, by embracing the precautionary principle, Cartagena made it easier for countries to block imports of GMOs. Because of long-standing regulatory restrictions within the EU and consumer resistance to genetically modified foodstuffs, few European firms produced such genetically modified seeds or foodstuffs and few farmers grew them. As a result, these European commercial interests had little to lose from a Treaty like the Cartagena Protocol that would restrict trade in GMOs. They did, however, stand to benefit if such restrictions raised costs or reduced demand for their GMO-dependent American competitors. By institutionalizing its own standard at the international level, the EU also significantly enhanced the legitimacy of the precautionary principle and increased the chance that EU rules might withstand scrutiny before the WTO. A domestic standard, like the precautionary principle, can hardly be treated as arbitrary or a completely unjustifiable trade barrier once it is enshrined in an international treaty signed by dozens of states.

Ultimately, the EU was at best partially successful. In 2003, the US, together with Canada and Argentina, brought a WTO action charging that the EU's de facto moratorium on GMOs between 1999 and 2003 violated world trade rules. In 2004, the EU lifted its moratorium, put in place a new system for the evaluation and authorization of GMO products, and began to approve a handful of genetically modified foodstuffs (principally grains for animal feed). The WTO finally issued a ruling in February 2006, declaring that the EU's moratorium between 1999 and 2003 had been illegal. The EU accepted the ruling, but emphasized that the ruling did not invalidate the new system of GMO regulation it had put in place in 2004, which was based on scientific evaluation of GMOs, but still applied the precautionary principle (Alden and Grant 2006). The EU's strategy of shielding its own GMO policies by promoting the spread of the precautionary principle in the Cartagena Protocol had not prevented the US – which had refused to sign up to the Cartagena Protocol – from attacking it. However, it is likely that the existence of the Cartagena Protocol, endorsed by more than 130 countries, made the WTO panel less willing than it might otherwise have been to undertake a frontal assault on the new EU regulatory regime and the precautionary principle that underpins it.

Climate change

As in the case of GMOs, the interaction of domestic politics and regulatory competition also encouraged the EU to take on a leadership role in addressing climate change. As awareness of the threat posed by climate change increased in the late 1980s and early 1990s, domestic political pressure for action to curb greenhouse gas emissions mounted in Europe. National governments in the greenest member states acted first, with the Dutch, German and Danish governments making commitments to CO_2 reductions in 1989 and 1990 (Porter and Brown 1991: 95). Quickly, the EU stepped in to develop a common approach, and the Council of Ministers announced that the EU as a whole, working through a 'burden-sharing' or 'bubble' approach, would seek to stabilize its CO_2 emissions at 1990 levels by 2000. National commitments within the EU would be differentiated, with some member states (principally the most economically developed ones) making the substantial reductions, and others (principally the less developed EU members) actually being permitted to increase emissions.

Turning to the international arena, the calculus for European policy-makers was clear: the bold, costly domestic actions on climate change that European publics demanded would put European industry at a competitive disadvantage unless an international agreement was reached that would force the EU's competitors to undertake costly measures as well. After proposing that the EU introduce a carbon tax in order to achieve the target for CO_2 emissions reductions that it had set for itself in 1990, the Commission pushed for industrialized nations to adopt similar energy taxes in the run-up to Rio. After other states refused to do so at the Rio Earth Summit, the Commission abandoned its carbon tax proposal in 1992.

The EU assumed an even more pronounced leadership role in the negotiations over the Kyoto Protocol between 1995 and 1997. In the negotiations leading to Kyoto, it was clear that the EU was willing to commit to costly measures – indeed, the EU was committed to do so regardless of the outcome of Kyoto. It was also clear from early on in the negotiating process that the costs of implementing Kyoto promised to be substantially less for the EU than for some other industrialized states – above all the US. One crucial factor was that 1990 was to be used as the baseline year against which mandatory reductions (of 8 per cent for the EU and 7 per cent for the US) would be measured. Using 1990 as a baseline allowed the EU to take advantage of reductions in emissions that were occurring in any case for idiosyncratic reasons – the switch from reliance on coal to natural gas in the UK in the first half of the 1990s and the shuttering of polluting industries in former East Germany after reunification, which had led to massive reductions in CO_2 emissions (Schreurs and Tiberghien 2007). As the EU was allowed to use a differentiated 'bubble' or burden-sharing approach, the large 'exogenous' reductions occurring in Germany and the UK could be leveraged to ease the emissions reduction burden for other member states. Finally, the 1990 baseline had another advantage for the EU in that the European economy – and associated CO_2 emissions – had grown far more slowly in the 1990s than the US economy and US emissions. Therefore, by the time the Kyoto Protocol was signed in 1997, the US would have had to cut its projected emissions by 30 to 35 per cent to meet Kyoto's 2012 target, where the EU would have only had to make cuts of 15 to 20 per cent (Yandle and Buck 2002). Indeed, some observers have argued that the EU hoped to use climate change negotiations to pressure the US to raise its relatively low energy taxes and thus to create a more level competitive playing field (ibid.: 197).

The point here is not to suggest that the EU asserted leadership on Kyoto simply in an effort to raise costs for competitors. The point, rather, is that because the EU was going to take substantial, highly costly action on greenhouse gas emissions in any case due to domestic political pressure, EU leaders felt it imperative to press other states – particularly the advanced industrialized states – to join them in the fight against climate change.

Despite the EU's inability to secure US participation in the agreement, EU leadership on Kyoto should be viewed as a relatively successful case of managing globalization. Kyoto has 178 signatories, and the EU has played a pivotal role in persuading key hold-out states such as Russia to participate. Moreover, the EU has been able to use the framework provided by Kyoto and the UN Framework Convention on Climate Change (UNFCC) – with tools such as 'Clean Development Mechanism' (CDM) – projects to encourage developing countries to join the effort to combat climate change and to encourage them to adopt EU standards and technologies when doing so. For instance, within the UNFCC/Kyoto framework, the EU has worked closely with China, establishing the EU–China Partnership on Climate Change in 2005, which promotes the transfer of low carbon technologies and CDM projects involving European and Chinese partners.

Turning to the ongoing negotiations on a post-Kyoto framework for combating climate change, we can observe similar dynamics behind EU leadership. In

2007, when the Commission announced new plans to combat climate change, Commission President Barroso acknowledged that the new rules would raise production costs and damage the competitiveness of EU industries. Therefore, the Commission proposed imposing a carbon tax on imports from countries that do not maintain similar restrictions on carbon emissions. French President Sarkozy expressed strong support for carbon tariffs, as did a number of members of the European Parliament and environmentalists. The fate of such proposals remains uncertain, but it is clear that many EU leaders are hoping to use the threat of 'carbon tariffs' as a way to pressure reluctant developed states – such as the US – and developing states – such as China – to make binding commitments in a post-Kyoto framework. Having established its *bona fides* as an environmental leader in the earlier rounds of climate negotiations and in negotiations on other environmental issues, it seems that the EU is now likely to rely more heavily on leveraging its market power to press other states to join it in making substantial commitments to reducing emissions.

GREENING WORLD TRADE

The EU has attempted to manage the impact of globalization on environmental regulation through two principal strategies. First and foremost, the EU tried to 'globalize' the environmental standards it favors through MEAs, as illustrated above in the discussions of the Cartagena Protocol and the Kyoto Protocol. The EU's second strategy has been its broader effort to 'green' the international trade regime. The EU has pressed for changes to or interpretations of international trade rules (i.e., those of the WTO) that would allow them to accommodate EU environmental measures and commitments made by the EU under MEAs. Conflicts between free trade rules and EU environmental policy commitments have led the EU to a number of 'trade vs. environment' disputes before the WTO, including the Hormone Treated Beef and GMO disputes. The EU has defended itself vigorously in these cases, but the EU has also gone on the offense, attempting to manage globalization by greening global trade rules before it is forced to defend itself in a judicial setting.

The GATT's Article XX general exceptions clause provides for exceptions to its free trade obligations that enable signatories to restrict trade on environmental grounds. During the Uruguay Round, the US and EU demanded the additional agreements that would clarify their right to maintain domestic environmental rules. The Agreements on Sanitary and Phytosanitary Measures (SPS) and Technical Barriers to Trade (TBT) concluded during the Uruguay round elaborated these conditions (Steinberg 1997).

Beginning in the mid-1990s, the EU raised particular concerns regarding the relationship between trade obligations contained in MEAs and general free trade rules of the GATT/WTO. The problem that they highlighted was that MEAs contain various trade measures including, trade bans, export and import licensing procedures and notification, packaging and labeling requirements. For instance, the Convention on Trade in Endangered Species (CITES) restricts trade in endangered animal species, and the Montreal Protocol bans the import of CFCs from non-parties. The EU was concerned with how the WTO would resolve disputes between free trade requirements and trade restrictions called for in international environmental treaties.

In the Doha Round trade negotiations, the EU has taken a lead role in pushing for reforms to the GATT that would give trade measures contained in MEAs supremacy over WTO requirements in cases of conflict. The EU began promoting this position prior to Doha, when, in 1996, it pressed the WTO's Committee on Trade and the Environment to add a reference to MEA trade provisions and other 'measures necessary to protect the environment' to GATT's Article XX exceptions (Stoler 2004; see also Steinberg 1997). In recent negotiations the EU has retreated somewhat, but still calls for MEAs and the WTO to be treated as equal bodies of international law and for the WTO to defer to MEAs on environmentally related trade restrictions.

Taking a step back, we can see how the EU's drive to make trade restrictions required by MEA's effectively 'WTO-proof' meshes with its consistent leadership on MEAs. The EU recognizes that standing in isolation, many of its environmental policies – particularly those based on the precautionary principle – may not withstand scrutiny with the WTO. However, where the EU can internationalize its standards by convincing other countries to sign on to them in an MEA, then these standards gain international legitimacy and may withstand legal challenges at the WTO.

CONCLUSIONS

To be sure, many factors have contributed to the rise of the EU as the undisputed leader in global environmental governance. A series of legal and political reforms and the EU's broad commitment to developing common foreign economic policy increased the EU's capacity to act in a cohesive fashion in the environmental arena. Global environmental problems, by their very nature, call for multilateral solutions. Thus, the environment was a natural focus for the many EU leaders committed to the EU developing an identity as a 'civilian' or 'normative' power on the world stage. The US retreat from leadership made this more attractive, in that the EU could contrast its virtuous, environmental leadership with the US's rogue behaviour. While these factors certainly played a role, the roots of the EU's commitment to global environmental leadership may be found at the intersection of domestic politics and international political economy. In the 1990s, the dramatic increase in power of environmental interests across Europe, and the dynamics of EU policy-making that encouraged harmonization at high levels of environmental protection, led the EU to adopt the strictest, most ambitious environmental legislation in the world. Given that strict standards were being put in place across Europe, it was in the interests of European industry and European governments to see similar standards spread to other jurisdictions.

The role of the EU in championing MEAs is well illustrated above in the discussions of the Cartagena Protocol and the Kyoto Protocol. The most striking aspect of the EU's position on MEAs is the sheer consistency with which it has supported them in recent years. The EU has emerged as a leading supporter of every major international environmental treaty since 1989. By consistently positioning itself as an environmental leader, the EU has spread a number of its environmental standards to other jurisdictions and has built up a reservoir of credibility in this policy domain, which it may draw upon in defending new measures against accusations that they constitute veiled protectionism. The EU has also worked to 'green' the world trade regime, elevating the status of MEAs *vis-à-vis* WTO rules. In all of this, the EU has not idly waited for the pressures of globalization to undermine its commitment to environmental policy. Instead, the EU has taken a leadership role and gone on the offensive to manage globalization or – to paraphrase Woodrow Wilson in a very different context – to make the world safe for environmental policy.

These dynamics clearly extend beyond the specific cases discussed above and may be observed in other areas of environmental, consumer protection and economic regulation. For instance, as the EU developed its ambitious new regulatory regime for chemicals (REACH), it simultaneously sought to influence international debates concerning chemicals regulation (Fisher 2008; Pesendorfer 2006). In attempting to spread its strict chemical safety standards, the EU is both leveraging its market power by requiring all foreign manufacturers exporting to the European market to comply with REACH and is supporting strengthening international initiatives on chemicals regulation – above all, the 2001 Stockholm Convention on Persistent Organic Pollutants. Moving beyond the environmental field, in areas including data privacy regulation, securities regulation, telecoms regulation, accounting standards and pharmaceutical standards, we can observe similar processes at work with the EU harnessing its market power and multilateral agreements to 'globalize' its standards (Bach and Newman 2007; Glimstedt 2001; Mattli and Büthe 2003; Mitchener 2002; Shaffer 2002).

ACKNOWLEDGEMENTS

The author thanks Sophie Meunier, Wade Jacoby, Mark Pollack, David Vogel, Joseph Jupille, Paulette Kurzer, Orfeo Fioretos, Nicolas Jabko, Kate McNamara, Andrew Moravcsik and other participants in workshops at Princeton and Park City for comments and suggestions, and he thanks the Institute for Advanced Study for research support.

REFERENCES

Alden, E. and Grant, J. (2006) 'WTO rules against Europe in GM food case', *Financial Times*, 7 February.

Bach, D. and Newman, A. (2007) 'The European regulatory state and global public policy', *Journal of European Public Policy* 14(6): 827–46.

Bernauer, T. (2003) *Genes, Trade and Regulation*, Princeton, NJ: Princeton University Press.

Commission of the European Communities (2001) 'White Paper on the strategy for a future chemicals policy', COM, 88 final.

Depledge, J. (2000) 'The Cartagena Protocol on biosafety', *Environmental Politics* 9(2): 156–62.

DeSombre, E. (2000) *Domestic Sources of International Environmental Policy*, Cambridge, MA: MIT Press.

Duchêne, F. (1972) 'Europe in world peace', in R. Mayne (ed.), *Europe Tomorrow*, London: Fontana/Collins.

Environmental News Service (2004) 'Europe gets new leadership, ratifies POPS treaty', ENS-Newswire, 19 November, available at: http://www.ens-newswire.com/ens/nov2004/2004-11-19-04.asp (accessed November 2009).

Falkner, R. (2007) 'The political economy of 'normative power' Europe: EU environmental leadership in international biotechnology regulation', *Journal of European Public Policy* 14(4): 507–26.

Farrell, M. (2007) 'From EU model to external policy?', in S. Meunier and K. McNamara (eds), *Making History: The State of the European Union*, Oxford: Oxford University Press.

Fisher, E. (2008) 'The perfect storm of REACH', *Journal of Risk Research* 11: 541–63.

Frank, D. (1999) 'The social bases of environmental treaty ratification, 1900-1990', *Sociological Inquiry* 69(4): 523–50.

Franzen, A. (2003) 'Environmental attitudes in international comparison', *Social Science Quarterly* 84(2): 297–308.

Glimstedt, H. (2001) 'Competitive dynamics of technological standardization', *Industry and Innovation* 8(1): 49–78.

Hettne, B. and Söderbaum, F. (2005) 'Civilian power or soft imperialism?', *European Foreign Affairs Review* 10: 535–52.

Hofrichter, J. and Reif, K-H. (1990) 'Evolution of environmental attitudes in the European community', *Scandinavian Political Studies* 13(2): 119–146.

Jacoby, W. and Meunier, S. (2010) 'Europe and the management of globalization', *Journal of European Public Policy* 17(3): 299–317.

Jupille, J. and Caporaso, J. (1998) 'States, agency, and rules: the European Union in global environmental politics', in C. Rhodes (ed.), *The European Union in the World Community*, Boulder, CO: Lynne Rienner.

Kelemen, R. (2004) *The Rules of Federalism*, Cambridge, MA: Harvard University Press.

Kelemen, R. and Vogel, D. (2010) 'Trading places: the role of the United States and the European Union in international environmental politics', *Comparative Political Studies* 43(4): 427–56.

Kurzer, P. and Cooper, A. (2007) 'What's for dinner? European farming and food traditions confront American biotechnology', *Comparative Political Studies* 40(9): 1035–58.

Mair, P. (2001) 'The green challenge and political competition', *German Politics* 10(2): 99–116.

Manners, I. (2002) 'Normative power Europe: a contradiction in terms?', *Journal of Common Market Studies* 40(2): 235–58.

Mattli, W. and Büthe, T. (2003) 'Setting international standards', *World Politics* 56(1): 1–42.

Meyer, J., Frank, D., Hironaka, A., Schofer, E. and Tuma, N. (1997) 'The structuring of a world environmental regime, 1870–1990', *International Organization.* 51(4), 623–51.

Mitchener, B. (2002) 'Rules, regulations of the global economy are increasingly being set in Brussels', *Wall Street Journal,* 23 April.

Pesendorfer, D. (2006) 'EU environmental policy under pressure', *Environmental Politics* 15: 95–114.

Pollack, M. (1997) 'Representing diffuse interests in EC policy-making', *Journal of European Public Policy* 4(4): 572–90.

Pollack, M. and Shaffer, G. (2005) 'Biotechnology policy', in H. Wallace, W. Wallace and M. Pollack (eds), *Policy-making in the European Union,* Oxford: Oxford University Press.

Porter, G. and Brown, J. (1991) *Global Environmental Politics,* Boulder, CO: Westview Press.

Prodi, R. (2000) '2000–2005: shaping the new Europe', Speech/00/41 to the European Parliament, Strasbourg, 15 February.

Raustiala, K. (1997) 'Domestic institutions and international regulatory cooperation', *World Politics* 49(4): 482–509.

Recchia, S. (2002) 'International environmental treaty engagement in 19 democracies', *Policy Studies Journal* 30(4): 470–94.

Roberts, J., Parks, B. and Vásquez, A. (2004) 'Who ratifies environmental treaties and why?', *Global Environmental Politics* 4(3): 22–64.

Sbragia, A. (2000) 'Environmental policy', in H. Wallace and W. Wallace (eds), *Policy-making in the European Union,* Oxford: Oxford University Press.

Sbragia, A. and Damro, C. (1999) 'The changing role of the European Union in international environmental politics', *Environment and Planning C: Government and Policy* 17(1): 53–68.

Sbragia, A. and Hildebrand, P. (2000) 'The European Union and compliance', in E. Weiss and H. Jacobson (eds), *Engaging Countries,* Cambridge, MA: MIT Press.

Scheipers, S. and Sicurelli, D. (2007) 'Normative power Europe', *Journal of Common Market Studies* 45(2): 435–57.

Schreurs, M. (2005) 'Global environment threats in a divided northern community', *International Environmental Agreements* 5: 349–76.

Schreurs, M. and Tiberghien, Y. (2007) 'Multi-level reinforcement: explaining EU leadership in climate change mitigation', *Global Environmental Politics* 7(4): 19–46.

Scruggs, L. (2003) *Sustaining Abundance,* New York: Cambridge University Press.

Shaffer, G. (2002) 'Reconciling trade and regulatory goals', *Columbia Journal of European Law* 9: 29.

Steinberg, R. (1997) 'Trade–Environment negotiations in the EU, NAFTA and WTO', *American Journal of International Law* 91(2): 231–67.

Stoler, A. (2004). 'The Doha round negotiations on the MEA-WTO interface', Paper presented at the International Bar Association Conference, Auckland, NZ, 26 October.

Vogel, D. (1995) *Trading Up,* Cambridge, MA: Harvard University Press.

Vogel, D. (2003) 'The hare and the tortoise revisited', *British Journal of Political Science* 33: 557–80.

Vogler, J. and Stephan, H. (2007) 'The European Union in global environmental governance', *International Environmental Agreements* 7: 389–413.

Yandle, B. and Buck, S. (2002) 'Bootleggers, Baptists, and the global warming battle', *Harvard Environmental Law Review* 26: 177–229.

Young, A. (2003) 'Political transfer and "trading UP"?', *World Politics* 55(4): 457–84.

Zielonka, J. (1998) *Explaining Euro-paralysis,* Basingstoke: Macmillan.

Managed globalization: doctrine, practice and promise

Rawi Abdelal and Sophie Meunier

ABSTRACT   Two alternate visions for shaping and explaining the governance of economic globalization have been in competition for the past 20 years: an *ad hoc, laissez-faire* vision promoted by the United States versus a managed vision relying on multilateral rules and international organizations promoted by the European Union. Although the American vision prevailed in the past decade, the current worldwide crisis gives a new life and legitimacy to the European vision. This essay explores how this European vision, often referred to as 'managed globalization', has been conceived and implemented and how the rules that Europe fashioned in trade and finance actually shaped the world economy. In doing so, we highlight the paradox that managed globalization has been a force for liberalization.

INTRODUCTION

Est maître des lieux celui qui les organise. [He who organizes is master of the arena].

—Jean de la Fontaine

The sustainability of our era of globalization, circa 1983 to 2009, is in question, and not primarily because of a devastating financial crisis that dragged the real economy down with it. Rather, globalization – the free flow of goods, services and capital across country borders – is suffering a crisis of legitimacy, a crisis that began to emerge late in the twentieth century, the severity of which has been substantially worsened by the collapse of the American and European financial sectors.

Two central challenges have not been met. First, national models of capitalism have failed to legitimate openness to the global economy in the eyes of national societies. Skepticism has been on the rise. Second, the institutional foundations of global capitalism have not been made firm enough. It is this second challenge that we address. We argue that two alternate visions for shaping and explaining the governance of global capitalism have been in competition for the past 20 years.

One of those visions – what we call *ad hoc* globalization – largely ignores the need to legitimate the processes of cross-border market integration. The second of those visions – managed globalization – offers a compelling doctrine, significant influences on policy regimes, and, most importantly, the promise to enhance the legitimacy of the project of building global capitalism. Alas, the American approach, heretofore defined primarily by an *ad hoc* building of cross-border ties through unilateral choices and bilateral deals, has generally dominated the European emphasis on multilateral rules and organizations to 'manage', 'harness', and otherwise quite literally 'rule' global capitalism. The proliferation of hundreds of bilateral trade and investment treaties is emblematic of *ad hoc* globalization. The success of the European Union's 'open regionalism' represents best the triumph of managed globalization (Katzenstein 2005).

As influential as the European approach has been, those organization-building endeavors culminated primarily in the institutionalization of a large, possibly growing, European economic space. Outside the union of 27 European countries and the expanding but still modest influence of European-inspired initiatives in the international organizations that underpin global capitalism, *ad hoc* globalization continued to reign. Even as US current account deficits, financed largely by surpluses in developing Asia and the Middle East, threatened to promote an asset bubble within the United States and a dangerously imbalanced international financial system, *ad hoc* globalization muddled along. And it muddled until, finally, the absence of a coherent collection of institutions revealed fundamental weaknesses in unregulated, unsupervised financial transactions. The crisis of 2008 to 2009 was a failure of *ad hoc* globalization. That crisis also represented the limits of the European attempt to organize the world economy without the participation of the most important borrower and spender in the world – the United States – and perhaps the most influential exporter and saver – China.

Although the world economy is in tatters, 'Europe' – as metaphor or vision for globalization – is decidedly not. Even in Spain, which experienced its own current account deficits and debt-fueled housing boom, the financial sector enjoyed access to liberalized capital flows, but was still regulated in such a way that exotic mortgage-backed securities were undesirable and impractical for the country's banks. The impetus within Europe is towards even more regulatory capacity to accompany its liberalized markets. Whereas *ad hoc* globalization brought liberalization without organizing, or even supervising, markets, organized globalization in doctrine and practice made great progress towards combining market freedom with bureaucratic capability and responsibility.

Ad hoc globalization is indeed in trouble, but the international community's sudden embrace of managed globalization as insurance against future crises presents the best opportunity at the level of the international system to re-legitimate cross-border capitalism. National governments will still, of course, have to revisit their social bargains in order to reassure their societies that the gains from participating fully in the global economy outweigh the costs – and, more importantly, that those gains and costs will be shared according to each nation's principles.

In this essay, we build on this distinction between US-supported *ad hoc* globalization and EU-led managed globalization. The story of *ad hoc* globalization is the more familiar. According to conventional wisdom, globalization occurred because the United States and United Kingdom embraced *ad hoc* globalization during the early 1960s. Markets for goods and capital became international again, the first era of internationalization having ended during the interwar years. At various moments, American and British policy-makers adopted unilateral action, bilateral pressure, and even multilateral negotiations to foster this liberalization. Major corporations took advantage of this new-found liberalization by exporting and outsourcing, and in so doing reinforced the process of globalization. Thanks to economic and technological changes, globalization is seen as an ineluctable tidal wave crushing borders without which national policy initiatives became impotent.

The alternative vision, promoted over two decades by continental Europeans, is one where globalization is not formed only by striking down regulations, but also by making them; one where bureaucrats, rather than just managers and politicians, write the rules of the game. The markets for those freely flowing goods and capital are built upon institutional foundations, including the myriad formal rules that oblige governments around the world to embrace openness. This is a globalization made possible by codified rules and empowered institutions, not by deregulation and the elimination of institutional constraints. By the end of the 1990s, Pascal Lamy, the current head of the World Trade Organization (WTO) and for 20 years a prominent figure in French and European bureaucratic politics, had dubbed the emergent doctrine *mondialisation maîtrisée*, or 'managed globalization' (Gordon and Meunier 2001; Lamy 2004a). Variants have included the phrases 'harnessed globalization' and 'globalization by the rules'.

Former French foreign minister Hubert Védrine insists that the French government 'calls for more rules to frame globalization so that it doesn't only come down to a revival of "might makes right"' (Védrine 2001). *Ad hoc* globalization entails, in other words, Thrasymachean justice, merely the will of the stronger. Globalization managed by multilateral deliberations in international organizations may produce a conception of justice that is skewed. The justice of managed globalization would, however, at least be the product of dialogue, argument and deliberation.

For over two decades there has been a struggle between these two alternative visions. The story of liberalization is well known, but that of bureaucratization, an essential foundation of truly global markets, is largely unknown in the United States and deeply misunderstood within Europe. This essay explores how the European vision has been conceived and implemented, and how the rules that Europe fashioned in trade and finance actually contributed to shaping the world economy.

This alternative story of globalization is paradoxical, for managed globalization is no less liberal than *ad hoc* globalization; it is, in some important ways, more liberal. The rules codified a commitment to liberalism with just a few exceptions, and the bureaucracies empowered to enforce the liberal rules have become rather powerful, particularly within Europe. The Americans may have helped to create a more liberal world, but Europeans have formally proscribed and informally delegitimated many deviations from liberalism. That is, the European doctrine of managed globalization has left the world much more liberal than it otherwise would have become.

More importantly, by embracing procedural justice, the doctrine and practice of managed globalization have begun to legitimize the global project. True, the *ad hoc* globalization favored by the United States is under severe attack, and analysts worldwide lament the absence of regulation that led to the international financial meltdown. 'Managed globalization' may emerge to save the current era of globalization from its worst excesses. This essay explores the origins of the doctrine of managed globalization, how it was implemented in practice, and whether it has been successful in shaping a more liberal but also more legitimate and more equitable world.

THE GENESIS OF THE DOCTRINE OF MANAGED GLOBALIZATION: FRANCE AND EUROPE

'Managed globalization' entered the European discourse in September 1999, when Pascal Lamy introduced it in his hearings to the European Parliament as the ideological cornerstone of his future tenure as European Trade Commissioner (Lamy 1999).[1] Since then, the term has been used and abused by European politicians. The doctrine of managed globalization has existed without a name, however, for more than a decade prior to this official baptism. As policy doctrine, managed globalization demanded that rules for globalization be written and obeyed, jurisdictions of international organizations be extended, and the powers of the organizations themselves enhanced. For more than 20 years European policy-makers have, often successfully, sought to codify the rules of globalization and empower the European Union (EU), Organization for Economic Cooperation and Development (OECD), International Monetary Fund (IMF), and WTO.[2]

The doctrine's genesis remains somewhat obscure, but it is clear that it was heavily influenced by French policy-makers – not so much by the politicians and their inflamed discourse, but rather by the French bureaucrats, nourished in the cradle of etatism, who populate international organizations.[3] 'There is a paradox', observes Lamy, 'of the French role in globalization. There is an obvious difference between the traditional French view on the freedom of capital movements and the fact that French policy makers played crucial roles in promoting the liberalization of capital in the EC, OECD, and IMF' (Abdelal 2007: 13).

A great deal has been written about the famous *tournant*, the U-turn, of François Mitterrand in the spring of 1983 (Hall 1986, 1987; Levy 1999). One theme remains to be explored, however: a handful of French policy-makers who orchestrated the *tournant* and replaced socialization with austerity and *rigueur* derived lessons from the experience that would later comprise the doctrine of managed globalization.

The personalities who elaborated and implemented the doctrine of managed globalization are well known for their experiences in the Mitterrand administration. Jacques Delors was Mitterrand's finance minister, and he was later president of the European Commission for a decade. Pascal Lamy was Delors' advisor, his chief of staff in Brussels, the EU Trade Commissioner, and today the head of the WTO. Michel Camdessus was first director of the *Trésor* for Mitterrand, who then appointed him governor of the Banque de France; Camdessus was later the IMF's managing director. Hervé Hannoun was an advisor to Prime Minister Pierre Mauroy, and has since risen to prominence in the Banque de France. Henri Chavranski was in the *Trésor* in the early 1980s, and then chaired the OECD's influential Committee on Capital Movements and Invisible Transactions (CMIT). With the exception of Camdessus, who tends to identify himself as a Social Christian, the others are Socialists. Delors and Lamy played prominent roles in the Socialist Party's leadership (though Lamy never ran for elected office).

These policy-makers of the Left turned France towards the market, Europe and the world. In doing so, the French Left laid the groundwork for Europe's embrace of market integration, leading from the Single European Act of 1986 to the Treaty on European Union, signed in Maastricht in 1991. The central lesson learned by the French was that a global capitalism without rules required order to make it politically legitimate in the eyes of continental societies.

European policy-makers conceived and promoted the doctrine of managed globalization partly because of the necessity for pragmatism in an internationalizing world. As Lamy explains, he developed this doctrine as a pragmatic response to new events for which the old responses had no clue:

> We are currently in a historical phase of globalization, which is a phase of market capitalism, whether one likes it or not. There have been other such phases before .... Because it is a global phenomenon, we need global rules. This is a political statement, based on social-democratic ideology. But this happens within the framework of market capitalism, which, from a pragmatic point of view, is the only system that seems to work, even with its flaws.[4]

The doctrine was also developed by French politicians in response to societal demands that emerged in the 1990s. The U-turn in socialism, the collapse of communism, and the apparent unabashed victory of American-style liberalism had left many politically disoriented. The massive social protest movement that erupted in December 1995 against the proposed reforms of right-wing Prime Minister Alain Juppé showed that the French were not ready to embrace the liberal version of globalization. Over the next few years, anti-globalization discontent grew into a powerful force, which French politicians tried to channel in their rhetoric (Ancelovici 2002; Birchfield 2005; Gordon and Meunier 2001; Meunier 2003). Europeanization and globalization, often intertwined in the minds of the French public, had become politically toxic. Yet since there was only so much that France could really do against the tide of globalization,

French politicians, on the Left as well as on the Right, started to qualify globalization with adjectives: left alone, globalization was bad, but 'managed', 'harnessed' or 'tamed' globalization was beneficial for France and Europe. By the 2002 French presidential election, the idea that globalization had to be managed or it would implode had become conventional wisdom.

The most important conclusion the French socialists faced with the onslaught of liberal globalization in the late 1980s was that the internationalization of finance and trade required an institutional architecture. After all, the disorganized nature of globalization was anathema to the French belief that a centralized, *dirigisté* bureaucracy could manage the economy. Observes Lamy, 'One resolution of this paradox is the French approach to the problem of liberalization: If you liberalize, you must organize' (Abdelal 2007: 14). So, as with the French liberalized trade and capital flows, those same French policy-makers sought to empower the bureaucracies of international organizations and expand their competences.

Europe was, naturally, the first step. The French government, and in particular several policy-makers from the Mitterrand administration, strengthened the capacities of the European Commission and extended the obligations of European membership. They harnessed the continental embrace of neoliberalism for the purposes of market-based integration. Europe was thus built to organize and manage globalization. The EU, according to Lamy, 'is the only instrument for harnessing the forces of globalization to make it compatible with our model of society' (Gordon 2001: 102). 'Even if it was articulated by French people at the origin, [*mondialisation maitrisée*] is fundamentally a European concept'.

Even though globalization was a public obsession more prolific in France than elsewhere in the late 1990s, other European countries embraced the French vision that globalization ought to be accompanied by new regulations and flanked by policies to soften its impact. To be sure, the European vision on globalization was not monolithic. In many European countries, for instance, in Great Britain and in the Central and Eastern European countries who later joined the EU, globalization was seen not as a threat but as an opportunity. Yet the anti-globalization movement was gaining traction in public opinion with its widely publicized successes at the WTO conference in Seattle in 1999 and later at the World Social Forum. Many European politicians calculated that there was little to lose from supporting managed globalization, which could be presented as having one's cake and eating it too: managed globalization was not about shunting liberalization but about making it happen, yet at the same time it would be counterbalanced by multilateral, bureaucratic governance on the European model.

Thus managed globalization was a doctrine made up from a synthesis that began with the original French thesis. It was a consensus of the UK's liberalism, Germany's ordo-liberalism, continental statism, and the realities of late twentieth-century markets. Whereas the Americans preferred to liberalize without empowering international organizations, the Europeans embraced supranational rules and jurisdictions which would ensure that bureaucracies would continue to have supervisory and regulatory responsibilities for the long-term sustainability of market practices.

BUILDING INSTITUTIONS FOR GLOBAL TRADE

Globalization is inextricably linked with trade, and therefore the management of globalization starts with the management of trade. As EU Trade Commissioner from 1999 to 2004, Lamy moved managed globalization into the guiding doctrine of EU trade policy. He rallied states with diverse trade interests around 'managed globalization' – a notion vague enough to appeal to everyone, from individual member states to various social actors. This conceptual apparatus, mostly shaped by Lamy himself and his chief of cabinet Pierre Defraigne but agreed to consensually by the European Directorate General for Trade, was the result of deep ideological beliefs about the moral duties of the EU (Meunier 2007).[5] It was also shaped by a public relations imperative: given widespread anti-globalization protests, especially surrounding the December 1999 WTO meeting in Seattle, globalization had to be tamed in order to be palatable to most European citizens. Concretely, it meant building strong institutions applying to the largest possible number of countries covering the widest possible number of issues.

European policy-makers and technocrats have tried to manage globalization by building more constraining institutions for regulating global trade. At the end of the Uruguay Round of the General Agreement on Tariffs and Trade (GATT) in 1994, the signatories agreed to the creation of the WTO. The EU strongly supported clear rules for settling trade-related disputes in the WTO. This meant codifying rules for reporting violations, adjudicating disputes, and implementing resolutions to facilitate trade liberalization. As Lamy (2004b: 3) observed:

> Most of all, government has to ensure that globalization is not a zero-sum game. The right way forward is removing obstacles to trade gradually, settling disputes peacefully, building up a body of rules which allow for fair play and transparency in world trade, and always ensuring that our policies and politics help those who are affected by the 'globally' more efficient division of labor.

This approach was initially controversial in Europe, both among people concerned about national sovereignty and those involved in anti-globalization groups. The first set of criticisms focused on the way globalization decisions were being made, in particular the power granted to unelected judges in Geneva to rule against decisions of sovereign parliaments: why were multilateral rules better than national ones? The second set of criticisms focused on the nature of the decisions: the WTO was an institution designed to promote trade liberalization, and therefore the rulings would always create more globalization. To add insult to injury, the first two disputes in which the EU was implicated, namely the bananas case and the beef hormones case, were ruled in favor of the plaintiff, the United States. As a far-right member of the

European Parliament summed up in 1999: 'The Delors Commission ... accepted the rules and arrangements for settling disputes within the WTO, which subsequently enabled the United States win the infamous disputes over bananas and hormone meat' (quoted in Lamy 1999).

Yet the EU stayed the course of its 'harnessed globalization' policy by accepting the verdicts and either implementing the rulings of the WTO or suffering economic consequences (authorized sanctions) in exchange. Such a policy eventually paid off. After all, remarked Lamy in front of the European Parliament, 'With panels, you win some, you lose some. At present we are more often the plaintiff than the defendant' (Lamy 1999). Subsequently, the EU won major cases against the United States, forcing the US to change its policies in the cases of steel and the Foreign Sales Corporation tax scheme, for instance.

A related component of managed globalization in trade was the extension of the scope of these rules. The wider the scope to which the rules applied, the more managed globalization would be. Expanding this scope had indeed become an objective of EU trade policy even before 'managing globalization' was erected as formal doctrine. Between 1995 and 2003, the trade policy agenda of the EU was dominated by trying to bring non-trade issues into the WTO, with a particular focus on trade and trading conditions, trade and environment, and trade and culture (Howse 2003). During the 1996 Singapore WTO ministerial conference, four working groups were set up to analyze non-trade issues that affect trade: competition policy, transparency in government procurement, trade facilitation, and investment protection. The EU initially incorporated these 'Singapore issues' into a broad agenda for the Doha round, but it failed to impose them upon the other WTO members, especially the developing countries, which had acquired more voice in multilateral negotiations and insisted on retaining control over these key sectors of their economy. At the 2003 Cancun WTO ministerial meeting, negotiations collapsed without an agreement. Negotiations resumed in 2004 but with the Singapore issues, except for trade facilitation, dropped from the agenda.

To some analysts, the Singapore issues, originally launched under Trade Commissioner Leon Brittan, were neoliberal in nature (Cafruny and Ryner 2007). For the anti-globalization community especially, the Singapore issues shared the same ideological lineage as the earlier failed Multilateral Agreement on Investment (MAI), because they further expanded the reach of trade into realms which, until then, had resisted internationalization. Yet evidence for a distinct ideological lineage may be found in the fact that the Singapore issues were proposed by the EU, when the MAI was a US initiative that ended up being defeated by EU members (Devereaux et al. 2006). Thus, one can also interpret the Singapore issues as yet another instrument towards the objective of managing globalization because, if passed successfully, they could have expanded the scope of the multilateral framework and therefore be one further stepping stone towards global governance (Evenett 2007; Woolcock 2003).

In addition to building constraining organizations and expanding the scope over which the multilateral rules applied, the management of global trade also expanded the number of WTO members. For European policy-makers, the more members, the more countries subjected to the rules and the less anarchy in the trading system. The number of countries making, and subject to, the rules of the multilateral trading system has greatly expanded over time. From 23 original founding members, the GATT had 128 members at the time of its demise in 1994. Today, 153 countries are members of the WTO, and many more are involved in negotiations to join. From the WTO's creation in 1995, the EU has championed enlargement to more countries as part of its strategy of managed globalization.

Since the WTO and its expanded membership was the cornerstone of the EU's policy of harnessing globalization, the EU gave priority to multilateralism over bilateral agreements in the governance of trade in the past decade, going as far as instituting a de facto moratorium on bilateral agreements in the early years of the Doha round (Meunier 2007; Orbie 2008). This was in contrast to the stated policy of 'competitive liberalization' in the US during the same period, which involved the conclusion of a multitude of bilateral trade agreements (Sbragia, this issue).

Supporting multilateralism in the name of managing globalization put head-to-head two competing interests of the EU: on the one hand, defending its narrowly defined economic interests, such as agricultural subsidies under constant attack by WTO members; on the other hand, casting the net of global rules over a wider number of countries in a wider number of policy areas, therefore harnessing globalization more tightly. The problem for the EU, and for France in particular, is that it has not clearly prioritized one set of interests over the other. The policy of exclusive multilateralism proved so costly that the EU eventually abandoned it in 2006 (Meunier 2007; Sbragia 2010). Pushing WTO multilateralism has also been costly for the EU because more countries are now involved in playing a crucial role in WTO negotiations, often to the detriment of the EU position. Decisions are no longer made solely by the so-called Quad (EU, US, Japan, Canada). Instead, the current round of multilateral negotiations in the WTO is notable above all for the new-found strength of some developing countries, such as India and Brazil, intent on not letting the US and the EU run the show as they did in the previous GATT rounds.

Regulating global trade thus provided an opportunity for Europe to recapture some control and influence over the process of globalization over the past 15 years, but with only limited success. Many European policy-makers believe that the EU is itself an experiment in managed globalization. A crucial, additional step in implementing the doctrine of managed globalization in trade is to export the EU model to other regions (Farrell 2007; Meunier and Nicolaidis 2006). As Lamy (2004b: 12) wrote when he left his office as EU trade commissioner,

> Encouraging regional integration enlarges markets, reinforces healthy competition between neighboring countries of comparable levels of development and competitiveness, favoring industrialization, development and regional

stability. It is less an alternative to multilateral liberalization, and should rather be seen as complementary. In many respects, the regional dimension can serve as an opportunity to test out innovations, which, if successful, can then be applied to multilateral frameworks.

The doctrine of managed globalization states that clear rules of the game must be established, and the players must be constrained in a heavily regulated organization. As the case of the creation of the WTO suggests, once the rules were in place, globalization became more controlled, subjected to 'fair play' and transparency. But these rules also enabled globalization to progress even further, as they tore down barriers to trade not respecting the new rules of the game and thereby created more liberalization.

BUILDING THE INSTITUTIONS FOR GLOBAL FINANCE

European policy-makers also conceived and codified the most important institutional underpinnings of global financial markets. As with trade, they began with their own European project as the basis for pooling sovereignty and cultivating a process of globalization by the rules.

These European organizers of globalization did not inherit a principle of openness from the project's founding fathers, however. The European economy envisioned by the authors and negotiators of the Treaty of Rome was not unconditionally liberal. Goods, services and people were supposed to flow freely. Capital, however, was not, except, according to the Treaty of Rome, 'to the extent necessary to ensure the proper functioning of the Common Market', and without jeopardizing the internal and external financial stability of members (Bakker 1996: 42–3). The conditionality of the obligation to liberalize capital reflected, in part, the consensus that capital flows ought to be controlled in order to avoid financial crises.

This consensus, which drew upon the lessons that European and American policy-makers believed were evident from the financial chaos of the interwar years, was, along with fixed exchange rates, the basis of the postwar international monetary system. The conditionality of capital liberalization in the Treaty also reflected bargaining among Europe's founding members. Germany had been alone in pushing for capital liberalization, whereas France, Italy and the Netherlands had argued against codifying such an obligation.

The legal implication of the Treaty's wording was that members' obligations to liberalize capital could only be redefined by unanimity on what members agreed constituted 'the extent necessary' for the common market.[6] The Commission began to define and expand members' obligations to liberalize capital with two directives in 1960 and 1962, but little progress was made. Members were obliged to liberalize only those transactions deemed essential to the functioning of the common market, and that turned out to be a short list indeed.

Subsequently, for more than 20 years, not a single new directive for liberalizing capital was issued from Brussels. The Commission did submit a third directive to the European Council in 1967, but a decade of negotiations led nowhere. When the Germans' enthusiasm for liberalization was shared by the Dutch and British in the early 1980s, those three countries sought to bring capital liberalization again to the agenda in Brussels. The 'uncompromising, dogmatic attitude of France' blocked the initiative (Bakker 1996: 147–53).

Everything changed with the *tournant* of 1983 when French policy-makers began to reconsider their approach to the freedom of capital movements in Europe. Then, on 1 January 1985, the architect of *rigueur*, Delors, became Commission President, a post he would hold for a decade. Sensing that the time was ripe for an ambitious new integration initiative based on market principles, Delors moved quickly to produce the June 1985 White Paper that was the first outline of a plan to complete the European internal market by 1 January 1993 (Moravcsik 1998: 361–2). Between July and December, the Delors Commission decided to also push forward capital liberalization, well beyond what was originally conceived in the single market program. Ultimately these liberalizers would seek to balance market freedom with bureaucratic organization and a broader social agenda that would be embodied in the new European rules (Dinan 2004; Ross 1995). The promises and disappointments of that social agenda continue to be important in their own right, but the effects of the liberalization that was part of that grand bargain continue to define the contours of European markets.

In 1986 the Commission formulated a plan for a series of directives to oblige member governments to liberalize unconditionally. Delors' first big step was a November 1986 Directive that moved many of the capital transactions from the list that the 1960 Directive had placed on the conditional liberalization list to the unconditional list. In June 1988 the final capital movement directive 88(361) was issued. No capital transaction or transfer was exempt from this new obligation to liberalize (Bakker 1996: 211). Thus was the *acquis communautaire* made liberal, and the Community acquired jurisdiction over the capital account policies of its members. The Commission was empowered to oversee and promote the compliance of European countries with their new obligation to liberalize.

Alongside the emergent doctrine of managed globalization, other considerations influenced the French approach to the codification of the norm of capital mobility. Most important was a quid pro quo with the Germans, who accepted a more symmetrical European Monetary System (EMS) and a firm timetable for moving towards monetary union (Grieco 1995, 1996; Jabko 1999; Parsons 2003; Sandholtz 1993).

Having created a European institutional foundation for internationalizing financial markets, the organizers of globalization turned their attention to a broader club: the OECD. Membership in the OECD is only for the privileged (Chavranski 1997: 7). It is symbolic of having achieved the status of 'developed' country. The most consequential obligation of OECD membership is adherence to its Code of Liberalization of Capital Movements. Adherence to the Code is non-negotiable, and its commitments are taken very seriously. Until the Commission's 1988 Directive, the Code of Liberalization was the only multilateral instrument promoting the liberalization of capital movements.

The Code of Liberalization, when established in 1961, excluded short-term capital movements on principle. As noted, the CMIT oversaw amendments to and members' compliance with the Code of Liberalization. On each of the occasions when the Code's obligations were broadened in 1964, 1973 and 1984 to include other types and maturities of financial transactions, members could not reach consensus about the desirability of including short-term capital movements. The French presented the most forceful arguments against such 'hot money'. The CMIT spent the end of the 1980s working towards such a consensus in favor of the liberalization of all capital movements among members. Yet the French eventually joined this consensus, and in 1989 the Code was amended one last time to include all capital movements. The single most influential policy-maker during the CMIT's evolution was Henri Chavranski, Chair of the committee from 1982 until 1994 and a member of the French delegation to the OECD. One of the central but under appreciated stories of globalization is of the Code of Liberalization of Capital Movements, the CMIT, and the convergence of European finance ministers to a worldview that enshrined the freedom of capital movements.

The origins of the Code had much in common with those of the Treaty of Rome. Both documents were founded amidst a profound mistrust of short-term capital movements, or 'hot money'. Thus, according to Raymond Bertrand, a senior official in the OECD Secretariat, the Code's obligations were self-consciously limited to long-term capital flows, particularly foreign direct investment. The Code's omission 'stems from the recognition that short-term financial transactions, in particular those initiated by banks, can pose problems for the management of money and of exchange reserves, especially under fixed or managed exchange rates' (Bertrand 1981: 6).

On each occasion when the CMIT discussed an extension of the Code's obligations to new capital transactions, the Europeans worried about 'hot money'. When the Code was first amended in 1964, the OECD, according to the Secretariat's Pierre Poret, 'took an explicit decision not to extend the scope of the Code to short-term operations on the grounds that their liberaliza- tion would make their balances of payments vulnerable to shifts in market participants' sentiments and compromise the independence of their economic policies' (Poret 1998: 5). Throughout the 1960s the United States urged their OECD colleagues to embrace capital liberalization, and was met with the reluctance, and, in the case of France, outright opposition of the Europeans (Shafer 1995: 123). The 1973 amendment was again quite modest, and included only collective investment services, and in 1984 the Code's jurisdiction of foreign direct investment was amended to include the right of establishment for non-resident investors.

The late 1980s were a period of profound change in the OECD, and the rethinking of finance that marked the Delors Commission also found expression at the OECD. As Henri Chavranski recalls, 'The French position in the OECD had always been to slow down the expansion of the Code of Liberalization. When the French position changed in the middle of the 1980s, the CMIT could begin its work toward a truly liberal Code' (Abdelal 2006: 15). After 40 years of contention in la Muette about short-term capital flows, the CMIT discussions on a new amendment proceeded consensually. According to Chavranski, 'There was no strong opposition to the expansion of the Code. A few countries were reluctant, but there was no big fight. The idea was accepted' (Abdelal 2007: 102). By the late 1980s, the US no longer needed to take the lead in expanding the liberalization obligations of the OECD, and this was true for the Code.

By 1990, then, the institutional foundations of the internationalization of finance among developed countries had been laid. The new rules had been shaped primarily by French policy-makers, both at the EU and OECD levels. The only institutional void in the architecture of globalization was the codification of capital mobility in a truly global organization. While the EU is for the Europeans, the OECD is for the rich, the IMF is for everyone. The Fund's near-universal membership makes its codified rules the legal foundation of the entire international monetary system.

The effort to codify the norm of capital mobility at the Fund was a phenomenon of the mid-1990s. The proposed amendment represented a dramatic reversal. Although the Fund's rules have, since 1944, obliged members to move towards current account convertibility, they have also reserved for members the right to control capital movements: members 'may exercise such controls as are necessary to regulate international capital movements'.[7] The IMF's Articles of Agreement list among the organization's purposes the liberalization of trade, but not of capital.

The proposed amendment emerged within the Fund when Michel Camdessus arrived in Washington as the new Managing Director, a post he held between 1987 and 2000. In late 1993, Camdessus approached Philippe Maystadt, Chairman of the Fund's powerful Interim Committee, with a proposal that the Fund extend its jurisdiction to the capital account (Abdelal 2007: 140). Camdessus worked with Fund management behind the scenes until 1995 when the idea was presented to the Executive Board. The European executive directors embraced the proposal enthusiastically. The amendment had two parts – first, giving the Fund the purpose of capital account liberalization, and second, giving the Fund actual jurisdiction over capital movements. Listing capital account liberalization among the Fund's purposes would allow the organization to include liberalization in the conditions attached to Fund programs. Jurisdiction would mean that the Fund would have the authority to judge members' capital account restrictions as consistent or inconsistent with their obligations as members.

Many Fund critics saw the proposal as the complete codification of liberalism in the international financial system and assumed that Fund management was doing the bidding of the US Treasury, which in turn must have been following the orders of the big banks on Wall Street. But neither was true. As Charles

Dallara, Managing Director of the Institute of International Finance, insists, 'The proposal was by no means a Treasury or Wall Street initiative' (Abdelal 2007: 139). Rather, for Camdessus and Fund management, the amendment would adjust the Fund's authority to a global economy, a world in which capital flows vastly exceeded trade flows. Meanwhile, the view from Wall Street and the Treasury was that the Fund's management was desperately attempting to make the IMF more relevant to globalization. Former Treasury Secretary Lawrence Summers called the proposal 'a bureaucratic imperative'. Dallara saw the Fund attempting to 'enhance its role in the international financial system, to bring it back to the center of the financial universe, where it had not been for some time'. (Abdelal 2007: 141).

The proposal to amend the Fund's Articles almost succeeded. Startled by the financial crisis in Asia, however, a number of developing country directors on the Executive Board opposed the amendment. The possibility of a capital account amendment was destroyed ultimately by the US Congress, when powerful Democrats in the House of Representatives threatened to withhold support for an increase in US contributions to the Fund if the Treasury did not withdraw all US support for the amendment.[8] The US Treasury withdrew its already meager support. Without US support, not to mention a G-7 consensus, no proposal for dramatic change had a chance. With only a few European executive directors still in favor of the proposed amendment, Camdessus and Fund management were left without even the most putatively natural allies of the codification of capital mobility. By 1999 the proposal was completely dead, and it has remained so. Although the rules of the EU and OECD still organize the vast majority of the world's capital flows, the effort by Camdessus and his European colleagues to codify globalization in the rules of a universal organization failed. The US vision of *ad hoc* globalization remains the principle for capital that flows from developed to developing countries, while Europe has organized the rest.

CONCLUSIONS

'Unharnessed globalization', Lamy argued in 2006, 'is an export of American values without going through any negotiation phase. Harnessed globalization is much more consensual.'[9] The G20 meeting in London in April 2009 clearly showed that the rest of the world, starting with Europe, no longer wants to accept this export of American values without counterpart or oversight. The world's financial crisis has revealed the limits of *ad hoc* globalization. Managed globalization, presented publicly as a true alternative, may offer the promise to save the current era of globalization from its excesses and weakening institutional foundations. The doctrine remains useful, even essential, owing to its emphasis on deliberation and co-ordination. Although co-ordination of policy stances is necessary for avoiding the destructive instincts towards closure that inevitably emerge as national economies founder, many of the world's leaders continue to talk past each other in fora, including the G20, that are ill-suited to the task.

Interestingly, at the critical institutional juncture in which the world finds itself in 2010, the French are again present – even ubiquitous – in the very international organizations called upon to rescue and steer globalization. Indeed, these are the very French leaders who invented and pushed forward the doctrine of managed globalization. The G20 meeting, which was called at the insistence of French President Nicolas Sarkozy, was no exception. It has become a forum for countries to vent against the dangers of *ad hoc* globalization and a forum where France (and Germany) can sell the merits of their own vision to other economic powers. Also unexceptional was the usefulness of collecting many of the relevant authorities and insisting that they deliberate together. 'We went faster in six months than in twenty years', claims a French negotiator.

The presence of Frenchmen at the head of so many international organizations (Jean-Claude Trichet at the European Central Bank, Hervé Hannoun at the Bank of International Settlements, Dominique Strauss-Kahn at the IMF and Pascal Lamy at the WTO) has furthered these French and ultimately European ideas about the advantages of deliberation, co-ordination and the codification of rules. 'To reinforce this strategy, Mr. Sarkozy wishes that the current president of the French Financial Markets Authority, Jean-Pierre Jouyet, and the credit mediator, René Ricol, take the helm, respectively, of the International Organization of Securities Commissions and the International Accounting Standards Committees' (Leparmentier 2009a). 'These men are not there by chance. Their concern for multilateralism let them occupy these functions, often judged as not very strategic by their peers. The French are conceptual and cartesian. Their training distinguishes them from Anglo-Saxon pragmatism, which does not work well in these large organizations. It is the revenge of Colbert, ENA, and the Inspection des Finances,' claims Jean-Pierre Jouyet, President of the French Financial Markets Authority. 'France has been statist for an additional generation compared to other countries; elsewhere, people of this caliber are in the private sector,' adds Pascal Lamy (Leparmentier 2009b). Even Sarkozy, whom many Anglo-Saxon analysts had mistakenly labeled a neoliberal during the presidential campaign, has proven to be the epitome of a *dirigiste* leader, and he has been using international fora, such as the 2008 French presidency of the EU and the G20, to push this *dirigiste* agenda at the international level. The November 2009 nomination of Michel Barnier at the helm of internal market and financial services in the second Barroso Commission places one more Frenchman in a key position to attempt to manage globalization in the years to come.

In 2009, it was, as in the mid-1940s, up to people in the public sector to refashion the rules for a private sector preparing itself for an uncertain future, after having left behind a set of financial and business practices that would not soon return. The end of the neoliberal moment has witnessed a pendulum swing towards more rules, more regulations; in a word, more state. The remaining question is whether our era of globalization will survive the process.

The promise of managed globalization as doctrine and practice is to retain the many advantages of our economically interconnected world.

ACKNOWLEDGEMENTS

We would like to thank the participants of the Princeton and Park City workshop, Suzanne Berger, Darren Hawkins, Peter Katzenstein and Alberta Sbragia, for comments on an earlier version of this essay, as well as two anonymous reviewers for their useful suggestions.

NOTES

1 Author's interview with Pascal Lamy, 25 July 2006 and with Matthew Baldwin, 13 June 2006. Matthew Baldwin was Pascal Lamy's Deputy Head of Staff at the European Commission.
2 For an account of the organization of trade in the EU and the WTO, see Meunier 2005. For an account of the organization of finance in the EU, OECD and IMF, see Abdelal 2006, 2007.
3 Author's interview with Lamy; Author's interview with Baldwin.
4 Author's interview with Lamy.
5 Author's interviews with DG Trade officials, June 2007 and April 2009.
6 Article 69 of the Treaty specified this role for the Commission (Padoa-Schioppa 1994: 27).
7 Articles of Agreement of the International Monetary Fund, Article VI, Section 3, 'Controls on Capital Transfers'.
8 Letter to the Honorable Robert E. Rubin, Secretary, Department of the Treasury, from Reps. Richard Gephardt, David Bonior, Nancy Pelosi, Barney Frank, Maxine Waters, and Esteban Edward Torres, 1 May 1998.
9 Author's interview with Lamy.

REFERENCES

Abdelal, R. (2006) 'Writing the rules of global finance: France, Europe, and capital liberalization', *Review of International Political Economy* 13(1): 1–27.
Abdelal, R. (2007) *Capital Rules: The Construction of Global Finance*, Cambridge, MA: Harvard University Press.
Ancelovici, M. (2002) 'Organizing against globalization: the case of ATTAC in France', *Politics & Society* 30(3): 427–63.

Bakker, A. (1996) *The Liberalization of Capital Movements in Europe*, Dordrecht: Kluwer.

Bertrand, R. (1981) 'The liberalization of capital movements – an insight', *Three Banks Review* 132: 3–22.

Birchfield, V. (2005) 'José Bové and the globalisation countermovement in France and beyond: a Polanyian interpretation', *Review of International Studies* 31: 581–98.

Cafruny, A. and Rymer, J.M. (2007) *Europe at Bay: In the Shadow of U.S. Hegemony*, Boulder, CO: Lynne Rienner.

Chavranski, H. (1997) *L'OCDE: Au coeur des grands débats économiques*, Paris: La Documentation francaise.

Devereaux, C., Lawrence, R. and Watkins, M. (2006) *Case Studies in US Trade Negotiation: Making the Rules*, Institute for International Economics, Washington, DC.

Dinan, D. (2004) *Europe Recast*, Basingstoke: Palgrave Macmillan.

Evenett, S. (2007) 'Five hypotheses concerning the fate of the Singapore issues in the Doha round', *Oxford Review of Economic Policy* 23(3): 392–414.

Farrell, M. (2007) 'From EU model to external policy? Promoting regional integration in the rest of the world', in S. Meunier (ed.), *Making History: European Integration and Institutional Change at Fifty*, Oxford: Oxford University Press.

Gordon, P. and Meunier, S. (2001) *The French Challenge: Adapting to Globalization*, Washington, DC: The Brookings Institution Press.

Grieco, J. (1995) 'The Maastricht treaty, Economic and Monetary Union, and the neorealist research program', *Review of International Studies* 21(1): 21–40.

Grieco, J. (1996) 'State interests and international rule trajectories: a neorealist interpretation of the Maastricht Treaty and European Economic and Monetary Union', *Security Studies* 5(3): 176–222.

Hall, P. (1986) *Governing the Economy: The Politics of State Intervention in Britain and France*, New York: Oxford University Press.

Hall, P. (1987) 'The evolution of economic policy under Mitterrand', in G. Ross, S. Hoffmann and S. Malzacher (eds), *The Mitterrand Experiment*, New York: Oxford University Press.

Howse, R. (2003) 'Enhancing WTO legitimacy: constitutionalization or global subsidiarity?', *Governance* 13(1): 73–94.

Jabko, N. (1999) 'In the name of the market: how the European Commission paved the way for monetary union', *Journal of European Public Policy* 6(3): 475–95.

Katzenstein, P. (2005) *A World of Regions*, Ithaca, NY: Cornell University Press.

Lamy, P. (1999) 'Hearings of commissioners-designate', European Parliament, Brussels.

Lamy, P. (2004a) *La democracie monde: pour une autre gouvernance globale*, Paris: Seuil Le République des idées.

Lamy, P. (2004b) *Trade Policy in the Prodi Commission 1999–2004: An Assessment*, Brussels: European Commission.

Leparmentier, A. (2009a) 'G20, OTAN: le pari diplomatique de M. Sarkozy', *Le Monde*, 31 March.

Leparmentier, A. (2009b) 'Les dirigeants français des grandes institutions internationales remis en selle', *Le Monde*, 2 April.

Levy, J. (1999) *Tocqueville's Revenge: State, Society, and Economy in Contemporary France*, Cambridge, MA: Harvard University Press.

Meunier, S. (2003) 'France's double-talk on globalization', *French Politics, Culture and Society* 21(1): 20–34.

Meunier, S. (2005) *Trading Voices: The European Union in International Commercial Negotiations*, Princeton, NJ: Princeton University Press.

Meunier, S. (2006) 'The EU as a conflicted trade power', *Journal of European Public Policy* 13(6): 906–25.

Meunier, S. (2007) 'Managing globalization? The EU in international trade negotiations', *Journal of Common Market Studies* 45(4): 905–26.

Meunier, S. and Nicolaidis, K. (2006) 'The European Union as a conflicted trade
power', *Journal of European Public Policy* 13(6): 906–25.

Moravcsik, A. (1998) *The Choice for Europe*, Ithaca, NY: Cornell University Press.

Orbie, J. (2008) 'The European Union's role in world trade: harnessing globalization',
in J. Orbie (ed.), *Europe's Global Role: External Policies of the European Union*,
Aldershot: Ashgate.

Padoa-Schioppa, T. (1994) *The Road to Monetary Union in Europe: The Emperor, the Kings,
and the Genies*, New York: Oxford University Press.

Parsons, C. (2003) *A Certain Idea of Europe*, Ithaca, NY: Cornell University Press.

Poret, P. (1998) 'The experience of the OECD with the code of liberalization of capital
movements', IMF seminar on Current Legal Issues Affecting Central Banks.

Ross, G. (1995) *Jacques Delors and European Integration*, Oxford: Oxford University
Press.

Sandholtz, W. (1993) 'Choosing union: monetary politics and Maastricht', *International
Organization* 47(1): 1–39.

Sbragia, A. (2010) 'The EU, the US, and trade policy: competitive interdependence in
the management of globalization', *Journal of European Public Policy* 17(3): 368–82.

Shafer, J. (1995) 'Experience with controls on international capital movements in
OECD countries: solution or problem for monetary policy?', in S. Edwards (ed.),
Capital Controls, Exchange Rates, and Monetary Policy in the World Economy,
Cambridge: Cambridge University Press.

Védrine, H. (2001) *France in an Age of Globalization*, Washington, DC: The Brookings
Institution Press.

Woolcock, S. (2003) 'The Singapore issues in Cancun: a failed negotiation ploy or a
litmus test for global governance?', *Intereconomics* 38(5): 249–55.

The EU, the US, and trade policy: competitive interdependence in the management of globalization

Alberta Sbragia

ABSTRACT   Competitive interdependence characterizes the EU–US relationship *vis-à-vis* third markets. Each defines success in relation to the other while each also views the other as its key geo-economic competitor in the world economy. CI has developed as the EU has attempted to manage globalization in the field of trade policy by focusing on the multilateral level and then by reversing course and privileging the regional, which in turn has expanded the EU's territorial influence. The reversal occurred largely because the Bush Administration in Washington pursued free trade agreements (FTAs) in a process of 'competitive liberalization'. The US outflanked the EU by negotiating FTAs that favored US firms in third markets. The EU, to protect its own firms, then began to negotiate FTAs itself. Geo-economic competition between the EU and the US is thus key to shaping EU trade policy.

INTRODUCTION

Within the global economy, the European Union (EU)[1] and the United States (US) are engaged in a form of structural competition in which each uses bilateral, regional and multilateral agreements to protect and advance their respective economic interests. Globalization has made such competition more complicated. The EU, for its part, has attempted to manage globalization by combining liberalization with 'formal and informal practices to bind market players and their governments' (Jacoby and Meunier 2010). But in trade policy the EU has found its options limited. European traders and investors must operate within a competitive environment shaped by US as well as EU trade policies.

Free trade agreements (FTAs) negotiated by the US can disadvantage European traders and investors in third markets unless the EU protects them by negotiating its own corresponding FTAs. When EU Trade Commissioner Pascal Lamy's approach towards managed globalization downgraded FTAs in favor of multilateralism (Meunier 2007), the EU risked losing privileged access to markets covered by US FTAs. Similarly, the empowering of international institutions, the World Trade Organization (WTO) in particular, does not guarantee that the EU will be able to pursue its own interests. Competitors can use such institutions to restrain the EU just as easily as the EU can use them to advance its own economic interests.

The EU and the US are simultaneously competitors and interdependent because, to a significant degree, each defines success *vis-à-vis* each other. Market access granted to one typically provokes the other to seek similar access. Since both parties have substantial economic interests and diplomatic power, they find themselves in a structural relationship of competitive interdependence (CI).

That relationship became noticeable in the 1995 to 2009 period. Since both the EU and the US have major stakes in third markets, neither can afford to ignore the other's inroads into such markets. Competition between US and EU firms for access to those markets, indeed, underpins much of the external politics of trade in both the US and the EU, and that structural competition represents an important driver of trade policy in both.

The EU and the US are analyzed here as geo-economic actors each interested in maximizing its geo-economic power and in using 'trade policy as a strategic instrument to enhance its international power *vis-à-vis* other states' (Zimmerman 2007: 817). They pursue this strategy by using international institutions which provide opportunities to constrain competitors. Both parties also try to expand their territorial reach by negotiating FTAs that establish advantageous rules of trade. The implication is that, rather than emphasizing the domestic and intra-institutional politics of trade policy (as existing literature does), scholars should consider how 'positional competition' between the EU and the US shapes the trade policies of both (Zimmerman 2007: 817; see also Aggarwal and Fogarty 2004: 13; Hirschman 1980).

EU AND US STRATEGIES

The EU's trade strategy has gone through two phases. Managed globalization, pursued by Trade Commissioner Lamy (1999-2004), privileged the multilateral level over the bilateral or the regional. It viewed the WTO as particularly central. Multilateralism trumped its competitors (Meunier 2007; Abdelal and Meunier, this issue). The WTO constitutes 'a central site for global governance' (Schaffer 2005: 130) and is an arena in which the EU (along with the US) has been able to exert disproportionate power. Ideally, it could permit the EU to temper the negative effects of globalization.

The EU, under the rubric of managed globalization, and the US, under the aegis of 'competitive liberalization', formulated alternative conceptions of global governance in the area of trade policy. The EU was trying to temper, shape and channel the process of economic liberalization so as to cushion its impact on society. The US, by contrast, favored market-driven outcomes and focused on opening markets by removing barriers to the movement of goods, services and capital.

Competitive liberalization of foreign markets represented the US response to Lamy's managed globalization strategy. Rather than privileging the WTO as a regulator of globalization, the US prioritized FTAs as instruments to accelerate the pace of economic liberalization both regionally and multilaterally (Woolcock 2008). Lamy's refusal to initiate new FTAs contrasted sharply with the almost frenetic pace at which the US pursued them – a difference that reflected sharply different approaches to globalization.

The expansive FTAs negotiated by the Bush Administration both benefited US firms and established a template for future agreements. Further, Lamy's simultaneous pursuit of managed globalization permitted the US to make gains in market access without a corresponding European gain. The US adoption of an FTA strategy indeed changed the negotiating landscape.

In 2006, however, the EU tried to regain lost ground by changing its trade strategy. The Commission's publication of *Global Europe: Competing in the World* (Commission 2006) symbolized a new era in EU trade policy and revealed the EU's new geo-economic ambitions. First implemented by negotiating FTAS with trading partners in both Asia and Latin America, the new EU strategy exemplified the type of competitive interdependence now characteristic of the EU–US relationship in third markets. By 2009, the EU had become willing to negotiate FTAs even with OECD countries such as Canada, once viewed as off-limits.

MECHANISMS UNDERLYING COMPETITIVE INTERDEPENDENCE

Competitive interdependence entails both the extension of territorial influence through FTAs and using the authority of the WTO. These two mechanisms – identified by Jacoby and Meunier (2010) as implementing the EU's management of globalization – are used by both the US and the EU in response to each other's initiatives. Given that competitive interdependence characterizes US–EU trade policy, it is not surprising that both parties would use the same mechanisms to further their own views of globalization. But the convergence occurred mostly after 2006, by which time the Bush Administration already had five years' experience of negotiating FTAs. The territorial spread of US and EU trade agreements indicates that states seeking access to the largest markets now accept the economic models and rules favored by the strong.

Both the US and the EU had previously used the WTO to pursue their interests while trying to constrain the other. However, the EU's use of the WTO to implement managed globalization did not stop the US using it to defend its own interests and to challenge those of the EU. Once institutions are in place, they cannot be monopolized by one actor and may be used for a variety of goals. Institutional rules can restrict either party. The competitive interdependence that binds the US and the EU rests on both the WTO and FTAs. Both parties use the WTO to constrain the other while trying to expand their influence through the use of WTO-compliant trade agreements. Since both are key players in international trade, the opportunity structure of each is shaped by a structure created and changed by both.

Competitive interdependence has developed over time. In phase one, the EU challenged the US in General Agreement on Trade and Tariffs (GATT) negotiations while spreading its territorial influence through enlargement and constructing a special relationship with most former European colonies. In phase two, the US used the WTO to force the EU to reshape that special relationship while simultaneously extending its own territorial influence. In phase 3, the EU has begun to once again extend its influence, this time in Latin America and Asia. The remainder of this essay examines how the EU and the US have interacted while implementing their strategy of working simultaneously within the WTO and extending their territorial influence outside it.

THE EUROPEAN UNION AS A GLOBAL ACTOR WITHIN THE MULTILATERAL SYSTEM

The Treaty of Rome empowered the EU to operate as a unitary actor within the GATT with the European Commission (at least formally) acting as the sole negotiator. The Six accepted a unitary trade policy partially because they wished to increase their effectiveness within the GATT. The Commission, for its part, supported the participation of the Six in the Kennedy Round because it wished to strengthen its position as the EU's negotiator in the face of reluctance on the part of the member states to allow the Commission to play that role (Winham 1986: 318; Johnson 1998; Coppolaro 2006).

The EU (along with the US) has played a key role in delaying, launching and closing multilateral trade rounds. It did not initially support the Uruguay Round of trade negotiations – strongly backed by the US – and had to be convinced to support it before the Round could be initiated (Davis 2003: 274; Meunier 2000; Paemen and Bensch 1995: 32–6; Woolcock and Hodges 1996: 305–6). By contrast, the EU strongly supported – in contrast to a reluctant US – the launch of the failed Millennium Round (Commission 1999; Council 1999: 13) and the subsequent Doha Round of negotiations (Kerremans 2005).

The EU and the US, when collaborating, were able to wield enormous power during the Uruguay Round. The two 'agreed in October 1990 to use their market power to close the Uruguay Round on terms they favored' (Barton *et al.* 2006: 65–6). Not surprisingly, most states decided to join the WTO to ensure that the two largest markets in the world would not exclude them from the benefits of the Most Favored Nation (MFN) guarantee.

In the post-Uruguay period, the EU strongly supported both multilateral negotiations and the WTO, the institution to which EU trade officials have devoted most of their attention (Evenett 2007: 20). Such attention to the WTO has also been encouraged by the fact that, in Lamy's words, 'the WTO has too often been the sole focus for efforts to strengthen international governance' due to a lack of 'suitable multilateral reference point[s]' in other issue areas (Commission 2004: 5). Not surprisingly, Kerremans (2004: 371) argues that 'the idea of a new round of multilateral trade negotiations – the first one in the World Trade Organization – is largely a European one'.

EXPANDED TERRITORIAL INFLUENCE

The EU has also been very successful in extending the territorial range of its influence. Most notably, the Six gradually enlarged to the EU-27 (Jacoby 2004; Kelley 2004; Vachudova 2005). Such enlargement, while burdening the EU in some respects, allowed it to exercise greater geo-economic and geo-regulatory power (Damro 2006; Young and Peterson 2006). The EU–Turkey customs union (which excludes agriculture) came into force in 1996 and again added to the EU's territorial reach. The EU, however, has also expanded its territorial influence outside the European continent. Such influence shapes the opportunities and constraints faced by EU exporters, multinational firms and third party exporters desiring to penetrate the EU market.

The instruments used by the EU to expand its influence beyond Europe have included development aid (Holland 2008), conditionality (Lister and Carbone 2006), association agreements, free trade agreements, and inter-regional dialogue, including political dialogue. Former British and French colonies were organized into the African-Caribbean-Pacific 'region' (only recognized as such by the EU), and the various Lomé Conventions allowed the EU to institutionalize EU–ACP relations (Carbone 2007). For decades, the ACP grouping has represented a key link for the EU with the developing world (Holland 2002). However, over time EU interest in the ACP relationship waned (Crawford 2004; Ravenhill 2004: 126).

In the mid-1990s, the EU began to negotiate with non-ACP states. In 1995, the EU signed the EU–Mercosur Framework Agreement as well as the EU–Israel Association Agreement. The following year, an agreement was signed with Chile, in 1997 with Mexico, in 1999 with South Africa (Dur 2007; Frennhoff-Larsen 2007; Sanabuja 2000; Szymanski and Smith 2005). These agreements were largely negotiated in response to the North American Free Trade Agreement (NAFTA) and the Clinton Administration's proposed Free Trade Area of the Americas (FTAA) (Defraigne 2002). They were intended to extend the EU's influence as a counterpoint to the US strategy of reshaping economic geography.

Beginning in 1997, however, the EU stopped pursuing new free trade agreements. Once the WTO had been created in 1995, some EU members viewed bilateral free trade agreements as a threat to the newly institutionalized multilateral system. Lamy was so personally committed to multilateralism that he did not initiate new free trade agreements – although those already in progress were allowed to move forward (Defraigne 2002; Evenett 2007; Lamy 2002; Meunier 2007).[2]

THE UNITED STATES RESPONDS

The American response to the EU's policies and power has included actions at both the multilateral and regional levels. The GATT and subsequently the WTO have provided the US with a forum within which to challenge the EU, though often with mixed results. The US also found that WTO-compliant regional and bilateral responses were quite effective in extending the sphere of American influence. We discuss each of these responses in turn.

The US challenges the EU: multilalteral responses

The six founding members of the EU changed the structure of the global trading system of that era by adopting a common external tariff and by developing a Common Agricultural Policy (CAP). The United States was forced to respond. In the area of trade policy, therefore, the multilateral institution of GATT trade rounds and later the WTO have been crucial for both the US and the EU. Arguably, the importance of the GATT Rounds was that they represented a key mechanism by which the US and the EU could try to 'manage' each other.

The 1960–61 GATT conference (Dillon Round) was primarily concerned with addressing the consequences of European economic integration for exporters to the markets of the Six, with special concern being expressed by agricultural exporters (Swinbank and Tanner 1996). The United States was so concerned about the future shape of the CAP that during the Round the Kennedy Administration 'requested a "semi-seat" at the Community table' so that the US would be consulted as the CAP was being planned (Devuyst 2008: 97).

In 1962, President Kennedy, in calling for what came to be known as the Kennedy Round, identified the expansion of the European Common Market as one of the five new challenges which had made 'obsolete [America's] traditional trade policy' (cited in Metzger 1964: 1). The US, in fact, changed its negotiating strategy so as to more effectively negotiate with Brussels (Bauer et al. 1972: 74; Evans 1971). Kennedy hoped that trade liberalization would expand American exports to Europe's growing economies. It quickly became clear, however, that agriculture would, as feared, present a major stumbling block, and that 'the United States might eventually have to settle for a bad deal in agriculture to get the type of industrial agreement that would be in the American interest' (Schwartz 2003: 37). President Johnson decided to take agriculture off the table, but it would remain a very contentious issue.

While extremely disappointed by the CAP, the US continued to support European integration. It supported the Commission's role as the sole negotiator during the 'empty chair crisis' in spite of the GATT Director General's proposal that the Six negotiate as individual states. The US supported the position that 'the Kennedy Round had to be negotiated by the Community, represented by the Commission' (Coppolaro 2006: 229). Given the reluctance of the member states to allow the Commission to act as sole negotiator, American support for the Commission's role was significant.

From the Kennedy Round on, the US and the EU negotiated at the multilateral level. It was there that they negotiated as equals, and it was there that they came into conflict. The Tokyo Round (1973–79) announced the arrival of an international economic system 'principally managed by a US/EC partnership'

(Winham 1986: 11). Launching the Uruguay Round was initially supported by the US while opposed by the EU (Davis 2003: 272–4; Meunier 2000: 122). After the Round was launched, the US made it clear that it would choose to kill the Round rather than accept the kinds of agricultural reforms it had accepted in the Tokyo Round (Davis 2003: 286). Agriculture was indeed addressed in the Uruguay Round, although agreement was not finalized until the Blair House Agreement was modified so as to render it acceptable to France (Meunier 2000: 121–6). The Uruguay Round led to the establishment of the WTO, which, in turn, was used by the US to challenge the EU's long-standing preferential trade relationships with the ACP countries. The US thereby used an institution supported by the EU to arrive at a decision which forced the EU to change a long-held policy.

The EU–ACP relationship

The EU's single market program had led (after intense intra-EU conflict) to the unification of what had previously been a disparate nationally based approach to the market for bananas. When a new EU-wide framework was put in place in 1993, it violated WTO rules because it did not treat all developing countries' imports equally as required. Bananas from ACP countries received privileged access to the EU market *vis-à-vis* bananas from Latin American producers (Grynberg 1998: 6–7; Alter and Meunier 2006). Complaints to the GATT from the Latin American states were blocked by the EU, a permissible strategy under GATT rules.

However, when the WTO was established as agreed in the Uruguay Round, the weak GATT dispute settlement procedure was replaced by a much more authoritative procedure. At that point, the US (defending the interests of the US company Chiquita Brands) joined the legal battle. After a complicated set of legal maneuvers, the US and the Latin American producers won, and the EU was forced to begin dismantling the banana regime that privileged ACP producers (O'Connor 2004; Alter and Meunier 2006). The WTO, which the EU had so strongly supported, could clearly be used to constrain the EU itself.

The decision was instrumental in leading the EU to acknowledge that the preferential relationships represented by the Lomé Conventions had to be modified. The US had long viewed the non-reciprocal preferences which lay at the core of the EU–ACP relationship as violating the MFN principle that was so central to the GATT/WTO. The Cotonou Agreement, which replaced the Lomé Conventions, essentially accepted that development goals and trade liberalization *à la* WTO were indeed compatible.

Non-reciprocal preferences were no longer legitimate; preferential trade relations with selected developing countries were no longer acceptable. They were to be replaced by EU–ACP trade liberalization as well as development assistance funds (Michel 2008). As a result, the Commission began the arduous task of developing the WTO-compliant Economic Partnership Agreements (EPAs) which were to integrate the ACP states into the world economy.

EPAs were to be finalized with six 'regions' by 31 December 2007, the date when the waiver from MFN granted by the 2001 Doha Ministerial Conference was to expire (Thallinger 2007: 501).

The EU, by attempting to establish EPAs that involved 'regions', sought to be WTO compliant by using Article XXIV as its guide (Curran *et al.* 2008). However, the storm of criticism that it has faced from both civil society groups and national parliamentarians has demonstrated how difficult it is to mix development with trade (Mombrial 2008). Although negotiations began in September 2002, only 35 countries had initialed an EPA by the deadline of 31 December 2007. By that date, only one region – composed of the CARICOM states plus the Dominican Republic – had initialed a full EPA, which it subsequently signed in October 2008. The other countries initialed an 'interim' agreement, which included only trade in goods and excluded far more controversial areas such as services and investment. It is unlikely that those will be finalized soon. At the end of 2008, for example, only two of the 14 states making up the 'Pacific region' had signed provisional agreements.

Although the move from the Lomé Convention to a WTO-compliant EU–ACP relationship was strongly supported by those member states traditionally hostile to the ACP's non-reciprocal preferences, WTO decisions provided the trigger for the overhaul of the relationship. The US's role in the process represented a continuation of its previously unsuccessful efforts in GATT rounds to force the EU to transform the EU–ACP relationship by making it GATT compatible. Although the US and the EU had collectively given birth to the WTO, the US was not reluctant to use its power against the EU.

The US challenges the EU again: North American regionalism

American regionalism posed a particularly effective challenge to the EU. Partially in response to both the Uruguay Round's very difficult negotiations and the EU's '1992' single market program, the US negotiated NAFTA. The US joined Canada and Mexico in the largest regional trading bloc outside of the EU itself. The US had decided to extend its own sphere of influence by negotiating an expansive regional trade agreement encompassing trade in goods and services, investment, and intellectual property rights.

NAFTA represented the emergence of the US as a 'regional' power, one that was willing to use a far-reaching trade agreement to liberalize trade in North America. NAFTA bound the US, Canada and Mexico into a new form of economic regionalism, one that brought together members of both the developing and the industrialized world. Coming into force in 1994, it has been described as 'among the postwar period's most consequential and far-reaching international developments' within the field of global economic relations (Gruber 2001: 705). It marked the first time the US had definitively shown its acceptance of regionalism rather than maintaining its traditional loyalty to multilateralism (Sbragia 2007). In the tug of war between regionalism and multilateralism (Sbragia 2008), NAFTA struck a strong blow for economic regionalism.

In the pre-NAFTA period, the US had chosen only multilateralism to pursue liberalization while choosing a bilateral approach to pursue trade restrictions. In the post-NAFTA period, by contrast, the US negotiated a series of trade agreements with Latin and Central American states, Australia, Singapore, Jordan, and most recently South Korea. NAFTA, therefore, represented a key break in the US strategy of pursuing the liberalization of trade primarily through multilateral negotiations. Furthermore, NAFTA signaled the arrival of a 'WTO plus' very expansive form of regionalism. The incorporation of intellectual property rights and investment protection in a free trade area represented a milestone in the shaping of the international trading system. NAFTA, in brief, forced all trading states to eventually rethink their trade strategies. The EU was no exception.

As the EU moved towards enlargement to the East as well as initiating negotiations in Latin America, the US indicated that it wished to negotiate a Free Trade Area of the Americas (FTAA). Such an agreement would have represented a major challenge for the EU, for whom Latin America is a major export market (Hall 1998). However, the Clinton Administration was unable to obtain negotiating authority, and the effort to extend the American sphere of influence had to wait for the Bush Administration. Nonetheless, as the EU became more important globally, the US executive reacted by seeking to expand US influence in Latin America.

The Bush Doctrine: competitive liberalization

The Bush Administration successfully negotiated a relatively large number of free trade agreements: Chile (approved by Congress in 2003), Central America and the Dominican Republic (CAFTA) (approved by Congress in 2005), and Peru (approved by the then Democratically controlled Congress in December 2007 after changing provisions related to labor, the environment and access to medicines). Agreements were also finalized with Colombia in November 2006, Panama in December 2006 and South Korea in April 2007. The (very controversial) South Korean agreement, if implemented, would be the most important trade agreement since NAFTA (Cooper and Manyin 2007: 1). All three agreements, however, have run into stiff opposition in the Democratically controlled Congress, and as of February 2010 had not been approved.

The negotiations in Latin America and Asia provided the substance for a trade policy strategy known as 'competitive liberalization', articulated by Robert Zoellick, the United States Trade Representative in the Bush Administration's first term. Essentially, the US began negotiating very expansive (WTO plus) bilateral free trade agreements with those states eager to gain access to the US market. Such agreements would encourage 'the adoption abroad of US-style market-friendly business laws and regulations, or at least the adoption of regulations that US businesses can accommodate more easily' (Evenett and Meier 2008: 31). The Bush Administration hoped that such an approach would trigger a dynamic which would encourage other states to seek bilateral agreements with the US as well as move towards a multilateral agreement in the Doha Round (Evenett and Meier 2008).

The strategy of 'competitive liberalization' represented a clear-cut example of the Bush Administration's interest in enlarging the sphere of US influence. While the Clinton Administration had used some elements of the strategy so as to raise the likelihood of obtaining a multilateral agreement (Steinberg 1998: 4), the Bush Administration implemented the strategy in such a way that bilateral trade agreements increased rapidly. Zoellick was driven by a sense that the US had been 'falling behind the rest of the world in pursuing trade agreements' (Zoellick 2002), and the zeal with which the US pursued bilateral free trade (as well as competition and investment) agreements was directed at making up for lost time.

THE EU REACTS TO THE US CHALLENGE

NAFTA presented a serious regional challenge to the EU as it expanded American influence by using regionalism rather than multilateralism. It triggered the reshaping of the transatlantic relationship, one in which the EU – rather than dealing with the Americas exclusively at the multilateral level – began to develop bilateral relations with Mexico and Chile and 'interregional' relations with Mercosur and the six Central American states. The Americas would become a central focus for both the US and the EU; the two became rival suitors. The EU courted Mexico, Chile and Mercosur while the Clinton Administration pursued an 'all-Americas' strategy by trying to obtain 'fast-track' authority from Congress so as to negotiate a hemispheric free trade area, eventually to be known as FTAA.

The EU's response to NAFTA was clear-cut. Pierre Defraigne, Deputy Director-General in the Commission's Directorate-General for Trade, stated the dynamic clearly: 'In order not to be evicted from the NAFTA market, the EU immediately started a FTA negotiation with Mexico' (Defraigne 2002: 7). In May 1995, the EU began negotiating the EU–Mexico Global Agreement, its first transatlantic free trade agreement. The Commission's website (http://ec.europa.eu/trade/issues/bilateral/countries/mexico/ftapr_en.htm) makes explicit comparisons with NAFTA, since the US is the EU's major competitor in both trade and investment in Mexico.

In November 1999, the EU began negotiating a FTA with Mercosur (a regional customs union in the making created by Brazil, Argentina, Paraguay and Uruguay). In 2000, negotiations began with Chile, which had been expected to join NAFTA but was kept from doing so by President Clinton's lack of negotiating authority. In fact, due to that lack, the US was unable to initiate FTAA negotiations, as well as those with Chile. This respite allowed the EU to 'catch up' by finalizing the agreement with Mexico, negotiating a FTA with Chile, and initiating negotiations with Mercosur in November 1999. However, the Commission under Lamy did not use the time to move aggressively in the rest of Latin America. The EU was therefore not playing a leadership role in Latin America's commercial diplomacy.

However, the election of George W. Bush as President, coupled with the Republican control of the House and Senate, ended the EU's respite and initiated a period in which the US moved very quickly to begin negotiations for the FTAA as well as with Chile and Central America. The EU and the US have both failed to successfully negotiate with Brazil and Mercosur, both of which offer the most important markets in Latin America. In fact, the US began negotiating with individual Latin American states owing to Mercosur's resistance to the US agenda during the FTAA negotiations. Mercosur refused to accept the US position that FTAA negotiations should only be conducted bilaterally – that is, Mercosur could not act as a unitary negotiator. Furthermore, the US and Mercosur (read Brazil) could not agree on agricultural liberalization, and many observers concluded that progress would only be made after the Doha Round's successful conclusion.

The EU, for its part, has been negotiating with Mercosur since November 1999 with no end currently in sight. It has insisted on an 'interregional' relationship, negotiating with Mercosur only as a regional grouping and resisting any suggestion of negotiating with individual Mercosur members. However, it did designate Brazil a 'strategic partner' in 2007, thereby introducing some doubt as to its longer term commitment to interregionalism. Thus, both the EU and the US negotiations with Mercosur are stalled, as neither party is able to accept Brazil's demands for agricultural liberalization. The FTAA is considered dead, and the EU faces the prospect of perhaps fruitless negotiations unless an agreement on agricultural liberalization is reached in the Doha Round.

The EU, therefore, has turned its attention to Central America and to the Andean Community. In 2006, the six Central American states (which have negotiated an agreement with the US) and the EU began negotiating an association and free trade agreement which they hoped to sign by 2010. However, the EU–Andean Community negotiations, initiated in June 2007, have not gone as smoothly as those of their Central American neighbors. In fact, in November 2008, the EU abandoned its insistence on a 'region-to-region' negotiation and decided to negotiate with Columbia and Peru (Peru already has an FTA with the US).

Furthermore, the EU has turned to Asia. The EU's negotiators have been absent there until recently, while those from the US have been very visible. The competition between the US and the EU, in fact, has become quite intense in Asia. Whereas the US concluded a free trade agreement with South Korea, in 2007 the EU began negotiating free trade agreements with India, the ASEAN (Association of Southeast Asian Nations) bloc of ten Southeast Asian States (with the EU currently exploring some version of 'variable geometry' in the negotiations), and with South Korea.

Given the difficulties the US–South Korea trade agreement faced in Washington in 2008–09, coupled with the lack of ongoing US–India and US–ASEAN free trade negotiations, it may well be that the EU will outpace the US in trade liberalization in Asia. The implications of an EU–India FTA are particularly significant for the US, especially since agriculture will not be on the negotiating table. The concern with which American multinationals are following the EU–India negotiations was well expressed by Wal-Mart's director of international corporate affairs. In her words, 'if Carrefour gets better access to the Indian market than Wal-Mart, there will be hell to pay' (Stokes 2008: 26). Whereas the EU has been a 'follower' in extending its influence to Latin America, it may emerge as a 'leader' in Asia.

In the trade arena, the process of enlarging the EU's territorial sphere of influence in competition with the US is not static. The EU may appear to be a 'follower' at one point in time but may transform itself into a 'leader' in a subsequent period. Competitive interdependence incorporates an inbuilt dynamic in which the US and the EU necessarily compete, whether at the multilateral or regional level or both. They cannot ignore each other for long periods of time – the cost to them would be too high. That same dynamic furthers globalization as well as the attempt to manage – and to profit from – that same globalization.

CONCLUSION

Given the structure of the multilateral system in trade, the advantages that can be gained from negotiating free trade agreements, and the competitive interdependence that exists between the EU and the US, the process of globalization in the field of trade policy has an inbuilt dynamic. Conceptualizing the EU and the US as operating interdependently while acting as geo-economic competitors helps explain why the attempt to manage globalization actually stimulates and nourishes it. In fact, globalization would be much easier to regulate and channel if the EU were the only key actor. However, the role of the US changes the calculations of what 'managing' globalization actually means. In the field of trade policy, competitive interdependence shapes both strategies and outcomes. The EU's trade strategy in the context of globalization needs to be conceptualized and analyzed as intersecting with that of the US – its key geo-economic competitor.

ACKNOWLEDGEMENTS

The author would like to thank Suzanne Berger, Maurizio Carbone, Chad Damro, Martin Holland, Wade Jacoby, Sophie Meunier, Martin Rhodes,

Yen-Pin Su, Martin Staniland, Pascaline Winand and Alasdair Young, the participants in the Park City workshop, and the journal's referees who all gave me valuable help.

NOTES

1 For the sake of convenience, the term European Union (EU) will be used throughout the text.
2 Lamy did allow authorized regional trade negotiations such as the EU–Mercosur negotiations, launched in 2000, to proceed. The Lamy approach to managed globalization in the field of trade was thus clearer conceptually than in practice.

REFERENCES

Abdelal, R. and Meunier, S. (2010) 'Managed globalization: doctrine, practice and promise', *Journal of European Public Policy* 17(3): 349–66.
Aggarwal, V. and Fogarty, E. (2004) 'Between regionalism and globalism: European Union interregional trade strategies', in V. Aggarwal and E. Fogarty (eds), *EU Trade Strategies: Between Regionalism and Globalism*, New York: Palgrave Macmillan.
Alter, K. and Meunier, S. (2006) 'Nested and overlapping regimes in the transatlantic banana trade dispute', *Journal of European Public Policy* 13(3): 362–82.
Barton, J., Goldstein, J., Josling, T. and Steinberg, R. (2006) *The Evolution of the Trade Regime: Politics, Law, and Economics of the GATT and the WTO*, Princeton, NJ: Princeton University Press.
Bauer, R., De Sola Pool, I. and Dexter, L. (1972) *American Business & Public Policy: The Politics of Foreign Trade*, Chicago, IL: Aldine-Atheron.
Carbone, M. (2007) *The European Union and International Development: The Politics of Foreign Aid*, London: Routledge.
Commission (1999) *The EU approach to the Millennium Round*, COM 331 Final, Brussels: European Commission.
Commission (2004) *Trade Policy in the Prodi Commission 1999–2004: An Assessment*, Brussels: European Commission.
Commission (2006) *Global Europe: Competing in the World. A Contribution to the EU's Growth and Jobs Strategy*, COM 567, Brussels: European Commission.
Cooper, W. and Manyin, M. (2007) 'The proposed South Korea–U.S. free trade agreement (KORUS FTA)', *CRS Report for Congress RL33435*, Washington, DC: Congressional Research Service.
Coppolaro, L. (2006) 'The empty chair crisis and the Kennedy Round of GATT negotiations (1962–67)', in J. Palayret, H. Wallace and P. Winand (eds), *Visions, Votes and Vetoes: The Empty Chair Crisis and the Luxembourg Compromise Forty Years On*, Brussels: P.I.E.-Peter Lang.
Council (1999) *Presidency Conclusions, Cologne European Council, 3– 4 June 1999*, SN 150/99.
Crawford, B. (2004) 'Why the euro–med partnership? European Union strategies in the Mediterranean region', in V. Aggarwal and E. Fogarty (eds), *EU Trade Strategies: Between Regionalism and Globalism*, New York: Palgrave Macmillan.
Curran, L., Nilsson, L. and Brew, D. (2008) 'The economic partnership agreements: rationale, misperceptions and non-trade aspects', *Development Policy Review* 26(5): 529–53.
Damro, C. (2006) *Cooperating on Competition in Transatlantic Economic Relations: The Politics of Dispute Prevention*, New York: Palgrave Macmillan.

Davis, C. (2003) *Food Fights over Free Trade: How International Institutions Promote Agricultural Trade Liberalization*, Princeton, NJ: Princeton University Press.

Defraigne, P. (2002) 'New regionalism and global economic governance', UNI/CRIS, Bruges, e-Working Papers W-2002/2.

Devuyst, Y. (2008) 'Is Washington ready for the "equal partnership"? Kennedy's legacy for transatlantic relations', *Studia Diplomatica: The Brussels Journal of International Relations* 61(3): 91–109.

Dur, A. (2007) 'EU trade policy as protection for exporters', *Journal of Common Market Studies* 45(4): 833–56.

Evans, J. (1971) *The Kennedy Round in American Trade Policy: The Twilight of the GATT?*, Cambridge, MA: Harvard University Press.

Evenett, S. (2007) 'The trade strategy of the European Union: time for a rethink?', *Discussion Paper Series No. 6283*, London: Centre for Economic Policy Research.

Evenett, S. and Meier, M. (2008) 'An interim assessment of the US trade policy of "competitive liberalization"', *The World Economy* 31(1): 31–65.

Frennhoff-Larsen, M. (2007) 'Trade negotiations between the EU and South Africa', *Journal of Common Market Studies* 45(4): 857–88.

Gruber, L. (2001) 'Power politics and the free trade bandwagon', *Comparative Political Studies* 34(7): 703–41.

Grynberg, R. (1998) 'The WTO incompatibility of the Lome Convention trade provisions', *Asia Pacific School of Economics and Management Working Papers 98/3*, available at: http://dspace.anu.edu.au/bitstream/1885/40346/1/sp98-3.pdf.

Hall, K. (1998) 'As interest wanes, negotiators meet to invigorate trade talks', *Journal of Commerce*, 2 December.

Hirschman, A. (1980) *National Power and the Structure of Foreign Trade*, Berkeley: University of California Press.

Holland, M. (2002) *The European Union and the Third World*, New York: Palgrave.

Holland, M. (2008) 'The EU and the global development agenda', *Journal of European Integration* 30(3): 343–62.

Jacoby, W. (2004) *The Enlargement of the European Union and NATO: Ordering from the Menu in Central Europe*, Cambridge: Cambridge University Press.

Jacoby, W. and Meunier, S. (2010) 'Europe and the management of globalization', *Journal of European Public Policy* 17(3): 299–317.

Johnson, M. (1998) *European Community Trade Policy and the Article 113 Committee*, London: Royal Institute of International Affairs.

Kelley, J. (2004) *Ethnic Politics in Europe: The Power of Norms and Incentives*, Princeton, NJ: Princeton University Press.

Kerremans, B. (2004) 'What went wrong in Cancun? A principal–agent view on the EU's rationale towards the Doha Development Round', *European Foreign Affairs Review* 9(3): 363–93.

Kerremans, B. (2005) 'Managing the agenda – the EU's rationale for a new round of trade negotiations', *German Foreign Policy in Dialogue* 6(15): 29–34.

Lamy, P. (2002) 'Stepping stones or stumbling blocks? The EU's approach towards the problem of multilateralism vs regionalism in trade policy', *The World Economy* 25(10): 1399–413.

Lister, M. and Carbone, M. (eds) (2006) *New Pathways in International Development: Gender and Civil Society in EU Policy*, Aldershot: Ashgate.

Metzger, S. (1964) *Trade Agreements and the Kennedy Round*, Fairfax, VA: Coiner Publications.

Meunier, S. (2000) 'What single voice? European institutions and EU–U.S. trade negotiations', *International Organization* 54(1): 103–35.

Meunier, S. (2007) 'Managing globalization? The EU in international trade negotiations', *Journal of Common Market Studies* 45(4): 905–26.

Michel, L. (2008) *Economic Partnership Agreements: Drivers of Development*, Brussels: European Commission.

Mombrial, N. (2008) 'What if politics finally got involved with world affairs? The Taubira report on EPAs', *Trade Negotiations Insights* 7(6): 1–2.

O'Connor, B. (2004) 'Remedies in the world trade organization dispute settlement system – the bananas and hormones cases', *Journal of World Trade* 38(2): 245–66.

Paemen, H. and Bensch, A. (1995) *From the GATT to the WTO: The European Community in the Uruguay Round*, Leuven: Leuven University Press.

Ravenhill, J. (2004) 'Back to the nest? Europe's relations with the African, Caribbean and Pacific group of countries', in V. Aggarwal and E. Fogarty (eds), *EU Trade Strategies: Between Regionalism and Globalism*, New York: Palgrave Macmillan, pp. 118–47.

Sanabuja, J. (2000) 'Trade, politics, and democratization: the 1997 Global Agreement between the European Union and Mexico', *Journal of Interamerican Studies and World Affairs* 42(2): 35–62.

Sbragia, A. (2007) 'European Union and NAFTA', in M. Telo (ed.), *European Union and New Regionalism: Regional Actors and Global Governance in a Post-Hegemonic Era*, Aldershot: Ashgate.

Sbragia, A. (2008) 'Review article: comparative regionalism: what might it be?' *Journal of Common Market Studies* 46(s1): 29–50.

Schaffer, G. (2005) 'Power, governance, and the WTO: a comparative institutional approach', in M. Barnett and R. Duvall (eds), *Power in Global Governance*, Cambridge: Cambridge University Press.

Schwartz, T. (2003) *Lyndon Johnson and Europe in the Shadow of Vietnam*, Cambridge, MA: Harvard University Press.

Steinberg, R. (1998) 'Great power management of the world trading system: a transatlantic strategy for liberal multilateralism', *Law and Policy in International Business* 29(2): 205–56.

Stokes, B. (2008) 'Europe hungrily eyes India', *National Journal*, 12 January.

Swinbank, A. and Tanner, C. (1996) *Farm Policy and Trade Conflict: The Uruguay Round and CAP Reform*, Ann Arbor, MI: University of Michigan Press.

Szymanski, M. and Smith, M. (2005) 'Coherence and conditionality in European foreign policy: negotiating the EU–Mexico global agreement', *Journal of Common Market Studies* 43(1): 171–92.

Thallinger, G. (2007) 'From apology to utopia: EU–ACP Economic Partnership Agreements oscillating between WTO conformity and sustainability', *European Foreign Affairs Review* 12(4): 499–516.

Vachudova, M. (2005) *Europe Undivided: Democracy, Leverage, and Integration after Communism*, Oxford: Oxford University Press.

Winham, G. (1986) *International Trade and the Tokyo Round Negotiation*, Princeton, NJ: Princeton University Press.

Woolcock, S. (2008) 'The role of regional agreements in trade and investment regimes', in A. Cooper, C. Hughes and P. De Lombaerde (eds), *Regionalisation and Global Governance: The Taming of Globalisation?*, London: Routledge.

Woolcock, S. and Hodges, M. (1996) 'EU policy in the Uruguay round', in H. Wallace and W. Wallace (eds), *Policy-making in the European Union*, Oxford: Oxford University Press.

Young, A. and Peterson, J. (2006) 'The EU and the new trade politics', *Journal of European Public Policy* 13(6): 795–814.

Zimmerman, H. (2007) 'Realist power Europe? The EU in the negotiations about China's and Russia's WTO accession', *Journal of Common Market Studies* 45(4): 813–32.

Zoellick, R. (2002) 'Falling behind on free trade', *New York Times*, 14 April.

Europe and the new global economic order: internal diversity as liability and asset in managing globalization

Orfeo Fioretos

ABSTRACT The diversity of market economies that constitute the European Union (EU) presents both constraints and opportunities for Europe when it comes to shaping the post-neoliberal global economic order. Diversity is a constraint in that it often prevents strong common positions in global negotiations and thus undermines the ability of Europe to exercise its collective hard power resources. Paradoxically, however, the EU's enduring diversity over time has become the source of a different type of power that also provides Europe with opportunities to shape the nature of global economic governance. By reconciling commitments to greater economic openness and extensive multilateralism with national discretion, the EU enjoys 'model power'. This type of power is based in specific institutional innovations within the EU that accommodate internal diversity and allow the EU to exercise important, if limited, influence over the substantive content and rules guiding the management of globalization.

INTRODUCTION

The structure of the global economic order is under review. The gradual delegitimation after the early 2000s of the intellectual underpinnings that had informed the global economic order for two decades and the 2008 global financial crisis have combined to reignite a debate on what should be the structure of the global economic system. European leaders have been particularly vociferous in calling for a new arrangement. While Gordon Brown has called for a 'new global order', Nicholas Sarkozy for a 'new Bretton Woods' and Angela Merkel for a 'new global architecture', European Commission President José Manuel Barroso speaks of a 'new emerging world order'. But is Europe in a position to define the structure of global economic governance in the twenty-first century? Can Europe manage globalization by expanding the territorial scope of its imprints (Jacoby and Meunier 2010)?

An answer to whether Europe can shape the structure of global economic governance requires that a distinction be made between defining the form of specific rules and shaping the broader system of governance. '[T]here is no governance in general nor general governance,' Bob Jessop notes. 'Rather, there is only *particular* governance and the *totality* of governance' (Jessop 1997: 105, emphasis added). A growing literature, including contributors to this collection, shows that Europe has in recent years been able to shape particular global rules in several domains, including trade, finance and the environment (e.g. Abdelal 2007; Kelemen 2010; Meunier 2007; Posner and Veron 2010). While the European Union (EU) represents the largest share of world GDP (30 per cent), trade (18 per cent), and official development assistance (52 per cent), there are significant limits to its ability in exercising Europe's collective economic power.[1]

To realize the EU's joint economic power requires agreement among its major member states, a reality that has often proven elusive. Yet even when Europe's leading economies are able to pool their economic power, this may not be a sufficient foundation for shaping the substantive content or institutional architecture of the global economic order. To shape the latter and influence not only particular rules but also the totality of the global economic order, Europe must be able to complement its economic power with normative powers that foster a legitimate social purpose.[2] Only when states have been able to muster both forms of power have they been able to define a global economic order (Ruggie 1982).

Global economic orders are distinguished by the division of labor between markets and public authorities at the international and domestic levels, as well as by the particular priorities such arrangements are designed to foster. Answers to what role should be played by public authorities in sustaining and promoting economic openness in capital, goods, service and labor markets are the ones typically seen to define an economic order. But the underlying priorities of a particular arrangement, its 'social purpose' – for example, whether economic growth or employment are prioritized over other goals, and whether social progress and environmental sustainability are principles that are actively promoted – are also integral features that define an economic order (Ruggie 1982; Gilpin 2003).

Since the founding of the modern economic system after the Second World War, there have been two distinct global economic orders. One emerged following the Bretton-Woods conference and became the foundation of what is known as the 'compromise of embedded liberalism' and lasted until the early 1970s (Ruggie 1982). A second arrangement took form during the 1990s and has been described as a 'neoliberal' order or one of 'embedded neoliberalism' and was characterized by market fundamentalism (Cerny 2008; Stiglitz 2008). The period in between, much like that today, was marked by transition, and the question of what form the global economic order would take remained open. However, unlike that period when European integration was very much a work in progress and several of its member states had failed to undertake structural reforms at home, Europe's economies are now more united, and its largest economies have implemented structural reforms that have made their industry better placed to meet the challenges of global competition.

Institutional innovations within the EU were critical in facilitating these developments by both harnessing the disciplinary forces of market integration and by giving governments significant room in developing nationally specific adjustment strategies that ensured domestic support for economic openness. Notwithstanding challenges such as high unemployment and modest growth rates in some countries, the EU's success in creating the world's largest internal market, a strong euro, and in facilitating extensive structural reforms while maintaining commitments to a diverse set of social models have contributed to speculation that the EU will also be able to exercise significant influence over the structure of the global economic order. Such speculations gained currency as the American economic miracle of the late 1990s and early 2000s collapsed and its intellectual and regulatory foundations became widely questioned following the economic crisis that began in 2007.

Is the EU able to influence the structure of a new global economic order? I urge some skepticism on this score, but also identify reasons why the EU may exercise more influence over the nature of the global economic order in the post-neoliberal era than it did during the founding of the neoliberal one. I argue that the diversity of national economic systems that make up the EU presents practical and enduring limits to the ability of its member states in mustering their collective market power as a means of comprehensively rewriting the rules of globalization. But I also note that this diversity, which has been a feature of the EU since its inception, has led member states to adopt a set of pragmatic institutional innovations that have helped them reconcile open economy strategies and extensive multilateralism with significant levels of national discretion. These institutions give the EU a type of normative power that may be termed *model power*. This model power is a foundation on which the EU is able to influence the structure and ultimately features of the substantive content of the post-neoliberal global economic order.

The EU's normative power has been much debated in recent years, and scholars have shown how the EU has successfully shaped the substantive content of public policies in other states and multilateral organizations in numerous areas, including in human rights and economic domains (e.g. Laïdi 2008; Manners 2002, 2008; Zielonka 2006). However, such efforts are often met with little enthusiasm in other states, especially among other large economies whose support is necessary to establish a stable global economic order. This contribution suggests that in such cases, the EU may influence the nature of the global economic order by representing a set of institutional innovations as to how difficult governance problems between sovereign states can be overcome in ways that allow individual governments to sustain domestic support both for greater international co-operation and economic openness. The EU exercises model power when states beyond its borders are persuaded that its institutional designs are attractive and feasible solutions for joint governance. In other words, the EU's normative power is found not only when it serves as an aspirational ideal to others or when its member states project a common normative template. Normative power may also be exercised when the EU is internally divided if it offers practicable solutions to how major differences among member states can be overcome in ways that foster the realization of both nationally specific and common international goals. More specifically, this essay argues that the EU enjoys model power by representing a set of solutions to a long-standing governance problem for the modern open economy, namely how a diverse set of states successfully reconcile the steady expansion of joint governance with extensive national discretion in politically sensitive domains. It concludes that key institutional innovations on which the EU relies to resolve this problem have come to shape significant parts of the global economic order in the twenty-first century.

How to harness the benefits of global markets without undermining national institutions and practices that are essential to sustaining strategies of economic openness has been an enduring governance problem for the world's leading economies. During the Bretton-Woods conference and in the years that followed, the world's leading economies crafted solutions to this problem by introducing a set of multilateral organizations that encouraged international trade, economic reconstruction and which stabilized the international monetary system. Yet these organizations also gave extensive responsibilities to national governments in managing capital markets and in compensating losers from economic openness. This arrangement lasted until the 1970s when economic crises generated a gradual reassessment of the postwar order. Following a major shift in the dominant ideas of governance in the 1980s, a new global order emerged in the 1990s that altered both the scope and nature of economic governance within large multilateral organizations and redefined what were favored means of domestic intervention. Through its presence and its relative absence, respectively, Europe's normative power played a key role in shaping the two economic orders. It is also its normative power, specifically its model power, that is key to understanding in what ways the EU may contribute to a new consensus on what will be the structure of the new global economic order.

The Atlantic Consensus

The United States and its European allies formed an Atlantic consensus after the Second World War which established the underpinnings of the international economic order and the principles of domestic economic discretion. While the US has been described as a hegemonic power in this period, it relied on the support of Europe's large economies to establish a global economic order that ensured high levels of openness. The defining feature of the Atlantic Consensus and what has become known as the compromise of embedded liberalism was that the promotion of global market integration through multilateralism was 'predicated on domestic interventionism' (Ruggie 1982: 393). Specifically, the stability of an open trading system was dependent upon governments intervening in the domestic economy in ways that ensured political support for economic openness.

Two features were central to embedded liberalism. First, while a fixed exchange rate regime anchored by the dollar and international financial institutions like the International Monetary Fund (IMF) facilitated a stable international monetary system, governments enjoyed extensive authority in regulating national financial markets, and used such powers to promote employment and long-term structural adjustment programs. Second, complementing international organizations like GATT (General Agreement on Tariffs and Trade), which promoted free trade, governments established domestic institutions of social insurance (broadly speaking, the welfare state) to compensate the losers of economic openness. The latter arrangement was evident in the strong correlation between economic openness and the size of national welfare states in the early postwar period (Burgoon 2010; Cameron 1978; Rodrik 1997). The complementary relationship between the international and domestic sides of the compromise of embedded liberalism created historically strong cross-class coalitions and a self-reinforcing system that enabled the reconstruction and consolidation of open economy strategies among Europe's largest economies.

The postwar global economic order gradually fell apart as the fixed exchange rate regime at its center dissolved in the early 1970s, economic growth slowed in industrialized states, and a new normative order took root in the 1980s. The emphasis on Keynesian macroeconomics and extensive government regulation of domestic markets were gradually replaced by monetarism, by extensive deregulation and liberalization of capital, goods, service, and in some cases labor markets. The dominant view in the 1990s on the role of economic multilateralism and appropriate forms of domestic government intervention became known as the Washington Consensus and constituted the normative foundation of a new economic order.[3]

The Washington Consensus

Most directly associated with the policy priorities of the international financial institutions based in the American capital (IMF, World Bank, Inter-American Development Bank (IADB)) and the US Treasury, the policy template of the Washington Consensus represented a significant departure from that of the Atlantic Consensus. While international economic organizations such as the World Trade Organization (WTO), IMF and World Bank were given the task of facilitating integrated capital, goods and service markets, national governments were encouraged to liberalize financial markets and to deregulate product and labor markets. At the same time, a strong emphasis was put on reducing the size of state budgets, which translated into significantly lower investments in institutions that managed social risk and in lower subsidies to industrial sectors. In other words, the domestic mechanisms of compensation that had been so central to the compromise of embedded liberalism were gradually dismantled; the costs and responsibilities of adjusting to economic openness now fell less on public authorities than on individual citizens (Laïdi 2008; Rodrik 2007a).

In contrast to the era of the Atlantic Consensus, Europe did not play as apparent a role in directly shaping the social purpose of global economic governance in the 1990s and early 2000s. Although it tried and had some measure of success (Abdelal and Meunier 2010), its normative power was compromised by several factors. The majority of Europe's economies were experiencing economic stagnation characterized by high unemployment and low growth. Europe was also internally divided over the structure of the global order, with Britain more open to US designs and Germany and France often seeking alternatives. Moreover, European integration was itself in transition, and the consolidation of the internal market program and of the ambitious Maastricht Treaty were slow and contested processes. Finally, it was the US that enjoyed a period of extraordinary prosperity and dynamic growth, thus placing that country in the position of shaping a new legitimate social purpose for the global economic order after the Cold War.

By historical standards, however, the normative power the US exercised in shaping the neoliberal order proved relatively short-lived. If the embedded liberal compromise had had self-reinforcing properties by enlarging popular support for open economy strategies over time, the neoliberal model associated with the Washington Consensus came to have a self-undermining quality as fewer and fewer of its main features enjoyed political support in those countries adopting the model's principal features.[4] Between economic and political failures in developing countries that followed the prescriptions of the Washington Consensus and the reality that countries violating many of its core principles fared better (Rodrik 2007a), a debate was fueled in the early 2000s on what ought to define the social purpose of global institutions (e.g. Bhagwati 2004; Stiglitz 2002). That debate gathered new momentum with the 2008 financial crisis, which was widely attributed to the economic blueprint that US governments had promoted at home and abroad since the 1990s.

A new consensus?

Many reforms promoted by European governments in the wake of the 2008 global financial crisis have origins in a longer debate within Europe on how globalization is best managed. Responding to global concerns about the domestic consequences of economic globalization in the late 1990s, then Trade Commissioner of the European Commission Pascal Lamy outlined a doctrine of 'managed globalization' in the form of a set of principles that should guide Europe's approach to global market integration (Abdelal and Meunier 2010). Modeled on the example of the EU with particular attention to the organizational principles of subsidiarity and transparency and the substantive norms of social progress and environmental sustainability, Lamy sought to extend the territorial scope of this doctrine to the global level and spoke of a 'Geneva Consensus' while seeking the position of the WTO's Director General (Lamy 2005).

According to Lamy, the Geneva Consensus is a 'new basis for the opening up of trade that takes into account the resultant *cost of adjustment*' (2006). This is key, since it was that particular consideration that was so essential to making the compromise of embedded liberalism a self-reinforcing and stable system over time. 'The greatest risk of globalization', underscores Dani Rodrik, 'lies in the prospect that national governments' room for manoeuvre will shrink to such levels that they will be unable to deliver the policies and political support from those it is supposed to help' (Rodrik 2007b: 11). Governments under a Geneva Consensus would address this risk in different ways than was the case during the Washington Consensus. In particular, they would be encouraged to enhance popular support for economic openness through state-sponsored programs with compensatory mechanisms for those dislocated through open economy strategies.

International organizations would have a major responsibility in helping weaker countries make the transition to sustainable open economies (European Commission 2005). However, rather than embracing one-size-fits-all economic strategies and radical reform programs centered around rapid deregulation and liberalization, international organizations like the WTO, IMF and World Bank would become partners in developing nationally specific solutions that would make open economy strategies sustainable in the long term and thus a liberal international economic order more stable. Among other things, international organizations would assume a larger role in developing national institutions of social insurance and in sharing expertise that would help countries develop greater capacities in meeting new norms of what constitutes environmentally sustainable practice.

In responding to the global financial crisis of 2008, European governments widely condemned the market fundamentalism associated with the Washington Consensus and promoted the creation of a global economic order that is socially more just, environmentally more sound, as well as more representative of the diversity of opinions that characterize a globalized economy. In doing so, leaders on both the European Left and Right embraced the basic principles associated with the Geneva Consensus, though that is a term, much like that of the embedded liberalism compromise or the Washington Consensus, that is itself not much used by policy-makers. Thus, for example, during summits of the world's largest economies in the aftermath of the crisis, Prime Minister Brown called for securing a 'progressive era of international co-operation', President Sarkozy addressed the issue of global representation when remarking that 'it seems unreasonable that the most important international issues are dealt with without Africa, Latin America and China', and Chancellor Merkel called for 'securing the principles of a social market economy across the globe'.[5]

LIMITS AND FOUNDATIONS OF MODEL POWER

Can the goals identified by the leaders of Europe's largest economies realistically be expected to become part of a new global economic order? In promoting their goals, European leaders confront both significant constraints and opportunities that are due to EU's heterogeneous membership.

Internal diversity as liability

Europe is characterized by great internal diversity. Although it is often depicted as a unitary actor (e.g. Drezner 2007), the EU's defining feature is the long-standing variety of economic systems that characterize its members. In broad terms, the key division among its large member states is one between liberal and organized market economies (Hall 2007; Schmidt 2002). Governments representing these two types of economies have tended to respond to globalization in distinct ways and to hold divergent views on the nature of common international rules, including European and global regulation (Fioretos 2001; Hall and Soskice 2001). For example, governments in the UK, a liberal market economy, tend to oppose the extension of more stringent rules in the trade and labor areas, and especially in the financial domain. In contrast, governments in Germany and France, which are alternative versions of organized market economies, tend to be more willing to accept such arrangements, especially in matters affecting their social models.

Notwithstanding examples where the three countries have been able to come to agreement and shape global designs in areas such as the environment, financial and trade domains, the EU's internal diversity frequently undermines the ability of its member states to exercise their collective market power. The effect of internal diversity is apparent in many cases, including in recent ones where the three largest economies have been unable to adopt a common position in global negotiations. For example, efforts by Germany and France before and after the 2008 financial crises to introduce more stringent global financial regulations met with opposition from Britain, which sided with the US and supported more modest extensions of global regulation.

Although the positions of Europe's largest economies have been more closely aligned in matters of trade (they are jointly represented by the European Commission within the WTO), disagreements also exist here that can be traced to differences in their particular varieties of capitalism. For example, disagreements over the nature of global labor standards are attributable to such divisions (Johnson 2005). In addition, differences in other areas that directly affect the institutional core of their distinct economic models, such as competition policy and corporate governance, may be understood as consequences of their particular varieties of capitalism (cf. Hall and Soskice 2001). In cases where disputes over how to regulate global markets have persisted, Europe's largest economies have failed to agree on a common position and, consequently, the EU's collective ability to influence the structure of global rules has been undermined significantly.

Internal diversity as asset

The internal diversity that characterizes the EU has been an enduring feature of that organization and its predecessors, and has forced member states to find a set of institutional solutions to help them meet their commitment to economic openness and international agreements without undermining domestic designs that are held dear by national constituencies. With extensive harmonization of national designs ruled out after the 1970s due to persistent difficulties in securing agreements among member states, the EU has come to rely on a set of institutional innovations to accommodate its internal diversity. Since the 1980s, it has used the principle of mutual recognition to ensure that national non-discriminatory practices are respected and permissible. In addition, in order to prevent scenarios where a mutual recognition regime and greater openness generate the potential for egregious races-to-the-bottom, the EU has relied on the use of common minimum standards. Such standards have generally been acceptable to countries seeking low standards as well as to those with higher standards. In addition, the EU relies greatly on directives (rather than regulations) in sensitive economic areas and gives members discretion in what types of national designs are employed in meeting international commitments. In recent years, the EU has also come to rely extensively on peer review and on promoting non-enforceable best practice standards through a practice known as the open method of co-ordination that facilitates closer intergovernmental co-operation without undermining national discretion.

When some governments have been faced with particularly difficult challenges in agreeing to rules supported by a large majority of member states, or when the costs of quick adjustment have been particularly high, the EU has also employed the practice of variable geometry and allowed some states to opt out of common arrangements or have given these states more time to meet their obligations. They have done so sparingly, but effectively, as a means to ensure that collective objectives are reached without undermining long-term support within specific member states. Furthermore, partially to reassure national constituencies that the EU itself will not usurp powers that can unexpectedly be used later to enforce radical changes at the domestic level, member states made subsidiarity a formal principle of economic governance in the early 1990s. Finally, in response to criticisms that the EU's leadership lacked legitimacy, the organization enhanced transparency, expanded its membership and included more stakeholders in its deliberations.

Each of the solutions embraced by the EU to accommodate its internal diversity – mutual recognition and common minimum standards, the growing use of directives, the open method of co-ordination, variable geometry, subsidiarity and transparency – have aimed to resolve difficult governance problems between sovereign states in sensitive areas that are often directly traced to the core of national economic systems. With time, these solutions have become a foundation on which the EU has overcome significant differences among members while expanding openness and preserving substantial national discretion in economic policy. It is in this capacity that the EU enjoys potential *model power*, a form of normative power in which some specific EU institutional solutions are attractive to states beyond its own borders.

A substantial literature on EU's normative power is focused on the role played by principled norms and ideas associated with the EU, and how these serve as a foundation on which that organization is able to actively persuade other states to alter their political, economic and social policy commitments following deliberation and debate (e.g. Risse 2000; Manners 2002). Addressed more rarely are instances when normative power is exercised passively through demonstration.[6] Yet, the latter form may in the long term be more consequential in persuading others of the value of specific principles of conduct and institutional designs. For example, the adoption of ostensibly German designs for Economic and Monetary Union was neither due to coercive tactics by that country, nor to German officials actively persuading policy-makers in other countries to adopt such designs. Rather, it was the reality that Germany's postwar macroeconomic model had ensured price stability while alternatives had failed, which led other states to support a European arrangement that had strong German imprints (McNamara 1998).

Model power functions in indirect ways without there necessarily being actual dialogue over what should be the structure of common rules and principles. Indeed, in many cases model power rests not on making available an ideal arrangement of economic governance, but is a function of an organization producing a set of prospective alternatives that have not yet been conceived (Barnett and Duvall 2005). Moreover, in the context of international governance, model power can exist in the absence of a normative consensus among states on what is the preferred substantive outcome if the relevant international model is one that accommodates diverse preferences among these states. For example, the EU's model power does not require internal unity among member states on matters of economic or regulatory policy as long as there is agreement among these states on what type of international designs should be employed to accommodate nationally distinct economic and regulatory models.

THE COUNTOURS OF A NEW GLOBAL ORDER

The effects of model power are neither immediate nor universal. Whether states accept and adopt a model of governance associated with other entities is the outcome of a process where existing designs have first become deligitimated. Such processes do not occur quickly, and because some features of extant designs typically enjoy domestic support, the adoption of a new model, whether national or international, is rarely one that is a perfect facsimile of the demonstration case. In the context of global orders, moreover, any legitimate arrangement will be a compromise between states, and these are likely to be more extensive with larger numbers of participants. Yet, despite these realities, not only is there a window of opportunity for the EU to manage economic globalization by influencing key institutional features of a new economic order, but the early contours of that order include features that are closely associated with the EU example.

Restoring national discretion

If diverse market economies continue to respond to globalization in distinct ways, the critical task of a new global order is to adopt rules that accommodate diversity in national economic systems and differential speeds of reform in ways that make greater levels of international co-operation feasible and sustainable. Following the collapse of the Washington Consensus, this is in large part a matter of restoring national discretion in managing the process of economic globalization and is a premise of the Geneva Consensus described by Lamy. The EU is the only international organization to effectively and enduringly protect such discretion by formalizing means of overcoming internal diversity, and simultaneously expanding economic openness and support for a liberal international order. As such, the EU represents a feasible and tested solution to achieving substantive policy commitments. The EU thus represents a significant departure from the situation that prevailed under the neoliberal order. Rather than promoting a one-size-fits-all economic reform program as was the case with the Washington Consensus (Rodrik 2007a), the EU starts from the premise that governments must enjoy significant discretion in adopting programs that help them build support for economic openness.

Enhancing national discretion is not synonymous with allowing states to use discriminatory practices. Indeed, the economic blueprints supported by European leaders are based on the idea that national discretion in some specific areas is a necessary complement to sustaining non-discriminatory open economy strategies. In particular, there is support for institutions of social compensation for those dislocated by exposure to international markets. The particular ways in which countries do so varies, and the EU has underscored the importance of giving such programs greater support and reducing the emphasis within the IMF and the World Bank on cutting government budgets if it comes at the cost of developing social insurance mechanisms and support for economic openness (e.g. European Commission 2006). The EU has also shown more willingness to support transitional agreements for developing countries when it comes to meeting the obligations associated with repaying loans to international financial institutions, WTO membership or environmental treaties. In addition, such arrangements constitute an explicit rejection of the dominant policy prescriptions of the Washington Consensus when speedy reforms and high short-term costs were accepted with the expectation that the prospects for long-term stability were improved.

For an increasing number of states and observers, the principles of mutual recognition, subsidiarity, the open method of co-ordination and variable geometry are attractive means by which to promote a global economic order in which economic openness and high levels of international co-operation are reconciled with the protection of national discretion. In the case of mutual recognition, this was already the case in the 1990s when the EU example 'prove[d] contagious' and informed a rapidly growing number of multilateral trade agreements (Nicolaïdis 1997: 1). Although the principles of subsidiarity and variable geometry have not formally become part of the global economic order through treaties, they are apparent in practice and are frequently discussed as essential elements to managing the global economy in the absence of an international government (e.g. Trachtman 2006; VanGrasstek and Sauvé 2006).

Similarly, the emphasis that the G20 has placed on promoting peer review and concrete but unenforceable best practice standards in the domain of financial regulation since the 2009 London Summit has clear commonalities with the EU's open method of co-ordination.

Enhancing legitimacy

Transparency and representativeness in global governance are key to ensuring that the major economic multilaterals achieve and maintain legitimacy. Unlike in the era of the Atlantic Consensus, the major international economic organizations came under a great deal of criticism during the era of the Washington Consensus. That criticism was similar in nature to that levied against the EU in the 1990s and that occasioned several initiatives designed to enhance that organization's legitimacy, in particular through greater inclusion of non-governmental organizations. As in the EU, though with some variations among themselves, the IMF, World Bank, WTO and International Labour Organization (ILO) are now more committed than only half a decade ago to incorporating more stakeholders in their governance. The EU features prominently as a model in debates among policy-makers, international lawyers and scholars on how these organizations can be reformed to become more transparent. For example, in promoting the Geneva Consensus, Lamy speaks of creating 'nothing less than a new politics' in the management of the global economy and draws on the EU model to promote a more inclusive agenda that gives greater voice to developing nations and non-governmental groups (Lamy 2004: 13).

While there is often reason to be skeptical of how significant non-governmental groups are in altering the types of decisions taken by international organizations, the expansion of membership by states and shifts in rules of representation are vehicles that have recognizable effects on the management and legitimacy of organizations. The EU has a long history of expanding its membership and has used such processes to enlarge markets, assist in the consolidation of political transitions, and as a means of enhancing its representativeness (Jacoby 2010). In current debates about the management of the global economy, the EU has drawn on these experiences and embraced expanded membership in both the informal and formal governance of the global economy.

In line with the principles of the Geneva Consensus, the leading European economies and the EU argue that to ensure legitimacy, three sets of reforms must be undertaken. The reliance on the G7/8 platform should be replaced by the G20, an organization established in the late 1990s and which includes the largest developing economies. They have also called for an expanded voice for developing economies in the major international financial institutions, including greater voting shares, as well as potentially ending the US–European monopolies on senior positions. Following the EU example, the basic premise of these initiatives is that though developing economies may not gain equal voice within these organizations, they must be compensated for the relative power disparities that exist between large and smaller economies in order for joint governance to be legitimate. This is a well-established practice of the EU where small countries and economies enjoy representation that is much greater than strict proportional formulas would have produced.

Extending the types of reforms the EU has employed to address concerns over its transparency and representativeness at the global level, however limited, would mitigate legitimacy deficits associated with the neoliberal order. Enhancing representation also addresses the imbalance that existed during the Atlantic Consensus when the embedded liberalism compromise was not 'fully extended to the developing countries' (Ruggie 1982: 413). While these reforms may be slow and may not fundamentally alter the balance of international power – in no small part because those large developing economies which would benefit are themselves rarely united – such reforms would represent a significant shift in the management of economic globalization. When promoting these innovations, European government officials and individuals who have later come to occupy senior positions within multilateral organizations have frequently turned to the EU not as an example of what should be the normative priorities of a new global order as much as a reference point for how complex governance problems can be resolved among sovereign states.

CONCLUSION

It is easy to be skeptical both about whether the EU has normative power and whether there is progress in global governance; for example, whether major multilaterals have or will become more representative and change their policy prescriptions. It is, therefore, particularly easy to be skeptical about the ability of the EU to shape the social purpose of the latter. Yet there is much evidence in the growing literature on 'normative Europe' that the EU has been able to shape the content of consequential national as well as global institutions of governance in a wide-ranging set of areas, including the security, human rights, environmental and economic domains (e.g. Manners 2002; Birchfield 2008; Laïdi 2008). Much of this literature has focused on the EU as an entity that has actively sought to export its ideas as a means of persuading other states to accept its normative ideals. But the EU is not a 'normative empire' that can easily dictate to other states what practices they should adopt and, contrary to arguments that the EU could export its model of governance to other regions of the world, it does not with its many imperfections constitute an ideal that other states are ready to voluntarily emulate (see Zielonka 2006; Miliband 2007). Confronted by this reality, the EU's ability to manage globalization in the long term may be found neither in its ability to overcome its internal differences for the purposes of mustering its collective market power, nor in whether its normative priorities are attractive to other states.

In a globalized world with multiple centers of economic power, the structure of the global economic order will be a contested one – much like the EU itself. This contribution has argued that the manner in which the EU has resolved similar contestations internally while simultaneously expanding the scope of international co-operation and sustaining high levels of national discretion gives that organization a foundation on which to influence the post-neoliberal global economic order. In historical terms, the contours of the new global economic order and the EU are now more closely aligned than before. This is a process that has gradually been defined less by the EU altering its practices to be in conformity with global arrangements than one in which an emerging consensus on what ought to be the structure of the global economic order has moved closer to institutional arrangements and priorities associated with the EU.

What label is given to a post-neoliberal consensus and whether it invokes Geneva or a different name is not particularly significant. What is significant for the long-term sustainability of a new global economic order is the institutio-nalization of a set of practices through which states can achieve their joint inter-ests while retaining significant national discretion for the purposes of securing support for open economy strategies. It is here that the EU, through its empha-sis on institutional innovations such as mutual recognition, common minimum standards, the open method of co-ordination and variable geometry, offers par-ticularly valuable lessons beyond its borders for how diverse interests among sovereign states can be overcome while high levels of economic openness, inter-national cooperation and national discretion in economic management are sus-tained. Meanwhile, the lesson for Europe itself is that in the long term it is wiser to focus on perfecting its own imperfect union and to illustrate how difficult governance problems may be resolved among heterogeneous states than to actively attempt to export its values and organizational principles; it is by tending its own house – not rearranging that of others – that the EU may most successfully manage globalization.

ACKNOWLEDGEMENTS

For comments on earlier drafts of this article, I especially thank Sophie Meunier and Wade Jacoby, as well as Sheri Berman, Richard Deeg, Rachel Epstein, Wade Jacoby, Dan Kelemen, Ray Taras, the *Journal of European Policy* reviewers, and participants at workshops in Princeton and Park City.

NOTES

1 Rounded figures from Sapir (2007).
2 The term 'social purpose' comes from Ruggie (1982: 382).

3 The core of the Washington Consensus is discussed in Williamson (1989). For critical reappraisal of its original and 'augmented form', see Rodrik (2007a), and Serra
and Stiglitz (2008).
4 On the distinction between self-reinforcing and self-undermining institutions, see
Greif (2006).
5 Brown's words appeared in the press conference following the G20 meeting in
London (3 April 2009); and Sarkozy's and Merkel's following a G8 meeting in
Italy (10 July 2009).
6 Manners' notion of 'living by example' is one way in which the EU may influence the
preferences and behavior of others by means of demonstration. By contrast to
Manners (2008: 56) who focuses on the extent to which there is unity within the
EU and whether the EU is 'coherent' and 'consistent' in promoting a particular set
of substantive norms, the notion of model power stresses the *process* by which inter-
state conflicts are resolved. In cases where internal diversity is extensive, how conflict
is managed is an analytically distinct question and key in determining whether
substantive outcomes are achieved over time and whether or not the pursuit of
these may be said to be either consistent, coherent or both.

REFERENCES

Abdelal, R. (2007) *Capital Rules: The Construction of Global Finance*, Cambridge, MA:
Harvard University Press.
Abdelal, R. and Meunier, S. (2010) 'Managed globalization: doctrine, practice and
promise', *Journal of European Public Policy* 17(3): 350–67.
Barnett, M. and Duvall, R. (2005) 'Power in international politics', *International
Organization* 59(1): 39–75.
Bhagwati, J. (2004) *In Defense of Globalization*, New York: Oxford University Press.
Birchfield, V. (2008) 'The EU's development policy: empirical evidence of 'normative
power Europe?'', EUCE Symposium, Georgia Institute of Technology.
Burgoon, B. (2010) 'Betwixt and between? The European Union's redistributive man-
agement of globalization', *Journal of European Public Policy* 17(3): 433–48.
Cameron, D. (1978) 'The expansion of the public economy', *APSR* 72(4): 1243–61.
Cerny, P. (2008) 'Embedding neoliberalism: the evolution of a hegemonic paradigm',
The Journal of Trade and International Diplomacy 2(1): 1–46.
Drezner, D. (2007) *All Politics is Global: Explaining International Regulatory Regimes*,
Princeton, NJ: Princeton University Press.
European Commission (2005) 'European values in the globalised world. Contribution
of the Commission to the October meeting of heads of state and government', COM
525 final, Brussels.
European Commission (2006) 'The European consensus on development', *Official
Journal* C 46/01.
Fioretos, O. (2001) 'The domestic sources of multilateral preferences: varieties of capit-
alism in the European Community', in P. Hall and D. Soskice (eds), *Varieties of
Capitalism*, New York: Oxford University Press.
Gilpin, R. (2003) *Global Political Economy: Understanding the International Economic
Order*, Princeton, NJ: Princeton University Press.
Greif, A. (2006) *Institutions and the Path of the Modern Economy: Lessons from Medieval
Trade*, New York: Cambridge University Press.
Hall, P. (2007) 'The evolution of varieties of capitalism in Europe', in B. Hancke,
M. Rhodes and M. Thatcher (eds), *Beyond Varieties of Capitalism*, New York:
Oxford University Press.
Hall, P. and Soskice, D. (eds) (2001) *Varieties of Capitalism: The Institutional Foun-
dations of Comparative Advantage*, New York: Oxford University Press.

Jacoby, W. (2010) 'Managing globalization by managing Central and Eastern Europe: the EU's backyard as threat and opportunity', *Journal of European Public Policy* 17(3): 416–32.

Jacoby, W. and Meunier, S. (2010) 'Europe and the management of globalization', *Journal of European Public Policy* 17(3): 299–317.

Jessop, B. (1997) 'The governance of complexity and the complexity of governance: preliminary remarks on some problems and limits of economic guidance', in A. Amin and J. Hausner (eds), *Beyond Market and Hierarchy*, Cheltenham: Edward Elgar.

Johnson, A. (2005) *European Welfare States and Supranational Governance of Social Policy*, Basingstoke: Palgrave.

Keleman, R.D. (2010) 'Globalizing European Union environmental policy', *Journal of European Public Policy* 17(3): 335–49.

Laïdi, Z. (2008) 'The normative empire: the unintended consequences of European power', available at: http://www.telos-eu.com (accessed June 2009).

Lamy, P. (2004) 'Europe and the future of economic governance', *Journal of Common Market Studies* 42(1): 5–21.

Lamy, P. (2005) 'WTO Director-General selection process: statement by Pascal Lamy', Geneva: World Trade Organization.

Lamy, P. (2006) 'Humanising globalization', Speech delivered Santiago, Chile, 30 January.

Manners, I. (2002) 'Normative power Europe: a contradiction in terms?' *Journal of Common Market Studies* 40(2): 235–58.

Manners, I. (2008) 'The normative ethics of the European Union', *International Affairs* 84(1): 45–60.

McNamara, K. (1998) *Currency of Ideas: Monetary Politics in the European Union*, Ithaca, NY: Cornell University Press.

Meunier, S. (2007) 'Managing globalization: the EU in international trade negotiations', *Journal of Common Market Studies* 45(4): 905–26.

Miliband, D. (2007) 'Europe 2030: model power not superpower', Speech delivered at the College of Europe, Bruges, 15 November.

Nicolaïdis, K. (1997) 'Mutual recognition and regulatory regimes: some lessons and prospects', *Jean Monnet Papers*, No. 7, New York University.

Posner, E. and Véron, N. (2010) 'The EU and financial regulation: power without purpose?', *Journal of European Public Policy* 17(3): 400–15.

Risse, T. (2000) 'Let's argue! Persuasion and deliberation in international relations', *International Organization* 54(1): 1–39.

Rodrik, D. (1997) *Has Globalization Gone Too Far?*, Washington, DC: The Brookings Institution.

Rodrik, D. (2007a) *One Economics, Many Recipes*, Princeton, NJ: Princeton University Press.

Rodrik, D. (2007b) 'Cheerleaders threat to world trade', *Financial Times*, 26 March.

Ruggie, J. (1982) 'International regimes, transactions, and change: embedded liberalism in the postwar economic order', *International Organization* 36(2): 379–425.

Sapir, A. (ed.) (2007) *Fragmented Power: Europe and the Global Economy*, Brussels: Bruegel.

Schmidt, V. (2002) *The Futures of European Capitalism*, New York: Cambridge University Press.

Serra, N. and Stiglitz, J. (eds) (2008) *The Washington Consensus Reconsidered: Towards a New Global Governance*, Oxford: Oxford University Press.

Stiglitz, J. (2002) *Globalization and its Discontents*, New York: W.W. Norton.

Stiglitz, J. (2008) 'The end of neo-liberalism?', *Project Syndicate*, available at: http://www.project-syndicate.org/commentary/stiglitz101 (accessed June 2009).

Trachtman, J. (2006) 'The world trading system, the international legal system and multilevel choice', *European Law Journal* 12(4): 469–85.

VanGrasstek, C. and Sauvé, P. (2006) 'The consistency of WTO rules: can the single undertaking be squared with variable geometry?', *Journal of International Economic Law* 9(4): 837–64.

Williamson, J. (1989) 'What Washington means by policy reform', in J. Williamson (ed.), *Latin American Readjustment: How Much Has Happened*, Washington, DC: Institute for the International Economics.

Zielonka, J. (2006) *Europe as Empire: The Nature of the Enlarged European Union*, Oxford: Oxford University Press.

The EU and financial regulation: power without purpose?

Elliot Posner and Nicolas Véron

ABSTRACT   If the European Union (EU) has been an effective bulwark against ad hoc globalization in any economic domain, we may well find evidence from finance, the engine of cross-border economic activity. Yet our study revealed little indication of a distinctive EU approach for regulating financial services industries. Our findings suggest that European decision-makers tried mainly to secure full market integration inside the EU rather than shape regulation to meet a common public purpose, whether at the EU or global level. The policy framework adopted by the EU was essentially modeled on pre-existing United States (US) examples, and does not reflect a transatlantic difference in underlying values. We put forth several hypotheses about why the EU did not seek to manage globalization in the financial services area.

INTRODUCTION

European Union (EU) regulation of financial services industries poses a conundrum. From the standpoint of this volume, the governance of banking, insurance and investment ought to be an exemplary case of European efforts to 'manage' globalization. After all, if the EU has been an effective force shaping globalization in any economic domain, we ought to find evidence from finance, the engine of cross-border economic activity. Several authors identify a managed EU approach to globalization in a wide range of sectors (see Jacoby and Meunier 2010; this entire collection; and Newman 2008), including one closely related to the financial services industry – namely the liberalization of capital accounts (Abdelal 2007; Abdelal and Meunier 2010). Lastly, European policy-makers were in a position to project such an approach overseas, as post-euro EU regulatory reforms transformed the polity into a financial regulatory great power (Drezner 2007; Posner 2009a). Nevertheless, our findings suggest that European decision-makers tried mainly to secure full market integration inside the EU rather than shape regulation to meet a common public purpose.

The first section of this article reports on our empirical study, which examines EU regulatory policy and architecture since the mid-1990s. Our findings show that despite the availability of policy instruments and the presence of motivated actors to steer the regional polity towards using regulation to manage the globalization of financial services, EU policy-makers adopted a limited agenda to ease cross-border financial activity in the EU and to level the transatlantic and global playing fields. They also passed legislation that harmonized rules largely in sync with United States (US) and British approaches, which cannot be adequately described as aiming at managing globalization. These conclusions run contrary to expectations that regulatory harmonization is 'market-correcting' (Scharpf 1999: 45–7). Our evidence, in contrast, suggests that EU financial regulation is a case of 'positive' yet 'market-making' integration.[1]

The second section evaluates plausible explanations for the observed absence of a managed approach. We evaluate three possible explanations invoked in this volume: (1) an irreducible diversity of national approaches that prevented the expression at the EU level of aggregated preferences to manage globalization; (2) US dominance on the 'battleground of ideas'; and (3) EU politics and institution-building that favored regional integration over a regulation embodying a common public purpose. Our analysis helps to explain why diversity among European financial arrangements led neither to paralysis nor to managed globalization, thus addressing a central question posed by the editors. In the conclusion, we discuss implications for EU reactions to the financial crisis.

ACCESS AND NON-INTERFERENCE, NOT MANAGEMENT

Approaches to regulation may be categorized by the concerns preoccupying policy-makers at the moment of decision. On the one hand, policy-makers, determined to reduce or raise transaction costs for some economic players, may create rules to ease or limit market access.[2] In these terms, rules may be thought of as more or less protectionist. EU measures that reduce cross-border discrimination exemplify, to use Scharpf's terminology, 'market-making', 'negative integration' (Scharpf 1999: 43–83).

On the other hand, policy-makers pursuing public goals may devise rules to constrain or expand firm discretion on a non-discriminatory basis. In terms of firm discretion – the focus of discussions about managed globalization – rules reflect the degree to which public authorities consider the private pursuits of firms to be in the public interest, however defined. At least in principle, the aim of managing globalization leads policy-makers to create rules to ensure that private behavior is consistent with public goals – a process that in the EU context would embody Scharpf's notion of 'market-correcting', 'positive integration' (ibid.).[3] In finance, classic examples include regulations requiring banks to hold designated amounts of reserve capital (i.e., prudential regulation) and to limit the financial products they sell to prevent unwanted exposure of risks to customers (i.e., customer/investor protection). Variance in financial disclosure requirements (such as accounting standards), to illustrate further, may impose more or fewer constraints on firm discretion. Policy-makers may also use firm discretion rules to achieve a host of other objectives, including national security, environmental or labor goals, with varying degrees of effectiveness

(Seabrooke 2006; Steil and Litan 2006). Thus, in applying the managed globalization idea to EU financial regulation, we use a restricted meaning, captured in Jacoby and Meunier's '[public] tinkering with free market outcomes'.

Using these two lenses for categorizing regulatory approaches, we examined three areas of EU financial services regulation: the international objectives, the content, and the rule-making procedures.

International objectives[4]

In the early 2000s, EU representatives found themselves with new abilities to constrain US behavior. The post-Monetary Union push to further harmonize regulations and shift more rule-making authority to the regional level (however incomplete) was enough to change US perceptions about the EU's capacity to affect the costs of doing business in Europe. In brief, new EU legislation enabled Brussels and national authorities to impose Europe-wide regulation on the European affiliates of US financial companies. Expecting a narrower scope for regulatory arbitrage and fearing transatlantic divergence in approaches (and therefore higher transaction costs), these US firms lobbied for Washington–Brussels co-ordination. One result was that EU representatives gained bargaining leverage *vis-à-vis* their US counterparts in achieving their goals. But what were these goals?

EU representatives sought to resolve a host of transatlantic regulatory conflicts by reducing asymmetries in cross-border market access. This was the case when EU officials sought easier US access for newly modernized (and internationally competitive) European exchanges, or when they strove to eliminate the prior lopsided regime under which American companies issuing securities in Europe were generally allowed to report in accordance with US accounting standards, whereas European companies had the expensive obligation to reconcile their accounts with US standards. The EU goal in a third dispute, over deregistration of foreign companies, was to remove what appeared from Europe's shores to be a costly burden that kept companies (even long after they delisted from US exchanges) under the regulatory authority of US officials. Similarly, in reaction to provisions in the 2002 US Sarbanes-Oxley Act, EU officials wanted mutual recognition of rules governing corporate board composition to eliminate the potential undesirable effects of incompatible regulations.

The EU Financial Conglomerates Directive (FCD)[5] and the auditing provisions of Sarbanes-Oxley were more complex cases. On the one hand, EU officials sought transatlantic mutual recognition arrangements to ensure equal cross-border market access. On the other hand, the resolutions of the disputes involved an apparent ratcheting up of regulation. In the following section, we assess the extent to which the FCD, requiring that a single regulator have the power to oversee all parts of financial conglomerates, represents a move in the direction of the management of globalization through financial regulation. Here, we note that whatever the original intent, EU authorities (mainly the UK Financial Services Authority) accepted an extremely lax US holding company regime as the equivalent to the new EU arrangements. Because the existing US net capital rule did not meet the new EU standards, the SEC added a new holding company oversight regime for investment banks, which on paper met the letter of FCD.[6] In practice, however, the new US rule gave investment banks more not less discretion. After switching to the new holding company status in 2004, major US investment banks were able to increase their leverage.[7]

Another development, the EU's new auditing legislation,[8] likewise had clear external goals for EU policy-makers and their Brussels representatives. The measure was designed to sufficiently match the new US rules in order to make mutual recognition possible, following the significant extra-territorial implications of enhanced public oversight in the US, an outcome of the 2002 Sarbanes-Oxley Act.[9] In other words, at its conception, the content of the EU law was more about eliminating asymmetries in the transatlantic market (or in the latter cases, preventing its fragmentation) than advancing any particular regulatory agenda. In addition, contrary to Abdelal and Meunier's (2010) finding regarding capital account liberalization, European representatives were satisfied with financial regulatory dispute resolutions without formal agreements or codification.

Content of EU regulation

Between 1999 and 2001, EU policy-makers took a giant leap towards the long-declared goal of integrated financial regulation. The 2001 Lamfalussy process, discussed below, changed the legislative and rule-making procedures, while the Financial Services Action Plan (FSAP), adopted by the European Commission in 1999, provided the content: the proposed legislation deemed necessary to integrate European national financial services industries.[10] The new legislation partly centralized regulatory authority by harmonizing national rules to a much greater extent than in the past. What trends characterize the content of the new pieces of legislation?

Our survey suggests several themes. First, some new EU legislation builds on previous efforts to ease cross-border financial services activity. The Markets in Financial Investments Directive (MiFID),[11] passed in 2004 and fully effective in November 2007, is perhaps the most important example. Its underlying principle, albeit imperfectly actualized, is to remove barriers that remained intact despite the passage of a previous EU directive,[12] also aimed at expanding cross-border competition in securities trading. The politics of MiFID were highly contentious, with a 'Southern European', 'market-shaping' coalition promoting rules that could be categorized as a 'managed' approach (Quaglia 2008a, 2009).[13] Our point, here, is that the outcome favored the 'Northern European', 'market-making' agenda, which gave firms a wide degree of discretion.

Second, the content of many new EU directives and regulations reflect 'best practice' as developed in international forums. The borrowed underlying principles tended to reflect hybrid models advocated by financial regulators of the leading financial centers (mainly Britain and the US) and, as a rule of thumb, give financial services firms significant discretion over what services to provide, prices to charge, capital to maintain and investments to make. A first example is the Capital Requirements Directive of 2006,[14] which transposes principles developed under the Basel II prudential framework into EU law (Quaglia 2008b; Christopoulos and Quaglia 2009).[15] A second example is accounting standards, with the adoption in 2002 of a regulation[16] mandating that publicly listed EU companies report their consolidated financial statements in accordance with International Financial Reporting Standards (IFRS), broadly speaking a mix between British and American approaches with a clear orientation towards investors' information needs. By contrast with other accounting traditions such as France's, IFRS do not include sector-specific standards and are less susceptible to being used as a tool for 'industrial policy'; the private sector nature of the standard-setting organization, the International Accounting Standards Board, means that the EU cannot readily leverage its adoption of IFRS in 2000 to 2002 to effectively manage globalization through this instrument (Véron et al. 2006; Véron 2007a). James Perry and Andreas Nölke go further and argue that IFRS favor financial over productive sectors (Nölke and Perry 2007; Perry and Nölke 2006). According to this view, the actors favored by the switch to IFRS would be mostly US-based financial intermediaries and audit networks, which are associated with ad hoc globalization.

One major piece of EU financial legislation appears, at least on the surface, to be an exception. The 2002 Financial Conglomerates Directive (FCD), intended to improve prudential regulation, arguably reduces firm discretion by giving authorities a panoramic view of conglomerates' operations. As noted above, US conformity to the FCD equivalence requirements did not result in a more 'managed' approach by the SEC. Was this also true in Europe? Or does the FCD mark an EU shift towards an attempt to manage globalization by means of financial regulation?

We are skeptical. The particular form of the FCD was more an accident of history than an indicator of a willingness to manage globalization. The FCD fits the mold of previous national arrangements for regulating the universal banks of continental Europe. The modern US banking industry has been largely defined by the 1933 Glass-Steagall Act (repealed in 1999), which mandated the separation of investment and commercial banking. By contrast, continental European banks generally kept both types of operations under one roof. Foreign purchases in the 1980s and 1990s of British merchant banks (in part by continental European universal banks) extended the universal banking model to the UK and facilitated EU agreement on a regional template that acknowledged universal banking as a key component of the financial system. Furthermore, the continental regulatory framework had, arguably, been less rigorous and intrusive than the SEC's net capital rule or the regime for governing other types of banks in the US. Finally, the more important indicators of the aim to manage globalization through financial regulation are the capital adequacy rules. In the EU, those rules are laid out in the Capital

Requirements Directive, itself largely shaped by the Basel II Accord. In addition, similar to IFRS, Basel II (more so than Basel I and despite successful German efforts to protect small and medium-sized enterprises (SMEs) in the negotiations (Quaglia 2008b)) gives large financial services companies significant discretion to determine the levels of capital reserves (Claessens *et al.* 2008; Underhill and Zhang 2008).

Altogether, the consequences of the FCD, essentially a loosening of solvency and liquidity requirements on large investment banks in the US and an expansion of bank autonomy over risk-assessment analyses, appear much more a case of ad hoc globalization in the transatlantic arena than of managed globalization stemming from Europe. Finally, the EU's application of the 'universalist' approach to managing insolvent cross-border banks may have improved resolution proceedings in the regional polity (Hadjiemmanuil 2005). Nevertheless, even Hadjiemmanuil's measured, though generous, reading of the 2001 Winding Up Directive[17] describes an uneven enhancement of prudential regulation, and the 2007 to 2009 crisis revealed its inadequacies.

Rule-making procedures

The Lamfalussy process altered the procedures for creating, implementing and enforcing EU financial legislation and rules (Coen and Thatcher 2008; Posner 2010; Quaglia 2007, 2008a).[18] To meet one of the stated goals of the reform – to improve accountability in rule-making procedures – EU policymakers borrowed US-style (or UK-style) public consultation as well as other transparency-improving mechanisms. These foreign legislative tropes had at least two effects in Europe. First, they helped to turn newly created bodies of national financial authorities into influential EU political players.[19] Because of their members' legal authorities, existing expertise and relations with market participants, CESR,[20] and to a lesser degree CEBS[21] and CEIOPS,[22] immediately enjoyed legitimacy in the eyes of private and public actors in spite of not having autonomous powers to make binding decisions. Holding public hearings and open consultations reinforced these perceptions. Second, the consultation mechanisms favored organized interests and London-oriented coalitions.[23] The European Commission's efforts to construct a consumer voice[24] were clearly no match for the logic of collective action (Olson 1965).[25] Conflicts among highly organized firms with concentrated interests dominated rule-making processes.[26] In addition, CESR, CEBS and CEIOPS became fairly reliable allies of industries seeking more, not less, discretion (Mügge 2006).

By contrast, company groups favoring a more restrictive approach to financial regulation – such as German small and medium-sized enterprises and auditing firms (Eberle and Lauter 2009; Nölke and Perry 2007; Quaglia 2008b) – won some battles but only recently found a stronger foothold in the EU legislative process, mainly through the European Parliament (EP). In general, as discussed below, voices in favor of striving for managed, as opposed to ad hoc, globalization had a difficult time framing debates and formulating policy alternatives.

In sum, our survey of international objectives, content of legislation and rule-making procedures revealed little evidence of the EU trying to manage globalization using financial regulation as a lever. These conclusions suggest that EU financial regulation belongs to the least discussed of Sharpf's types of EU integration: 'market-making' (as opposed to 'market-correcting') 'positive integration' (i.e., cross-border regulatory harmonization) (Scharpf 1999: 45–7). In most of his discussion of negative and positive integration, Scharpf more or less equates positive integration with market-correcting regulatory harmonization. Yet in his introduction of the concepts, he points out that positive integration need not be market-correcting:

> While all measures of negative integration should probably be classified as being market-making, measures of positive integration may be either market-making (e.g. if divergent national product standards are being 'harmonized' in order to eliminate existing non-tariff barriers to trade) or market-correcting (e.g. process-oriented regulations of working conditions or pollution).
>
> (Scharpf 1999: 45)

A further twist in the story is that EU reforms, sometimes inadvertently, gave European market authorities new bargaining heft, which was then used not to promote a social or normative European model, but rather to pressure US authorities to level the playing field through mutual recognition arrangements. Unlike in data privacy and the environment, sectors mentioned in Jacoby and Meunier's discussion of mechanisms (Jacoby and Meunier 2010), EU financial regulation tended towards an international consensus that was shaped by a normative framework developed under de facto hegemony of international financial intermediaries and US officials.

EXPLAINING THE LACK OF REGULATORY PURPOSE

There are several possible explanations for these empirical conclusions. One is that embedded differences in national political economies made EU consensus impossible on the most important areas of financial regulation (Fioretos 2010). By this logic, rooted in the varieties of capitalism literature (Hall and Soskice 2001), our investigation suffers from a selection bias: we look at the regional level, rather than at a range of 'managed approaches' that would reflect differing national purposes, each sensitive enough to impede EU-level agreement. In contrast to the 1980s when a 'battle of the systems' kept ad hoc regulation at bay (Story and Walter 1997), according to this type of argument, the default position in today's Europe of cross-border financial activity is expanded discretion for firms, via regulatory arbitrage, not harmonization.

If this explanation were correct, our findings would suggest that member governments and the EP could not agree on EU-level arrangements in most areas where countries have historically limited firm discretion in order to advance national aims. The supportive evidence is fairly strong in two well-known cases: prudential supervisory institutions and corporate governance. Critics have long warned that new levels of regionalization in banking rendered existing prudential supervision (largely at the national level) unable to meet the public interest in a stable financial system (Véron 2007b). Yet until the crisis, several governments successfully resisted increasing sovereignty-sharing schemes, let alone new EU-level regulatory bodies. The corporate governance example follows a similar story-line, with Germany's last-minute sabotage of an EU overhaul that would have constrained national governments' freedom to set domestic company law (Cioffi 2006).

These high-profile cases notwithstanding, the broader trend shows that governments did manage to co-operate extensively by the turn of the millennium in many if not most areas of financial regulation considered too sensitive for sovereignty-sharing in the 1980s. Policy-makers succeeded in making important EU-level bargains, which suggests that the absence of a managed approach was not accidental. Areas that followed this trend include accounting standards, stock exchanges, auditing and financial conglomerates. In short, the 'incommensurability' thesis appears to lack strong evidence.

A second possible explanation points to the dominance of US ideas for organizing finance (Gill and Law 1989; Simmons 2001).[27] Two types of evidence support this argument. First, in terms of the degree of firm discretion, there has been considerable congruence between the US regulatory approach and the raft of new EU legislation during the decade to 2008. Second, one can identify specific mechanisms through which US ideas made their way into EU legislation: international bodies (Finnemore 1996), firm lobbying (Coen and Richardson 2009; Quaglia 2008b) and European national-level reforms (Boyer 1996). Reluctant to adopt regional-level regulation based on a particular national model, EU policy-makers have been drawn to regulatory principles developed within international financial bodies, long dominated by officials overseeing the world's largest financial markets. Not surprisingly, such principles, accepted as 'neutral' or 'technical' in terms of EU politics, tended to rely on self-regulation, private authority and other governance modes used in the US and the UK that gave considerable discretion to financial services firms. Prime examples of this transmission mechanism include IFRS, created by the IASB as a purely private-sector body,[28] and EU capital reserve requirements based on Basel II.

Firm lobbying at the national and regional levels has been a second mechanism through which US ideas seeped into EU legislation. By the end of the 1990s, the largest European financial services companies had become supporters of regional regulation (Mügge 2006), and along with their US counterparts, encouraged co-ordinated transatlantic rules. Finally, even before the late 1990s push to integrate financial regulation, national lawmakers had been borrowing US ideas and arrangements – a pattern facilitating EU-level co-operation along an ad hoc approach to financial globalization. London followed New York's equity market liberalization in 1986, Paris followed after Mitterrand's U-turn, and Frankfurt followed in the early 1990s

(Cerny 1989; Loriaux 1991; Lütz 1998; Moran 1991). Initially considered 'big bangs', these domestic reform packages were in fact slow-moving transformations that gradually expanded firm discretion. Accounting is a good example from the 1990s, with the German government allowing its firms to shift to US GAAP or IFRS on a voluntary basis, under rules adopted in 1998.

Despite this supportive evidence, not all of the historical record supports the explanation. Solutions forged in international forums, for example, often reflected positions advocated by large countries other than the US. For example, Germany successfully won protections for SMEs in the Basel II agreement (Christopoulos and Quaglia 2009; Quaglia 2008b). More to the point, the argument emphasizing the domination of US ideas is insufficient in at least three critical respects. First, it does not address core questions about the role of the EP. EU-level regulatory solutions not only had to overcome national differences but also a balance of powers problem – the ongoing struggle among the member governments (organized in the Council), the EP, the Commission and, more recently, the European Central Bank. By the late 1990s, member governments had signaled their willingness to delegate authorities over financial rule-making to the European Commission (Almer 2006). MEPs, concerned about their institution's relative position, posed the main obstacle. Why did the EP, with Europe's strongest voices in favor of managing globalization, ultimately accede to the FSAP, adoption of IFRS, and Lamfalussy process? Second, as the other contributions here attest, financial regulation is somewhat of an outlier. The domination of US ideas hypothesis does not address why finance was more susceptible to US ideas than other regulatory areas. Finally, European leaders had long been familiar with US ideas about how to organize finance. The domination explanation does not account for why the EU regulatory shift occurred between 1998 and 2008.

Answers to these questions lie in a third explanation, one that recognizes the European integration process – the politics and institutionalization of the polity – as a distinct historical causal force (Meunier and McNamara 2007; Pierson 1996; Posner 2009b; Stone Sweet *et al.* 2001). We argue that a constellation of developments – all tied to the regional integration project – came together to form a consensus in favor of intensified integration at the turn of the millennium. During this period, policy-makers made financial integration their top priority, selecting legislative content and rule-making procedures that posed the least resistance to this aim.

What led to the consensus? First, policy entrepreneurs, prominent among them Mario Monti in his capacity as EU Single Market Commissioner (1995–1999), then as Competition Commissioner (1999–2004), took advantage of the euro's introduction and the apparent acceleration of US financial dominance to promote the European Commission's decades-old goal of integrated financial regulation (Posner 2007). In framing the debates, Brussels officials argued that the benefits of the new currency would be lost if barriers to cross-border finance remained in place, or even that permanently fragmented financial markets could become a threat to the sustainability of the single currency. Moreover, there was a concern that, without a single financial market in Europe, EU firms would never be on an equal footing with US financial services companies.[29]

Second, previous integration efforts contributed to the shift in the policy positions of European firms. The remaining obstacles to cross-border competition, reinforced by existing legislation, became a source of frustration and a motivation for firm-driven reforms. Such lingering regulatory obstacles were without parallel in other large industries, with the possible exception of energy utilities, defense and railways, in which incumbents, because of their monopolist status, tended to be more resistant to integration than in finance. The nearest equivalent to such monopolies in banking would be the German savings banks and *Landesbanken*, whose local positions are protected under the so-called regional principle (*Regionalprinzip*). These banks have opposed integration more than any other group of market participants (Grossman 2006). From this standpoint Monti's taming of Landesbanken in the early 2000s may be seen as emblematic of Europe's financial integration.

Finally, EU legislation from the 1980s and early 1990s also helps to explain France's and Germany's willingness to intensify financial regulatory co-operation, even if it meant the adoption of British and American approaches. Directives that partly put a stamp of approval on existing protectionist measures, such as the 1993 ISD, allowed Germany and France to employ infant-industry strategies to modernize their stock exchanges and other capital markets. Along with their apparent success came a palpable hubris that Frankfurt and Paris could compete with London in a single EU marketplace (Posner 2007). There is also reason to believe that German Finance Minister Hans Eichel and British Chancellor of the Exchequer Gordon Brown (both thinking that the UK would one day adopt the euro) favored an alternative EU regulatory apparatus to prevent the encroachment of the ECB. The governments in both countries had gained new political controls over financial regulation by shedding authorities from their respective central banks (Westrup 2007). In the UK, the reform was a bargain giving the Bank of England greater independence while many supervisory tasks were entrusted to the newly created FSA. In Germany, the new dispensation was part of the shift from the Bundesbank to the ECB and the creation of a new financial regulatory and supervisory agency, BAFin. The FSAP framework, which essentially preserved national implementation and enforcement of EU legislation and rules, simultaneously kept hard-won political controls over financial regulation, while preventing future ECB expansion.

These three developments contributed to a broad-based consensus about further integration and to a pragmatic moment in EU financial history. No one wanted to be seen as slowing the integration momentum, and the results were extraordinary[30] – around 40 pieces of legislation and an overhaul of financial rule-making. Within this political context the EP picked its battles carefully, choosing to hold out on issues of institutional power rather than fighting for the management of financial globalization through EU legislation. In some cases, this choice was made easier by the failure of opposing coalitions to frame comprehensive alternative principles for guiding financial regulation. The promoters of the accounting standards regulation, for example, presented the measure as international best practice and a technical matter for experts; whereas the opponents were unable to put forth a tractable alternative, and the regulation was passed by an overwhelming majority. However, in more contentious cases, MEPs were forced to make difficult choices. On one side were the more integrationist measures that both provided opportunities for new inter-institutional bargains to expand EP powers but also tended to correspond with Anglo-style rules. On the other side were regulatory approaches that, while promoting elements of managed globalization, were widely perceived as protectionist. The heated political contests surrounding MiFID and the Prospectus Directive exemplify these tensions (Quaglia 2009), and the coalitions in favor of tighter controls over firm discretion lost in both cases in large part because the EP supported the positions of the London-based interests.

In the absence of a vision of how to manage the global financial system that could be easily shared by all main EU countries, the path of least resistance was the one that was most easily embraced by the EU's large financial companies (which by 2000 had become well organized) and by US-based banks with large operations in Europe. The dissenting voices – inside and outside the EP – did not put forth an alternative that could as compellingly serve the prevailing objective of cross-border financial integration.

CONCLUSION

In the decade to 2008, the diversity of European financial regulatory approaches did not lead to a series of weak and watered-down directives as it had in the years following the 1986 Single European Act. Nor did it lead to a consistent drive to manage financial globalization. Our analysis helps to explain this outcome. A constellation of factors, largely endogenous to the EU project's evolution, gave rise to a consensus for regulation that would enable financial market integration. A strong political tide thus swept EU decision-makers towards international practice as established in US-dominated bodies and Anglo–American regulatory models that allowed financial services firms large degrees of discretion.

A major question at the time of writing is whether the ongoing financial crisis has changed this situation in a lasting way. In the short term it undoubtedly has. The collective failure of a financial system that was perceived as largely modeled on an Anglo–American approach has provoked a widespread rhetorical rejection of ad hoc financial globalization. This is evident at the level of national political leaders such as France's President Nicolas Sarkozy or Germany's Finance Minister Peer Steinbrück, and on the part of the European Commission, by Internal Market Commissioner Charlie McCreevy's new discourse targeting a range of financial industry participants who until 2008 viewed him as 'business-friendly'. More significantly, EU policy-makers have adopted more stringent regulation in areas including credit rating agencies, capital requirements and securitization, and are negotiating tighter regulations for hedge funds and asset management firms. All of these legislative efforts are likely to constrain to some extent the activities of financial services firms operating in the EU.

In the medium term, a managed approach to financial regulation would require institutional arrangements promoting better regional co-ordination to match the tighter rules – at least so long as cross-border financial activity continues at current levels. At the time of writing, the public discussion concerning institutional reform, largely shaped by the Larosière Report commissioned by the European Commission,[31] has resulted in Commission proposals for the creation of more centralized EU supervisory authorities,[32] but it remains too soon to assess whether the severity of the current crisis has weakened the intergovernmental and inter-institutional constraints that long defined the evolution of EU financial regulatory bargains.

There is of course a possibility that a more managed approach could be achieved through a de-integrative process, albeit in that case it would be about the management of regional or national financial systems rather than the global one. Indeed, national bank rescue plans have repeatedly seemed to favor reversals in the previous drive towards cross-border banking integration, but the hard evidence so far remains ambiguous. Looking forward, the increase in risk aversion tends to reduce cross-border credit flows, while the impending restructuring of the entire banking sector is set to create cross-border merger or acquisition opportunities. Here too, it is still too early for a reliable assessment of the respective strengths of such conflicting trends.

Meanwhile, the three successive summits of the G20 group of heads of state and government, beginning in November 2008, have exemplified an effort to manage globalization in times of financial crisis. But while Europeans claim leadership in having made them happen,[33] they were somewhat overshadowed by the United States and China, especially in the second and third meetings in London and Pittsburgh, for reasons that include the impact of visible intra-European divisions on key policy issues. Thus, while there is no doubt that the crisis is altering the previous decade-long pattern of regulatory integration, it is too early to map out the direction European financial regulation will follow in the aftermath of the massive financial and economic turmoil.

ACKNOWLEDGEMENTS

The authors thank Wade Jacoby, Erik Jones, Patrick Leblond, Sophie Meunier, Lucia Quaglia, Gillian Weiss and two anonymous reviewers for their useful comments on previous drafts of this essay.

NOTES

1 While not engaged in the debates about the management of globalization, some legal scholars imply that regulatory harmonization is market-correcting (Hadjiem-manuil 2006).
2 To the extent possible, we avoid the term 'liberal', 'liberalization' and other related terms to avoid confusion between two possible meanings in the EU context. In the first, analysts use liberal to connote non-discrimination across borders. In the second, they use the term to mean the absence of public interference in the business decisions and behavior of firms.
3 Here, for the sake of clarity, we leave aside the possibility of achieving a managed approach in the EU through the sum of the efforts of member states.
4 This section is based on Posner (2009a).
5 Directive 2002/87/EC of the European Parliament and of the Council of the European Union.
6 See Posner (2009a) for details.
7 See 'Agency's '04 rule let banks pile up new debt, and risk', *New York Times*, 3 October 2008: 1. On how the EU directive affected US regulation, see Cox (2008).
8 Directive 2006/43/EC of the European Parliament and of the Council of 17 May 2006, on statutory audits of annual accounts and consolidated accounts.
9 Eberle and Lauter (2009) argue that a backlash by European auditors against US-style oversight has hindered the European Commission's goals of transatlantic mutual recognition.
10 European Commission, 'Financial Services Action Plan', Brussels: Commission of the EU, 1999, COM (1999) 232; and 'Single Market in Financial Services Progress Report, 2004–2005', Brussels, SEC (2006) 17, 5 January 2006.
11 Directive 2004/39/EC of the European Parliament and of the Council of 21 April 2004 on markets in financial instruments.
12 Council Directive 93/22/EEC of 10 May 1993 on investment services in the securities field, known as the Investment Services Directive (ISD).
13 As Quaglia (2009) points out, it is difficult to decipher between protectionism of material interests and positions derived from beliefs rooted in a distrust of markets.
14 Actually a combination of two simultaneously adopted directives: Directive 2006/48/EC of the European Parliament and of the Council of 14 June 2006 relating to the taking up and pursuit of the business of credit institutions, and directive 2006/49/EC of the European Parliament and of the Council of 14 June 2006 on the capital adequacy of investment firms and credit institutions.
15 The CRD includes investment firms and all banks, thus going beyond Basel II, which is limited to internationally oriented credit institutions, and made a few important adaptations (Quaglia 2008b: 56–8).
16 Regulation 1606/2002 of the European Parliament and of the Council.
17 Directive 2001/24/EC of the European Parliament and of the Council, 4 April 2001.
18 The Lamfalussy process was introduced in the securities sector in 2001 and in the banking, insurance and occupational pensions sectors in 2004. It defines four levels of decision-making, each corresponding in principle to a specific stage in the elaboration or implementation of financial legislation.

19 Posner makes this argument in 2010. See also Quaglia (2008a) for a different though not incompatible interpretation.
20 The Committee of European Securities Regulators.
21 The Committee of European Banking Supervisors.
22 The Committee of European Insurance and Occupational Pensions Supervisors.
23 See, for example, the remarks by Alexandre Lamfalussy (2005).
24 See ec.europa.eu/internal_market/finservices-retail/fscg/index_en.htm (accessed December 2009).
25 See Quaglia (2008a: 574) which notes that consumer groups, in particular, have been absent from the processes.
26 For example, examine the participants in CESR's consultation process. Go to the 'consultation' icon at www.CESR-eu.org (accessed December 2009).
27 On normative frameworks in the context of international regimes, see Rugge (1983). See also McNamara (1998).
28 The IASB was formally submitted to a 'Monitoring Board' of public authorities in 2009, well after the adoption of IFRS in the EU. Furthermore, this new arrangement is unlikely to be permanent in its current form, as suggested by the refusal of EU Commissioner Charlie McCreevy to formally sign the Monitoring Board's founding texts on behalf of the EU (as of July 2009).
29 An early European Commission communiqué along these lines is *Financial Services: Building a Framework for Action.* ip/98/941, 28 October 1998.
30 Author's interview with European Commission official, 9 June 2004, Brussels.
31 'The High-level Group on Financial Supervision in the EU', chaired by Jacques de Larosière, Brussels, 25 February 2009.
32 Conclusions of the European Council meeting of 18–19 June 2009.
33 Until then, G20 meetings had been regularly held since 1999 but only at the level of finance ministers and central bank governors, with no participation of heads of state and government.

REFERENCES

Abdelal, R. (2007) *Capital Rules: The Construction of Global Finance*, Cambridge, MA: Harvard University Press.
Abdelal, R. and Meunier, S. (2010) 'Managed globalization: doctrine, practice and promise', *Journal of European Public Policy* 17(3): 350–67.
Almer, J. (2006) 'The reform of comitology and the parallel reform of the European financial services sector', New Modes of Governance Project, CIT1-CT-2004-506392, 7/D05a rev, 12 December.
Boyer, R. (1996) 'The convergence hypothesis revisited: globalization but still the century of nations?', in S. Berger and R. Dore (eds), *National Diversity and Global Capitalism*, Ithaca, NY: Cornell University Press.
Cerny, P. (1989) 'The "little big bang" in Paris: financial market deregulation in a *dirigiste* system', *European Journal of Political Research* 17(2): 169–92.
Christopoulos, D. and Quaglia, L. (2009) 'Network constraints in EU banking regulation: the capital requirements directive', *Journal of Public Policy* 29(2): 179–200.
Cioffi, J. (2006) 'Building finance capitalism: the regulatory politics of corporate governance reform in the United States and Germany', in J. Levy (ed.), *The State after Statism: New State Activities in the Age of Liberalization*, Cambridge, MA: Harvard University Press.
Claessens, S., Underhill, G. and Zhang, X. (2008) 'The political economy of Basel II: the costs for poor countries', *World Economy* 31(3): 313–44.
Coen, D. and Richardson, J. (2009) *Lobbying the European Union: Institutions, Actors and Issues*, Oxford: Oxford University Press.

Coen, D. and Thatcher, M. (2008) 'Network governance and multi-level delegation: European networks of regulatory agencies', *Journal of Public Policy* 28(1): 49–71.

Cox, C. (2008) Address to the Security Traders 12th Annual Washington Conference, Washington, DC, 7 May, 2008. Available at www.sec.gov (accessed December 2009).

Drezner, D.W. (2007) *All Politics is Global: Explaining International Regulatory Regimes*, Princeton, NJ: Princeton University Press.

Eberle, D. and Lauter, D. (2009) 'Domestic private interests and the EU–US dispute on audit regulation: the role of the European accounting profession', unpublished paper.

Fioretos, O. (2010) 'Europe and the new global economic order: internal diversity as liability and asset in managing globalization', *Journal of European Public Policy* 17(3): 383–99.

Finnemore, M. (1996) *National Interests in International Society*, Ithaca, NY: Cornell University Press.

Gill, S. and Law, D. (1989) 'Global hegemony and the structural power of capital', *International Studies Quarterly* 33(4): 475–99.

Grossman, E. (2004) 'Bringing politics back in: rethinking the role of economic interest groups in European integration', *Journal of European Public Policy* 11(4): 637–54.

Grossman, E. (2006) 'Europeanization as an interactive process: German public banks meet EU state aid policy', *Journal of Common Market Studies* 44(2): 325–48.

Hadjiemmanuil, C. (2005) 'Europe's universalist approach to cross-border bank resolution issues', in D. Evanoff and G. Kaufman (eds), *Systemic Financial Crises: Resolving Large Bank Insolvencies*, Hackensack: World Scientific.

Hadjiemmanuil, C. (2006) 'Financial services', in D. Chalmers, C. Hadjiemmanuil, G. Monti and A. Tomkins (eds), *European Union Law: Text and Materials*, Cambridge: Cambridge University Press.

Hall, P. and Soskice, D. (eds) (2001) *Varieties of Capitalism: The Institutional Foundations of Comparative Advantage*, Oxford: Oxford University Press.

Jacoby, W. and Meunier, S. (2010) 'Europe and the management of globalization', *Journal of European Public Policy* 17(3): 299–317.

Lamfalussy, A. (2005). 'The four-level approach to financial regulation in Europe: origins, main features, achievements, concerns', in The Euro: One Currency, One Financial Market, Conference Proceedings, New York, 19–20 April.

Loriaux, M. (1991) *France after Hegemony: International Change and Financial Reform*, Ithaca, NY: Cornell University Press.

Lütz, S. (1998) 'The revival of the nation-state? Stock exchange regulation in an era of globalized financial markets', *Journal of European Public Policy* 5(1): 153–68.

McNamara, K. (1998) *The Currency of Ideas: Monetary Politics in the European Union*, Ithaca, NY: Cornell University Press.

Meunier, S. and McNamara, K. (2007) *Making History: European Integration and Institutional Change at Fifty*, Oxford: Oxford University Press.

Moran, M. (1991) *The Politics of the Financial Services Revolution: The USA, UK and Japan*, New York: St Martin's Press.

Mügge, D. (2006) 'Reordering the market place: competition politics in European finance', *Journal of Common Market Studies* 55(5): 991–1022.

Newman, A. (2008) 'Building transnational civil liberties: transgovernmental entrepreneurs and the European Data Privacy Directive', *International Organization* 62(1): 103–30.

Nölke, A. and Perry, J. (2007) 'The power of transnational private governance: financialization and the IASB', *Business and Politics* 9(3), Article 4.

Olson, M. (1965) *The Logic of Collective Action: Public Good and the Theory of Groups*, Cambridge, MA: Harvard University Press.

Perry, J. and Nölke, A. (2006) 'The political economy of international accounting standards', *Review of International Political Economy* 13(4): 559–86.

Pierson, P. (1996) 'The path to European integration: a historical institutionalist analysis', *Comparative Political Studies* 29(2): 123–63.

Posner, E. (2007) 'Financial transformation in the European Union', in S. Meunier and K. McNamara (eds), *Making History: European Integration and Institutional Change at Fifty*, Oxford: Oxford University Press.

Posner, E. (2009a) 'Making rules for global finance: transatlantic regulatory cooperation at the turn of the millennium', *International Organization* 63(4): 665–99.

Posner, E. (2009b) *The Origins of Europe's New Stock Markets*, Cambridge, MA: Harvard University Press.

Posner, E. (2010) 'The Lamfalussy process: polyarchic origins of networked financial rulemaking in the EU', in C. Sabel and J. Zeitlin (eds), *EU Governance: Towards a New Architecture?*, Oxford: Oxford University Press.

Quaglia, L. (2008a) 'Financial sector committee governance in the European Union', *European Integration* 30(4): 563–78.

Quaglia, L. (2008b) 'Setting the pace? Private financial interests and European financial market integration', *British Journal of Politics and International Relations* 10: 46–63.

Quaglia, L. (2009). 'Completing the single market in financial services: the politics of competing advocacy coalitions', in EUSA Conference Proceedings, April.

Ruggie, J. (1983) 'International regimes, transactions and change: embedded liberalism in the postwar economic order', in S. Krasner (ed.), *International Regimes*, Cambridge, MA: Cornell University Press.

Scharpf, F. (1999) *Governing in Europe: Effective and Democratic?*, Oxford: Oxford University Press.

Seakbrooke, L. (2006) *The Social Sources of Financial Power: Domestic Legitimacy and International Financial Orders*, Ithaca, NY: Cornell University Press.

Simmons, B. (2001) 'International politics of harmonization: the case of capital market regulation', *International Organization* 55(3): 589–620.

Steil, B. and Litan, R. (2006) *Financial Statecraft: The Role of Financial Markets in American Foreign Policy*, New Haven, CT: Yale University Press.

Stone Sweet, A., Fligstein, N. and Sandholtz, W. (2001) 'The institutionalization of European space', in A. Stone Sweet, N. Fligstein and W. Sandholtz (eds), *The Institutionalization of Europe*, Oxford: Oxford University Press.

Story, J. and Walter, I. (1997) *Political Economy of Financial Integration in Europe: The Battle of the Systems*, Cambridge, MA: MIT Press.

Underhill, G. and Zhang, X. (2008) 'Setting the rules: private power, political underpinnings, and legitimacy in global monetary and financial governance', *International Affairs* 84(3): 535–54.

Véron, N. (2007a) 'The global accounting experiment', *Bruegel Blueprint* 2: 1–86.

Véron, N. (2007b) 'Is Europe ready for a major banking crisis?', *Bruegel Policy Brief* 3: 1–8.

Véron, N., Autret, M. and Galichon, A. (2006) *Smoke & Mirrors, Inc.: Accounting for Capitalism*, Ithaca, NY: Cornell University Press.

Westrup, J. (2007) 'The politics of financial regulatory reform in Britain and Germany', *West European Politics* 30(5): 1096–1119.

Managing globalization by managing Central and Eastern Europe: the EU's backyard as threat and opportunity

Wade Jacoby

ABSTRACT   As European voters and politicians increasingly demanded in the 1990s that the European Union (EU) 'manage' globalization, managing the new member states of Central and Eastern Europe (CE) emerged as an important precursor. To richer areas like the old EU-15, poor areas next door often appear as both threat and opportunity. Some EU-15 actors – mostly corporations, but also many European liberals – saw in CE a chance for new markets, new workers and new investment opportunities for the core EU-15 economies. They tried to codify new conditions of production and sale that they thought beneficial, but other EU-15 actors worried about competition from CE on capital, labor and product markets. The fearful – mostly EU-15 states and the EU itself but sometimes firms headquartered in the EU-15 – acted to try to minimize these potential threats. I show that, as a broad proposition, actors motivated by the threats seem to have shaped conditions more than those motivated by opportunity. Data from financial flows, trade in goods and services, and labor migration illustrate this central point. I conclude with speculations on how this pattern is affected by the economic downturn after 2008.

Southeast Asia begins 70 kilometers east of Berlin.

–German trade union official, 1993

You think we don't know what you say? East Europe...where you pick up masterpiece for string of beads.... And what we spend on meal for you is tip. And you can buy our whole machine tool industry for thirty second ad on NBC.

–David Edgar, 'Pentecost'

INTRODUCTION

How did the Eastern enlargements of the European Union (EU) in 2004 and 2007 fit with Europe's broader efforts to manage globalization? A substantial literature focuses on EU efforts to manage the behavior of economic rivals, but how does the EU manage *prospective* members who are not yet major economic rivals? Managing Central and Eastern Europe (CE) seems a prerequisite for managing globalization, and it is also an important issue in its own right. As the two epigraphs above suggest, poor areas next door often inspire both feelings of threat and opportunity in rich areas (and the EU-15 are very rich indeed). The threat notion captures the worry (often on the part of the very same actors in the old EU-15) that competition from the region might actually threaten them.

One core question about CE mirrors Europe's core question about globalization: are potential new economic partners more of an opportunity or more of a threat to us? I argue that the CE states have emerged as a clear opportunity for the EU, and one reason is that the EU and its then 15 member states took them seriously as a potential economic threat almost from the very outset. I show that emerging potential threats were attenuated, weakened and managed, often in ways that put the EU at the very center of the politics between the Western and Eastern parts of Europe. I also show that actors from the old EU-15 often used the EU to increase their business opportunities in CE.

My main goal here is to flesh out the point that 'enlarging the sphere of EU influence' is an important mechanism for managing globalization (Jacoby and Meunier 2010). This is a novel claim, and it may have broader relevance since several authors – many among those optimistic about the EU as a rising power – have made the claim that the EU will increasingly impact upon a very large sphere of geographically proximate countries (McCormick 2006; Reid 2004; Schnabel 2005).[1] It seems useful, then, to look back on the EU's engagement with CE as a source of clues about how the EU deals with economically weaker states whose proximity can be both an opportunity and a threat to its member states.

To do so, I investigate the three most commonly cited areas of globalization, namely flows of capital, labor, and goods and services. In my account, actors from the EU's 15 pre-2004 'old member states' plus EU officials are the managers, while the 10 CE new member states are the managed.[2] I focus my attention on the period from the collapse of communism to the onset of the financial crisis in late 2008, the effects of which are too new for inclusion here. My core intuition is that managing global challenges begins by managing one's own backyard. To the extent that there is a perception that much lower costs lie in close geographic proximity, this should induce some actors to try to exploit that and some to restrict it. I show that this is exactly what has happened since 1990.

CE sparked two primary responses among West European economic and political actors: a feeling of threat and one of opportunity. Some actors – mostly corporations, but also many European liberals – saw a chance for new markets, new workers and new investment possibilities for the core EU-15 economies. The underlying logic was that these actors could use the physical, human and legal assets of the CE region to diversify (generally not abandon) their own economic model.[3] On the other hand, many EU-15 firms, labor unions and many politicians worried openly about competition from CE on capital, labor and product markets or the cost of fiscal transfers to the much poorer region. They sought to defend their economies against threats emanating from CE by proposing barriers to immigration and trade and measures to moderate the amount of investment that flowed from EU-15 to CE sites.

Broadly, I argue that EU-15 actors exercised remarkable control over the economic transformation in CE. That is, EU-15 actors used the EU to manage the CE states. They have done so in ways that provided new opportunities while carefully managing threats. Sometimes, this has involved very conventional EU tools – such as trade agreements – so that the outcome is not surprising. In other cases, however, the EU has acted creatively to manage flows of both capital and labor with new instruments. None of this is to deny that CE actors – including national governments – were crucial to the economic reforms of post-communism, a prominent theme in my other work (Jacoby 2004, 2006). But in a collection devoted to EU efforts to manage globalization, it seems important to focus more light on some of the EU's less understood policies towards CE.[4] In the interest of space, it is also regrettably necessary to downplay the very important national and subnational differences among these 10 states (Bohle and Greskovits 2007) in an effort to give a general account of such diverse policy reforms.

I show that private actors from the EU-15 hit the ground early in CE, and their effects have generally pre-dated an active interest by the EU in the regulatory system of CE economies. But where private actors have provoked relatively decentralized policies, the EU, while coming late to the table, enjoyed substantial leverage, especially during the run-up to enlargement. In broad terms, the EU (and some of its member states) sought to displace private practices geared towards exploiting new opportunities with more defensive 'fear-driven' policies as the dominant management approach in the region. I elaborate this central point through materials drawn from a growing secondary literature and from my own decade of research into these issues. I begin with an account of FDI, followed by immigration and trade.

CAPITAL INVESTMENT: PROMOTING OPPORTUNITY, ATTENUATING THREATS

In capital, the EU was fairly quiet in the face of early post-communist investment debates but asserted key EU-15 interests against perceived threats that arose later in the transformation. Immediately after communism collapsed, many Western corporate managers saw investment in CE as a chance to build a low-wage platform to complement or replace high-cost home production, exploiting new conditions that would make their firms more fit for global competition. The first epigraph – that Southeast Asia begins 70 kilometers east of Berlin – captures the sense of many actors that CE was a natural low-cost region no matter what political actions were taken there. Yet it is incorrect to imagine that capital flowed East quickly and easily. Almost all CE states started out strongly protective of their national capital stock, partly for reasons crystallized in the second epigraph, taken from a character in David Edgar's brilliant 1995 stage play, 'Pentecost'.

Ironically, just as Edgar was writing foreign direct investment (FDI) saw its first real surge into the region. Even at that time, however, more than twice as many CE respondents told pollsters that 'Foreigners should not be allowed to own land in (respondent's country)' as in the Organization for Economic and Co-operative Development (OECD) states (69 per cent versus 33 per cent) (Bandelj 2008: 55). Yet by 2004 FDI as a percentage of gross domestic product (GDP) was 39 per cent in CE – almost twice the world average. In banking, the picture was even starker, as more than half the CE financial sector was in foreign hands by the end of 2004, as opposed to an OECD average closer to 20 per cent (Epstein 2008: 70–2). Clearly, something had overcome these sceptical attitudes.

This market did not emerge spontaneously but was fostered by three sets of policies driven by, respectively, the international financial institutions (IFIs), transnational corporations (TNCs), and the CE states themselves. First, when CE governments had initial reservations about selling state firms to Western investors, the Western-dominated IFIs that played a role in encouraging privatization could point to the EU's 'free movement of capital' as a component of eventual membership (Kaminski 2000). So while the EU itself had little involvement in the basic design of privatization programs, its famous Annual Reports often mentioned specific targets of privatization and encouraged the various CE governments to sell properties for whom the most plausible buyers were generally from the EU-15. Even Czech 'voucher privatization' came only *after* the conservative Czech government initially resisted selling the perceived jewels of the Czech economy into foreign hands (Appel 2006). Drahokoupil shows that the EU 'narrowed the space for attempts at promoting domestic accumulation' (2008a: 26), and multivariate regressions of the determinants of openings to FDI flows across all post-communist states show large and significant 'EU effects' (Bandelj 2008: 84–5).[5] Although hardly the central actor in privatization, the EU thus broadly sought to increase investment opportunities in CE.

TNCs were a second source of policy innovation. Far from merely responding to CE states' privatization tenders to buy and revitalize aging communist firms, many TNCs were willing to make expensive greenfield (i.e., brand new) investments. A detailed study of seven major greenfield projects – six from EU-15 firms and a seventh from Kia – confirms that far from taking conditions as given, TNCs launched structured bidding wars among potential investment locations. When BMW announced plans to build a major car plant, it called upon officials in prospective locations to answer over 70 questions about the conditions of investment there. It received proposals from about 150 locations in CE. BMW also hired a CE-based consulting firm, Svoboda & Partner, to encourage localities to put their best fiscal foot forward. One Svoboda official recalled, 'We would knock on the closed doors of various [Czech] authorities, trying to persuade them that the state had to make a real effort. It was not enough to offer land; it was necessary to fulfill even the unexpressed wishes and expectations of the car-maker' (quoted in Drahokoupil 2008b: 204). While such demands have become standard global practice for TNCs, in CE the TNCs could help set the broad initial rules of the game, rather than the more general pattern of seeking exceptions to those rules.

The third source of policy innovation has been the CE states. In the hunt for investment capital, they have often offered very lucrative investment incentives targeted at foreign investors (Drahokoupil 2008a, 2008b; Ellison 2007; O'Dwyer and Kovalcik 2007). Where large car firms are arguably policy 'makers',[6] smaller Western investors are policy 'takers', and good general conditions are meant to lure them East. In that sense, we can imagine CE policy-makers solving the collective action problems of smaller foreign investors, who may be too dispersed to effectively lobby CE states. The basket of policies includes tax cuts for foreign investors, a simplified tax code, tax holidays, land grants, loose restrictions on labor relations, and even long-term commitments to reduced social spending as a credible commitment to sustained low taxes. Clearly a function of aggressive governments seeking to lure hard-to-identify potential investors, these policies have proliferated more in some CE states than in others.

These policies were coterminous with a second boom in FDI in the early part of the 2000s, but then a backlash ensued against hyper-liberal policies ensued.[7] The backlash was led by actors worried about EU-15 competitive disadvantage and by EU officials keen to prevent behavior that might undermine the legitimacy of the single market. Some sought to prevent capital from flowing from the EU-15 by pressuring CE states to raise standards quickly so that CE tax rates soon approximated those on capital in the EU-15 and to end very attractive tax holidays. This reaction came despite the fact that EU-15 states did not see major capital outflows to CE (except, perhaps, from Austria and, even then, major Austrian banks were reaping well over half of their profits in CE markets by 2005 (Epstein 2008: 70)).

In this reaction, the leading instrument of EU-15 actors has been the EU, with its detailed single market *acquis* and enforcement mechanisms.[8] As a leading target of FDI, Hungary's policies have come in for particular scrutiny.[9] EU-15 corporate tax rates have come down markedly in recent years, at least partly in response to CE tax competition, a development generally welcomed by managers.[10] On the other hand, the EU screening process stripped CE states of some potentially useful national tools for managing the political economy – tools that were judged by the Commission to be in contradiction to the *acquis* (Appel 2006; Ellison 2007; Gabrisch and Werner 1999). Some tax tools were outlawed altogether as violations of the state aids section of the *acquis*; others were trimmed substantially, such as the length and extent of tax holidays. When the EU tried to void favorable conditions between Slovakia and US Steel, the American company resisted, and the EU wrote an exception into the Slovakian accession treaty. In most cases, however, the EU was pushing to remove or limit concessions won by EU-15-based actors in CE.[11]

CE states know that the EU has relatively few tools to constrain the corporate tax policies of CE states and are often allied with well-informed and powerful Western firms poised to defend their policy discretion.[12] That said, with the controversial 'flat taxes' in six EU members (Estonia, Latvia, Lithuania, Slovakia, Romania and Bulgaria), only the Bulgarian choice for the flat tax came after EU membership, with the Baltic States moving already in the mid-1990s. Smaller and poorer CE countries were attracted to the flat tax to draw FDI flowing to Poland, the Czech Republic and Hungary, and the EU-15 could do little to stop them.[13]

At the same time, FDI allows EU-15 states new options, including some that leave them better prepared to face globalization pressures. Without fundamentally changing their own national models of capitalism – a deeply contentious process with uncertain results – many large and small EU-15 firms are able to do things complementary to (not alternative to) production at home. Suzanne Berger notes that some EU-15 firms (her examples are drawn from Italian textiles) tend to use CE investment for new business and expansion while their core business stays in the home location.[14] Becker and Muendler (2008) use a German dataset to show that job separation at TNCs who invested abroad was substantially lower than with comparable jobs at non-TNCs. Among other things, this may be because FDI allows better matching of worker to comparative advantage, thus increasing overall firm efficiency and perhaps global market share. Bandelj (2008) shows that investment opportunities in CE allow EU-15 firms to alter the 'make versus buy' decision in many cases.

In short, CE is both a platform for EU-15 business expansion and also a pressure valve to diminish tension over domestic regulations on the grounds that investors can escape some regulations by going to CE. CE politicians play to both sides of this: they offer preferential terms for foreign investment, defend those deals against skeptical EU Commission officials, and hope to use the resulting investment to catch up to EU-15 standards.

LABOR MIGRATION: VARIETIES OF ANXIETIES

If the capital movement case revealed a structural advantage for EU-15 actors who saw opportunity in CE, the labor case reveals an advantage for those who felt threatened. Moreover, the capital side showed substantial diversity across the region, suggesting that CE states clearly are not all responding in the same way to EU-15 management efforts. The labor case adds the important dimension that the EU-15 vary significantly in *what they want from CE*. In explaining this variation, geography clearly matters in the case of labor. Germany and Austria had quite poor CE states on their immediate border while none of the other EU-15 did.[15] Their politicians judged the potential for migration flows very differently than did politicians in, say, the UK.

Broadly, the EU-15 have both a tradition of very low labor mobility internally and a de facto 'low-skill bias' in their immigration policies. This combination brings somewhat fewer economic benefits than would high mobility and a high-skill immigration bias, but it also exacerbates the political tensions that surround immigration. In comparative perspective, moreover, Europe is more skeptical towards low-skilled immigrants than is the US since it has a more generous welfare state (Brücker and von Weizsäcker 2007: 248).

While some EU-15 actors placed priority on getting access to labor (especially skilled labor) from CE, others focused on walling off immigration from CE. Initially, it seemed as if the primary management here would involve the Commission walking the CE states through a welter of well-established (if patch-work) regulations regarding free movement of persons, which had become a core principle of the single market in both theory and deed by the 1990s (Grabbe 2006: chs 6 and 7). But technocratic debate over mutual recognition of things like professional certificates was soon swamped in the late 1990s by the high politics of member states. Germany and Austria, in particular, raised strong objections to immediate free movement of CE workers. In Austria, the temporary work of CE migrants was often likened in the coarse public debate to prostitution. Indeed, the places where day laborers waited for work in Vienna were called the '*Arbeitsstrich*' – roughly the 'work brothel'. Between 2000 and 2004, the number of residents of the accession states living in the EU-15 increased from 700,000 to over 900,000. At that stage, gross monthly wages in the immediately acceding CE countries generally ranged from less than 15 per cent of German wages (Latvia and Lithuania) to about 30 per cent (Hungary and the Czech Republic) (Zimmerman 2007).[16]

Faced with severe pressure from Germany and Austria, the EU was ultimately obliged to negotiate the right of individual EU-15 states to limit entry of workers from CEE states for up to seven years after membership. Once the possibility was opened, 12 of the 15 took advantage of it – all but the UK, Ireland and Sweden. To many observers this majority position seemed politically comprehensible, but economically (and morally) shortsighted.[17] The Commission unsuccessfully advocated more openness to CE immigration. Frits Bolkestein, Internal Market Commissioner, was blunt about the defensiveness of these walls: 'In a healthy economy it is better to prepare for competition than to draw up new barriers' (Grabbe 2006: 146). In the event, Polish immigration to Germany barely budged with enlargement, though there seems little doubt that many Poles who emigrated to the UK might otherwise have gone to Germany.[18]

Yet despite their significant miscalculation in the number of arriving immigrants, there was, up until the time of the downturn in 2008, no evidence of declining native wages in the UK, Ireland or Sweden 'even in the sectors with the largest share of new immigrants' (Zimmerman 2007). There has also been little evidence of a growth in 'welfare tourism' (Kvist 2004). Zimmerman's 2007 data show that after enlargement, Irish unemployment trended very slightly downward while UK and Swedish unemployment trended slightly upward until, with the financial crisis of 2008, it rose sharply everywhere in Europe. Interestingly, the public perception of immigration (share who agree that 'immigration is good for the country's economy') long tracked these disparate political decisions. In both the UK and Ireland, the share of respondents who agreed with the statement rose in the wake of enlargement. In both Germany and Austria, the share fell (Zimmerman 2007).

In keeping with these heightened anxieties, Austria and Germany announced their intention to sustain migration bans through 2009 (Austria) and 2011 (Germany). Meanwhile, Greece, Spain, Portugal and Finland lifted the bans entirely after the first period, while Belgium, Denmark, France, Italy, the Netherlands and Luxembourg modified the restrictions, especially in sectors with tight labor markets. In short, anxiety over immigration has varied substantially across the EU-15, but the broad picture is that most used the EU to legitimate time-limited immigration bans on citizens of fellow member states in order to buy time for adjustment to challenges from CE.

TRADE PATTERNS: BUYING MORE TIME

In trade, the EU initially used protectionism, treating the post-communist states as it would other non-members. Controlling access to its market is, of course, one of the key EU assets for managing globalization on behalf of its members (Drezner 2007). Soon, however, the EU began negotiating the so-called Europe Agreements (EAs) with the CE states. While most observers saw the EAs as a substitute for offering the CEs any perspective on quick membership, the EAs did contain much more favorable trade provisions than were available otherwise.[19] Giving up on pure protectionism, however, meant moving to a more subtle mix of management strategies.

As protectionism gave way to the managed trade of the EAs, the EU-15 determination to avoid competition in sensitive sectors was evident from the outset. On the surface, the bilateral deals between the EU and the CE states seemed tilted towards the latter: Europe would remove its trade barriers within five years, while the CE states would get ten years. The fine print, however, contained exclusions for many products where CE states were most competitive, including iron, steel, some chemicals and several agricultural products (Mayhew 1998: 62–71). This asymmetry bought the EU-15 time to respond to areas of CE comparative advantage, and an obvious response was to buy heavily in those areas. By the time general openness arrived, a surge in EU-15 FDI after 1995 (described above) left many key assets in foreign hands.

The point is that trade deepened in ways that substantially softened the blow to EU-15 economies. Recent scholarship paints a vivid picture of trade developments up to enlargement in which the CE economies grew deeply dependent on that of the EU-15. For example, Baldone *et al.* (2007) show that CE states' revealed comparative advantage is likely much lower than previously thought. Using EU data on firm registration of intermediate goods flows, the authors decompose trade statistics in a way that takes account of two facts: first, that many products that originate in non-EU countries go through at least one phase of their production in the EU (called 'inward processing trade' (IPT)); and second, that many products that originate in the EU undergo a phase of production outside the EU ('outward processing trade' (OPT)). For example, German and Austrian firms often temporarily exported to CE and then re-imported the goods for final finishing.[20] EU countries' OPT shares were virtually always highest with the CE states, rather than with American or Asian states who were their leading trade partners and with whom their IPT shares were highest. Yet CE states had a trivial position as temporary exporters to the EU, accounting for about 2 per cent of total IPT in the EU. Thus trade in semi-finished goods was essentially a one-way street. The data also show that apparent CE strength in exports was, in some sectors, derivative of German and Austrian production that conventional trade statistics counted as CE trade, even though most of its value added occurred elsewhere. This means that CE comparative advantage is overstated in most existing trade datasets.

Another indicator of dependency in CE economies takes off from the distinction between two basic forms of intra-industry trade (IIT). Vertical IIT occurs when developed countries control all the highest value added parts of the product cycle, while horizontal IIT characterizes peer-to-peer trading regimes of differentiated products of roughly equivalent value added. Gabrisch and Werner (1999) showed that Visegrad (e.g. Poland, Hungary, the Czech Republic and Slovakia) IIT did rise during the 1990s, but that it tended to have much higher vertical levels than in EU-15 states (1999: 147). The same data also showed that relative unit values (essentially, within sector variation in price–quality measures for EU-15 and Visegrad production) showed that consistently large gaps in favor of EU-15 producers in most sectors liberalized quickly. In only six of the 30 sectors measured were Visegrad producers more competitive (146–7). Finally, in the few cases of CE advantage in price–quality ratios, fewer than 10 per cent are in 'high-quality' imports.[21] Broadly, the Visegrad states are specializing in areas of 'standard goods of labor- and scale-intensive production' (148). This certainly can raise incomes but in a way less likely to fundamentally challenge EU-15 models of production, which I have argued is the essence of managed globalization in the context of enlargement.

My interpretation of these results is that the EU-15 have managed the trade aspects of integration with CE successfully from their perspective. They have diversified EU-15 production by investing in CE but without (so far) provoking any major backlash against enlargement.[22] As noted above, EU-15 firms could insist on steps to open CE markets while protecting themselves from competition from there. For example, though illegal under EU law, many investors imposed 'vertical restraint agreements' prohibiting their own CE affiliates from using technology transferred to them for any production activities outside the framework of their joint-venture agreement with their Western partners (Lorentzen and Mollgard 2000). Moreover, Volkswagen (legally) limited reimports to the EU-15 of its Skoda products out of fear of cannibalizing its VW brands there.[23] This management strategy dampened the potential for unwanted competition that did occur.

So far, CE producers have posed few really stiff competitive challenges to EU-15 producers. There are two factors behind this pattern. First, the trade strategy described above meant that potential direct competitive challenges from CE could be largely managed by EU rules and policies. The EU allowed access to its market only on its own terms and at its own pace. Second, global liquidity was so high since the second wave of FDI that ample investment capital could flow to CE without thinning the capital base of the EU-15. This 'win-win' pattern is easiest to see in the auto sector, where very clear upgrading did take place in CE (already by 1999, CE producers had caught up with EU-15 producers in unit values in autos) (Scepanovic 2009: 6). Even as CE producers increased employment and exports of both high- and low-value-added production in the auto sector, the sector also showed stable or growing production in Southern Europe (especially Spain) and Germany (Scepanovic 2009).

While the first factor – limits to market access – dampened CE growth into high value-added markets, the second – high liquidity – promoted such growth. Both of these factors have changed, however. First, the EU-15 regulatory strategy depended very heavily on the CEs' non-member status, which ended in 2004. Should CE-based firms – aided by propitious tax, investment and labor market policies in CE – launch new challenges, it is harder to see how this pattern could be repeated.

Second, the financial crisis has manifested, in part, as a liquidity crisis, and lending is down substantially since 2008. FDI inflows to the CE member states fell 9 per cent in 2008, and FDI inflows for 2009 may be an estimated 50 per cent lower than in 2008 (Hunya 2009). CE exports have been devastated, falling around 30 per cent year-on-year in several CE economies in 2009. Industrial production is down. Year-on-year growth reversals between 2008 and 2009 ranged from a low of −5 per cent (Poland) to −28 per cent (Latvia), and Poland was the only CE member to register positive growth in 2009 (0.8 per cent). Poland's relatively favorable growth reversal numbers are equal to that of the EU-15 average, so all other CE states are doing worse than the EU-15 and some far worse. Still, growth reversals are lower in CE states that trade heavily with the EU-15 than in states like Russia and Ukraine, suggesting some buffering role for intra-European trade (WIIW 2009: 4). While a fragile recovery is forecast for some states, most predictions see growth remaining below 3 per cent in even the best performers through 2011 (WIIW 2009: 11–12).

CONCLUSION: FOUR PARADOXES OF FRAGILE ECONOMIES

'Enlarging the sphere of EU influence' is one of five mechanisms that this collection puts at the core of managed globalization. I argue that the EU-15 have been highly risk-averse during this enlargement. Their management efforts allowed EU-15 actors to exploit investment opportunities in CE but without immediately exposing EU-15 economies to large increases in migration or trade pressure in sectors where CE had comparative advantage. Slowly, CE states shifted from a domestic growth strategy to one based more on attracting FDI and boosting exports. This transformation was aided, abetted and channeled by the EU-15. In finance, the EU eventually stripped CE states of some of the tools they had been using to attract foreign capital, and the EU paved the way for the EU-15 to delay trade opening in sensitive sectors until FDI patterns increased EU-15 influence and, later, to put up barriers to labor mobility. Emphasizing that the EU-15 bought time to adjust, the CE states also played important (and quite understandable) roles in promoting FDI. The result was neither a neoliberal invasion (Aligica and Evans 2009) nor a pure 'manager's paradise' (Bluhm 2007), but a carefully managed economy closely tied to those in Western Europe.

Four paradoxes emerge. First, even though CE states have been thoroughly managed by the EU-15, the result has still been broadly perceived as a win-win situation, at least until recently. Even though the EU-15 states won all the key disagreements prior to enlargement – over issues like agriculture funding, the size of the structural funds, the time to membership, the stretching of the *acquis* to novel areas – the wide gap in living standards between EU-15 and CE states means that even small concessions were meaningful in CE. More-over, their status as potential and then actual EU members has helped lower CE borrowing costs, which stimulated a long consumption boom. In most places, between 2000 and 2008, employment, growth and investment were up while inflation was down. The financial crisis that began in 2008 may only further cement CE interest in joint EU policies even if costs are asymmetric. For example, while most CE states have taken a cautious approach to future eurozone membership, it has not escaped notice that those states that did join – Slovenia, Slovakia, Malta and Cyprus – enjoyed a certain insulation from the currency fluctuations that roiled markets in late 2008, hammering even states like Iceland, let alone Hungary and Latvia.[24]

A second relevant paradox is that where Abdelal and Meunier (2010) show that the EU was more able to manage globalization in capital than in trade, the CE cases show roughly the opposite pattern: EU-15 governments more easily managed the trade aspects of enlargement than the FDI aspect, where they often resented the hyper-liberal policies designed to attract investment. These liberal policies emerged from an implicit coalition between CE reformers and EU-15 investors (Jacoby 2006). This coalition around finance was much harder for the EU-15 to control, but it also generated conditions under which the later move to free trade would be much less disruptive, since EU-15 actors soon came to own the CE firms exporting (or reimporting as in the above data) to the EU-15. Broadly, this pattern underscores again how powerful is the EU's gatekeeping leverage granted by virtue of the large internal market to which it controls access. By contrast, the EU has far fewer instruments to limit the outflow of capital from the EU-15.

The question is how well the EU deploys this leverage. Sbragia (2010) shows that the EU has often fared poorly, seemingly handcuffed by its commitment to multilateralism. In the current banking crisis, the EU seems often to have failed to exploit widespread disenchantment with American finance practices to play a central role in developing new global financial regulations (or even get its own house remotely in order) (Newman 2009; Véron 2009). Even in its own neighborhood policy, the EU has struggled to use economic leverage alone (without membership conditionality) to prompt radical reforms in 'deep' Eastern Europe or the wider Mediterranean areas (Vachudova 2008). However, in CE the EU did play its trade cards adroitly and to the clear benefit of EU-15 actors. Now that the CE states are full members (a situation that often improved conditions for previous waves of EU entrants), they can defend themselves far better. Yet what if access to consumption financing narrows dramatically and investment capital flows out of CE during a protracted economic downturn? Will the CE states, even as full members, find that they have left behind their status as geo-strategic buffer states for the USSR only to emerge as economic buffer states for the old EU?

A third paradox is that some level of liberal 'threat' from CE may actually be welcomed by generally conservative and risk-averse EU-15 governments. Initially, West European firms' efforts to attract generous investment subsidies seemed to empower CE states with whom these firms often worked very closely. EU-15 states often protested about the potential for social dumping and unfair tax competition. These complaints have grown quieter however, and part of the reason for this may be because CE liberalism both helps solve a collective action problem of West European firms and provides them with favorable conditions that reduce their demands on EU-15 governments. Many such corporations – not least large German firms – chafe at domestic regulations and are genuinely interested in using production abroad not just to cut costs but to put reform pressure on their home governments. Yet the ability to lower their costs in the short run by investing in CE may rather dampen their fervor for reforms that might lower their home costs in the long run. In that sense, CE investment seems to have functioned as a 'pressure valve' that, when released, somewhat deflates the pressure for domestic reform, something that might, for example, have threatened to tear apart the CDU–SPD grand coalition that governed Germany until the autumn of 2009. Post-election interviews in the German Ministry for Economics suggest no enthusiasm for reopening the contentious debate over 'tax dumping' in CE.[25]

A fourth paradox is that when EU membership was achieved, the resulting 'safety' seems to have led CE states to adopt some very risky new behaviors. This behavior is the subject of another paper, but some of its roots seem already to be clear enough. On the one hand, the very fact of prospective and then actual EU membership dramatically lowered borrowing costs for CE actors, but this was especially true to the extent that borrowing was denominated in foreign currencies like the euro or Swiss franc. Some of this debt was no doubt justifiable in the context of consumer prices that were converging on EU-15 levels quite a lot faster than were wages. Nevertheless, when domestic currencies came under severe pressure in the autumn of 2007, debt service became a crushing burden for both private and public actors. To this economic logic, we must also add an important note about politics that may well lie at the heart of this risky behavior: CE politicians of all stripes have been faced with relentlessly dissatisfied electorates, resulting in high electoral volatility, party death and exit, and high government turnover. In this context, the incentives are hard to resist for politicians to pursue policies with benefits in the here and now and costs that will be borne by the next government, almost certainly not by them.

What lies ahead? With the global economy in turmoil, it is exceedingly difficult to say. One hunch is that variations across European economic systems will become even more important. We already know that even the Europe of the EU-15 contained up to four fairly coherent economic models: (1) Nordic Co-ordinated Market Economies (CMEs); (2) Continental CMEs; (3) Liberal Market Economies (LMEs); and (4) a Southern European model (Pontusson 2005; Fioretos, this issue). A useful line of future research would ask the extent to which countries from each part of the typology have and sustain a distinct relationship with CE. For example, Germany is, by some distance, the largest investor in CE. On the other hand, the UK – well ahead of Germany and second only to the US in global FDI outflows – has been only a bit player in CE, accounting for less than 5 per cent of total FDI, except in Bulgaria (11 per cent) and Lithuania (7 per cent) (Bandelj 2008: 106–10). One hypothesis consistent with this data would be that LMEs have least to gain from CE (since their economies are already more liberal) and that they therefore invest less in CE. A corollary might, however, be that LMEs have allowed more immigration from CE, suggesting that they want something different, but not that they are less interested in CE. In other words, the EU-15 may use regionalization differently: Britain hosts CE workers, while Germany prefers to invest there instead.[26]

Variation in EU-15 objectives must also be matched analytically with substantial variation in CE capacities, a crucial theme that space limitations have obviously precluded here. Greskovits (2006) shows that behind broadly liberal policy regimes very different economic structures are still being reproduced. Distinguishing capital-intensive and non-intensive production regimes as well as skilled versus less skilled production produces a typology with four combinations: capital-intensive-low skilled (e.g. mining, Bulgaria), capital intensive-high skilled (e.g. autos, Slovakia), non-capital intensive-low skilled (e.g. textiles, Romania), and non-capital intensive-high skilled (e.g. electronics, Hungary). Surely, these sectors will respond differently to the ongoing turmoil, with the auto sector in especially difficult times. It is far from certain that the EU-15 can still use EU instruments to manage CE states now that they are all members, but given the history outlined above and the rough times ahead, it seems beyond a doubt that they will give it a try.

ACKNOWLEDGEMENTS

Thanks to the participants of the Princeton and Park City workshops, Suzanne Berger, Dorothee Bohle, Rachel Epstein, Bela Greskovits, Bob Hancké and Grigore Pop-Eleches for comments on an earlier version of this article, as well as two anonymous reviewers for useful suggestions.

NOTES

1 For example, Leonard (2006: 145–6) lists 82 non-member European, African and Asian, states in an emerging 'Eurosphere'.
2 This article does not treat Malta and Cyprus, which also joined in 2004.
3 This logic applies both to firms – which have a model of production – and to nations in the sense of national models of capitalism.
4 For important exceptions, see Gowan 1995; Zielonka 2006; Böröcz 2010.
5 This finding is based on a dummy for prospective membership. On the other hand, formal EU investment treaties seem not to explain much variation (Bandelj 2008: 123).
6 Audi resisted Hungarian efforts to impose a 4 per cent 'solidarity tax' on foreign capital and helped scuttled the whole measure (Ellison 2007: 25).
7 To be clear, my claim is not that liberal policies definitely attracted investment capital and jobs. Even when the Baltic states moved to the kind of hyper-liberalism just described, this did not redirect FDI away from the four 'Visegrad' states that had already been the main beneficiaries of the first FDI boom (see Bohle and Greskovits 2007: 457–9). My point is that the policy basket under discussion scared key EU-15 actors with visions of the proverbial 'race-to-the-bottom'.
8 The CE states appear to have been conscientious about passing EU legislation and resolving disputes with the EU subsequent to membership (Sedelmeier 2008).
9 For example, Volkswagen accounted for about 15 per cent of both Czech and Slovakian exports in the years leading up to enlargement (Pavlínek 2004).
10 A 2006 EU report found that corporate tax rates declined in 22 out of 25 EU states between 1995 and 2004. Weighted for country size, the average rate drop was from 43 per cent to 33 per cent (European Commission 2006: 82–4).
11 Van Aken (2008) shows that foreign investors provided a clear advantage when CE states sought temporary 'derogations' to set aside parts of the *acquis* for a limited time.
12 Former Estonian Prime Minister Juhan Parts spoke for many when he said, 'Estonia views any move to QMV on tax and social security as not acceptable.' *BBN Estonia*, 6 October 2003.
13 For a subtle but inconclusive analysis along these lines, see Aligica and Evans (2009: 185–203).
14 Even here, however, Berger (2005) stresses the low productivity in CE sites like Romania, while noting that firms there are often obliged to build much of their own infrastructure. Such hidden costs cut heavily into anticipated benefits. See also Sammarra and Belussi (2006).
15 Greece did by 2007, but not 2004 when the core policy space was contested. Italy was bordered by relatively well-off Slovenia.
16 Slovenia was an outlier at just over 50 per cent. Bulgaria and Romania (2007 accession) were under 10 per cent of German wages.
17 To be sure, Germany and Austria have the highest shares of non-nationals among their working-age populations (about 10 per cent – though few from CE states).

18 The UK received far more immigrants than anticipated (according to the BBC, 600,000 total rather than the Home Office's estimate of 13,000 per year (e.g. approximately 50,000 per year since May 2004), with Poland by far the biggest sender).

19 For the EAs, see Sedelmeier (2005). A more positive view is Kaminski (2000), who notes that many potentially protectionist measures were limited in practice. Still, Eurostat data show that aggregate CE trade deficits with the EU-15 jumped from just under €5 billion in 1994 to nearly €13 billion in 1996. Vachudova (2005: ch. 4) shows that stingy EU trade concessions in the EAs increased CE determination to seek full EU membership.

20 In the years the study was conducted – 1990 to 2003 – the CEs were non-EU countries.

21 In a later study, Mykhnenko (2007: 373) found that CE states (even those with very different growth levels) still showed similar comparative advantages in global markets, namely low and medium technology exports and resource-based manufacturing exports.

22 This claim is easier with the Lisbon Treaty finally ratified. That said, I am not aware of solid data linking prior French, Dutch or Irish rejection of the Constitutional or Lisbon treaties to frustration over enlargement.

23 I thank Bob Hancké for this information.

24 For the Hungarian case, see Szlanko (2008); for the Latvian case, see Raudseps (2008).

25 Interview with Hansjög Schaal, German Ministry of Economics, Berlin, September 2009.

26 Consistent with this proposition, Ireland has virtually no CE investment. On the other hand, Sweden – which also opened its labor markets from the start of enlargement – was actually the fifth largest investor in CE.

REFERENCES

Abdelal, R. and Meunier, S. (2010) 'Managed globalization: doctrine, practice and promise', *Journal of European Public Policy* 17(3): 350–67.

Aligica, P. and Evans, J. (2009) *The Neoliberal Revolution in Eastern Europe*, Cheltenham: Edward Elgar.

Appel, H. (2006) 'International imperatives and tax reforms: lessons from postcommunist Europe', *Comparative Politics* 39(1): 43–62.

Baldone, S., Sdogati, F. and Tajoli, L. (2007) 'On some effects of international fragmentation of production on comparative advantages, trade flows and the income of countries', *The World Economy* 30(11): 1726–69.

Bandelj, N. (2008) *From Communists to Foreign Capitalists*, Princeton, NJ: Princeton University Press.

Becker, S. and Muendler, M. (2008) 'The effect of FDI on job security', *B.E. Journal of Economic Analysis and Policy* 8(1), available at http://www.bepress.com/bejeap/vol8/iss1/art8

Berger, S. (2005) *How we Compete*, New York: Currency.

Bluhm, K. (2007) *Experimentierfeld Ostmitteleuropa? Deutsche Unternehmen in Polen und der Tschechischen Republik*, Wiesbaden: VS.

Bohle, D. and Greskovits, B. (2007) 'Neoliberalism, embedded neoliberalism and neocorporatism: towards transnational capitalism in Central-Eastern Europe', *West European Politics* 30(3): 443–66.

Böröcz, J. (2010) *The European Union and Global Social Change: A Critical Geopolitical-economic Analysis*, London: Routledge.

Brücker, H. and von Weizsäcker, J. (2007) 'Migration policy: at the nexus of internal and external migration', in A. Sapir (ed.), *The Fragmented Power: Europe and the Global Economy*, Brussels: Bruegel.

Drahokoupil, J. (2008a) *Globalization and the State in Central and Eastern Europe: The Politics of Foreign Direct Investment*, London: Routledge.

Drahokoupil, J. (2008b) 'The investment-promotion machines: the politics of foreign direct investment promotion in Central and Eastern Europe', *Europe-Asia Studies* 60(2): 197–225.

Drezner, D. (2007) *All Politics is Global: Explaining International Regulatory Regimes*, Princeton, NJ: Princeton University Press.

Ellison, D. (2007) 'Competitiveness strategies, resource struggles, and national interest in the new Europe', Carl Beck Working Paper.

Epstein, R. (2008) *In Pursuit of Liberalism: International Institutions in Postcommunist Europe*, Baltimore, MD: Johns Hopkins University Press.

European Commission Directorate-General for Taxation and Customs Union (2006) *Structures of the Taxation Systems in the European Union: 1995–2004*, Brussels: EC.

Fioretos, O. (2010) 'Europe and the new global economic order: internal diversity as liability and asset in managing globalization', *Journal of European Public Policy* 17(3): 383–99.

Gabrisch, H. and Werner, K. (1999) 'Structural convergence through industrial policy?', in J. Van Brabant (ed.), *Remaking Europe: The European Union and the Transition Economies*, Lanham, MD: Rowman & Littlefield.

Gowan, P. (1995) 'Neo-liberal theory and practice for Eastern Europe', *New Left Review* 213: 4–60.

Grabbe, H. (2006) *The EU's Transformative Power: Europeanization through Conditionality in Central and Eastern Europe*, London: Palgrave.

Greskovits, B. (2006) 'Leading sectors and the variety of capitalism in Central and Eastern Europe', Unpublished paper, Budapest: Central European University.

Hunya, G. (2009) 'FDI in the CEECs under the impact of the global crisis: sharp declines', Vienna: WIIW.

Jacoby, W. (2004) *The Enlargement of the European Union and NATO: Ordering from the Menu in Central Europe*, New York: Cambridge University Press.

Jacoby, W. (2006) 'Inspiration, coalition, and substitution: external influences on post-communist transformations', *World Politics* 58(4): 623–51.

Jacoby, W. and Meunier, S. (2010) 'Europe and the management of globalization', *Journal of European Public Policy* 17(3): 299–317.

Kaminski, B. (2000) 'The Europe Agreements and transition: unique returns from integration into the EU', in A. Antohi and V. Tismaneanu (eds), *Between Past and Future: The Revolutions of 1989 and their Aftermath*, Budapest: CEU Press.

Kvist, J. (2004) 'Does EU enlargement start a race to the bottom? Strategic interaction among EU member states in social policy', *Journal of European Social Policy* 14(3): 301–18.

Leonard, M. (2006) *Why Europe Will Run the 21st Century*, London: Public Affairs.

Lorentzen, J. and Mollgard, P. (2000) 'Exclusive agreements and technology transfer: competition policy and EU enlargement', Copenhagen Business School.

McCormick, J. (2006) *The European Superpower*, London: Palgrave.

Mayhew, A. (1998) *Recreating Europe: The European Union's Policy Towards Central and Eastern Europe*, Cambridge: Cambridge University Press.

Mykhnenko, V. (2007) 'Strengths and weaknesses of "weak" coordination', in B. Hancké, M. Rhodes and M. Thatcher (eds), *Beyond Varieties of Capitalism: Conflict, Contradiction, and Complementarities in the European Economy*, Oxford: Oxford University Press.

Newman, A. (2009) 'Flight from risk: unified Germany and the role of identity in the European response to the financial crisis', *European Politics Newsletter*, summer: 19–26.

O'Dwyer, C. and Kovalcik, B. (2007) 'And the last shall be first: party system institutionalization and second-generation economic reform in postcommunist Europe', *Studies in Comparative International Development* 41(4): 3–26.

Pavlínek, P. (2004) 'Regional development implications of foreign direct investment in Central Europe', *European Urban and Regional Studies* 11(1): 63–5.

Pontusson, J. (2005) *Inequality and Prosperity: Social European vs. Liberal America*, Ithaca, NY: Cornell University Press.

Raudseps, P. (2008) 'Bridge collapse', *Transitions Online*, 3 December.

Reid, T. (2004) *The United States of Europe: The New Superpower and the End of American Supremacy*, New York: Penguin.

Sammarra, A. and Belussi, F. (2006) 'Evolution and relocation in fashion-led Italian districts: evidence from two case-studies', *Entrepreneurship and Regional Development* 18: 543–62.

Sbragia, A. (2010) 'The EU, the US, and trade policy: competitive interdependence in the management of globalization', *Journal of European Public Policy* 17(3): 368–82.

Scepanovic, V. (2009). 'The battle of peripheries: positioning of East Central and South European industrial clusters within the European automobile industry networks', in Transnational Capitalism Conference Proceedings, 29–30 May, EUI.

Schnabel, R. (2005) *The Next Superpower?: The Rise of Europe and its Challenge to the United States*, Lanham, MD: Rowman & Littlefield.

Sedelmeier, U. (2005) *Constructing the Path to Eastern Enlargement*, Manchester: Manchester University Press.

Sedelmeier, U. (2008) 'After conditionality: post-accession compliance with EU law in East Central Europe', *Journal of European Public Policy* 15(6): 806–25.

Szlanko, B. (2008) 'Hungary: lost in economic space.' *Transitions Online*, 13 November.

Vachudova, M. (2005) *Europe Undivided: Democracy, Leverage, and Integration After Communism*, New York: Oxford University Press.

Vachudova, M. (2008) 'Trade and the internal market', in M. Baun, M. Smith and K. Weber (eds), *Governing Europe's Neighborhood: Partners or Periphery?*, Manchester: Manchester University Press.

Van Aken, W. (2008). 'The sectoral impact of enlargement', in Conference Proceedings, 2 May, University of Washington.

Véron, N. (2009) 'Die Neuordnung des europäisches Bankensystems is noch nicht abgeschlossen', *Börsen-Zeitung*, 20 October.

Wiener Institut für Internationale Wirtschaftsvergleiche (WIIW) (2009) 'Die globale Krise und die Länder Zentral- Ost- und Südosteuropas', WIIW Pressegespräch, 6 November.

Zielonka, J. (2006) *Europe as Empire: The Nature of the Enlarged European Union*, Oxford: Oxford University Press.

Zimmerman, K. (2007) 'Migration potential and its labor market impact after EU enlargement: a review', Unpublished paper, LoWER Workshop on Migration, London, 21 April.

Betwixt and between? The European Union's redistributive management of globalization

Brian Burgoon

ABSTRACT   The European Union's (EU) management of globalization includes redistributing or compensating for distributional consequences of globalization, using policies at different levels of governance (national, regional-European and supra-European). This contribution analyzes the extent and politics of such redistributive management. It emphasizes how redistributive management is meaningful and very popular, though less developed than EU policies setting the level and terms of openness. In addition, it suggests how EU policies that manage globalization through redistribution or other mechanisms and that operate at different levels of governance are causally interconnected. Existing national and EU policies of redistribution have strong but uneven effects for EU protections setting the level of openness. And national-level welfare provisions and EU redistributive policies, like the Structural Funds, sometimes undermine and sometimes reinforce one another. Case examples and analysis of public opinion develop these claims.

INTRODUCTION

Most of the mechanisms by which the European Union (EU) may be seen to manage globalization – such as EU regulation, EU empowerment of international institutions, or EU enlargement of its membership – involve managing the extent and terms of globalization. They regulate how much and what kind of international trade, investment and immigration Europeans experience. Yet perhaps the most basic mechanism for managing globalization involves redistributive management: redistribution or compensation for globalization's consequences instead of regulation of its extent and terms. Although modest compared to redistributive efforts by national governments, EU policies and institutions include meaningful redistributive or compensatory benefits, and these operate on several levels of governance: from benchmarking best practices of social policy at the national level; to dispensing Structural Funds at the regional-European level; to calling for aid transfers within the World Trade Organization (WTO) at the supra-European level.

That the EU's redistributive management of globalization takes place at different levels of governance and alongside other mechanisms for managing globalization makes it difficult to assess. It raises, in particular, two sets of questions. First, how substantial and politically sustainable are EU efforts to manage globalization through redistribution rather than other mechanisms of management and at one rather than another level of governance? Is EU redistribution as developed as EU regulation of the extent and terms of globalization? Are those EU redistributive policies operating at the regional-European level – such as Structural Funds – more or less developed than those EU policies operating at other levels, such as benchmarking of national policies? And how strongly do European publics support EU management of globalization, and redistributive management in particular?

Second, how does redistributive management at a particular level of governance affect and become affected by redistribution at other levels of governance or by other mechanisms for managing globalization? Might EU redistributive management, for instance, shape how EU provisions manage the extent of trade openness? How do redistributive policies at the national level affect and become affected by EU redistribution at the European level? Might generous redistributive benefits offered on the national level of governance lower support for more benefits at the regional-European level – and vice versa?

I answer these questions by focusing on established policies and public opinion towards globalization and redistributive policies in the EU. Actual policies capture existing redistribution effort. In addition, public opinion data help capture the political sustainability of such effort and provide common comparative metrics of support for various mechanisms for managing globalization.

As the first section discusses, policies and opinion suggest that the EU is an architect of redistribution for risks associated with globalization and is generally seen by European polities as a trusted manager of globalization's effects. But how much this is so clearly differs across mechanisms and levels of management. For instance, the EU does more to set the terms of globalization than to compensate for its costs; and among the EU's redistributive efforts, regional-European compensation is more extensive than EU efforts to either co-ordinate national-level redistribution or to set up redistribution at the supra-European level. In contrast to these patterns of actual policy development, public opinion data suggest that support for EU redistribution programs is higher than that for EU programs limiting the extent of globalization.

The second section addresses the second set of questions, focused on the politics of EU redistributive management. As we shall see, both actual policies and public opinion suggest that the depth of EU's managed globalization partly reflects how management policies influence one another. In particular, EU management via redistribution at one level of governance may be in tension or harmony with management via other mechanisms or at other levels of governance. Between mechanisms of management, for instance, EU-provided redistribution may obviate the need and diminish support for EU trade protections that limit the extent of globalization. And between levels of governance, redistribution at the national level might obviate the need and reduce support for redistribution at the regional-European level. Such dynamics help clarify the limits and possibilities of the EU's role in managing globalization.

MANAGING GLOBALIZATION BY SETTING EXTENT OF AND COMPENSATION FOR OPENNESS

Managing the effects of globalization with redistributive policy interventions has a long tradition in political-economic history. Karl Polanyi's *Great Transformation* focused on nineteenth- and twentieth-century industrialization, a process marked by a 'double movement' where polities intervened to make markets for labor, capital and goods, and then intervened again to protect society from the insecurities, risks and damage such markets might cause (Polanyi 1944). After the Second World War, industrialized democracies developed national policies and international institutions to re-establish trade and monetary openness and multilateralism, while protecting national societies from their risks by compensating for and setting limits on such liberalism (Ruggie 1982). These interventions involved policies that regulate and set the terms of openness, but also policies that redistribute or compensate for its uneven consequences – together constituting what has been called 'embedded liberalism'.

Given 50 years of European political–economic integration, we should not be surprised if management of the current wave of globalization might involve a mix of EU redistribution and other policies consistent with such embedded liberalism. Sure enough, EU institutions (Commission, Court, Parliament and Council) have developed redistributive as well as other kinds of management, and have done so by shaping national, regional-European and supra-European international policies. It is largely an empirical question, however, how substantially the EU manages globalization through redistribution rather than setting the terms of globalization and how much it does so at one rather than another level of governance. Although definitive answers are beyond my reach here, examples of EU policies and snapshots of public opinion clarify the practice of and support for EU redistributive management.

Redistributive management at three levels of governance

Much of EU management of globalization involves regulating how much, under what conditions, and what kinds of goods, services, investment and people flow across national borders – encompassing the most developed policy realms of the EU project, commercial and monetary policy. But meaningful redistributive management is taking place, including provision of actual social policies (e.g. European Social Fund or the new Globalization Adjustment Fund), as well as facilitating harmonization, benchmarking and consultation over national policies (e.g. Open Method of Co-ordination on pension, youth, childcare and other welfare policies in the post-Lisbon era). To be sure, most of these programs are not explicitly targeted at the costs of globalization. However, just as much of the national public economy can play an indirect or implicit compensatory role addressing globalization's risks (Rodrik 1997), so too can many EU provisions nominally delinked from globalization but which provide transfers or services relevant to economic risks. European citizens recognize the relevance of such programs for the victims of globalization. For example, 54 per cent of EU-27 citizens who say that EU Regional policies should address new issues name globalization as the first or second issue that such policies ought to address (European Opinion Research Group 2008, 25).

The EU engages in such redistributive management at three levels of governance: the supra-European international, European and member state levels. The significance of EU redistributive management is uneven across these levels. EU competencies remain modest compared to the national-level governments' redistribution. Indeed, it is not wrong to claim (for many, lament) that development of 'Social Europe' has long been eclipsed by 'negative' integration focused on market liberalization (e.g. Scharpf 2002; Streeck 1995). This implies that most of the globalization management involving compensation is done at the national level of governance, carried out by nation states rather than by the EU.

But EU-provided compensatory management at the national level is not absent. For instance, the EU has in recent years provided a framework for co-ordinating national social policy reforms in the context of the Open Method of Co-ordination (OMC), co-ordinated and institutionalized benchmarking in pensions, employment and family policies that partially fulfill a compensatory role for globalization. How much this actually matters to learning and welfare reform among member states is still an open and debated question (Mosher and Trubek 2002; Zeitlin 2005), but such activity constitutes EU redistributive management.

The most extensive EU-led redistributive management, however, takes place at the regional-European level. The EU has long had redistributive budget programs in place at that level. All three of the current Objectives of the Structural Funds serve broadly redistributive or compensatory goals, though not directly tied to economic globalization. The most relevant, broad fund is the European Social Fund (ESF), but indirectly also the European Agricultural Guidance and Guarantee Fund (EAGGF) and the European Regional Development Funds (ERDF). These programs have all grown considerably since Delors I and II, by 2006 totaling nearly 30 billion euros and more than 30 per cent of the EU budget (EC 2007). Beginning in 2007, the EU introduced the European Globalization Adjustment Fund (EGF), budgeted to spend some 500 million euros annually to co-finance retraining and adjustment for those dislocated due to (mainly) extra-European trade or investment. In its first year, the EGF disbursed more than 21 million euros to programs in France, Germany, Finland, Malta and Portugal (EC 2008). Add to all these explicit budgetary programs that the EU has since the 1950s engaged in limited hard-law harmonization (e.g. in workplace safety), and regional-European compensation is no small endeavor.

Turning finally to the supra-European level of EU redistributive management, the story is much more modest, and in fact is almost an empty policy space. Even here, however, nascent EU redistributive management exists. Former EC Trade Commissioner Pascal Lamy and a number of EU member states made the EU a chief supporter and architect of the World Trade Organization (WTO) 'Aid for Trade' program, founded in 2005. With 2006 disbursements rising to 23 billion euros (3.1 from the EU), that program co-ordinates aid efforts to help developing country WTO members build state capacities and infrastructure, and to ease adjustment associated with trade liberalization (Garcia and Lammersen 2008). All told, the EU's redistributive management may be said to be less substantial than management of the terms and extent of openness but is meaningful at all levels of governance, particularly the regional-European level of governance.

Public opinion on EU-managed globalization

Public opinion patterns suggest the political viability and promise of redistributive management. Surveys suggest strong support for EU management of globalization, but also for a mix of redistributive and other mechanisms of management that stand in contrast to actual practice. A 2004 survey in the 27 (now) member states reveals surprisingly high levels of trust in EU-guided management of globalization's effects (European Opinion Research Group 2004). After asking about benefits and costs of globalization, the survey showed respondents a list of actors and institutions, and asked: 'who do you trust most to get the effects of globalization under control?' (Multiple answers were possible). The question does not specify what it means to get globalization's 'effects under control', which can imply various interventions. But it does gauge how citizens subjectively judge the EU rather than their national government or other 'actors' (e.g. international organizations or NGOs) to manage the globalization's *effects* – hence geared more to actions redistributing globalization's costs and benefits than to those shaping its extent.

Figure 1 presents the national averages for EU-15 and Central and East European Countries (CEEC-12), revealing that EU citizens tend to trust the European Union to manage globalization more than they do other 'actors'. On average, 27 per cent of EU-15 respondents named the EU, the closest second being consumer rights groups. This masks variation within the EU-15, with the highest trust in EU management in the Netherlands (43 per cent) and the lowest in the UK (16 per cent). But the only EU-15 polities *not* rating the EU highest were France (preferring consumer rights groups) and the UK (trusting WTO the most). Among CEEC-12 countries the pattern is similar, though not completely comparable with EU-15 results since CEEC-12 polities were not given the option 'don't know'. Still, a plurality (33 per cent) trusted the EU most to handle globalization's effects (with 'citizens themselves' being the distant second, at 25 per cent). Again, that average harbors variation: 43 per cent of Hungarians and Romanians were most trusting of the EU and

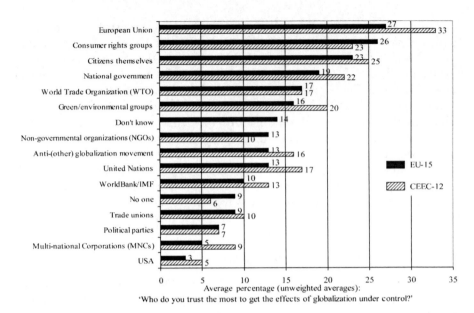

Figure 1 Support for EU to manage effects of globalization
Source: Eurobarometer, 61, own calculations.

only 19 per cent of Poles; and a few polities (Cyprus, Estonia, Malta and Poland) tended to choose the EU as only the second-most trusted globalization manager. Both EU-15 and CEEC-12 citizens see their national governments as only the fourth most trusted globalization manager (19 per cent for EU-15; CEEC-12, 22 per cent), behind consumer rights groups and 'citizens themselves'. In addition, they express even less trust in international organizations like the WTO and World Bank. Such results reveal strong citizen support for the EU to manage globalization's effects.

It is difficult to divine what European citizens expect or want such EU management to entail, not least because existing surveys do not explicitly compare relevant programs. The nearest alternative is to compare distinct surveys where respondents are asked to judge a particular goal or policy action of the EU relevant to globalization. Figure 2 summarizes citizen support for EU redistributive policies and for EU trade policies. The first three bars measure support for different faces of redistributive management. The first two involve support for making social policy activities 'a key priority of the EU': 'to develop joint policies to fight unemployment in Europe' (q.53.19); and 'giving more help to the poor and the socially excluded in the European Union' (q.53.21). Both from Eurobarometer 47.2, these questions broadly cover EU compensatory activity to address economic risks. The third measure involves support for a specific EU redistributive program: the European Social Fund, the EU program that funds training and other labor market assistance to Europe's unemployed, consuming almost 10 per cent of the EU budget. Based on a

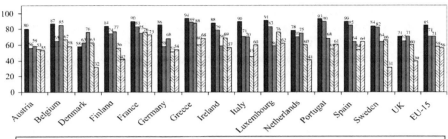

Figure 2 Support for EU management by redistribution or by trade regulation
Source: Eurobarometer 44.2; 47.2; 261.

2006 survey, the third bar of Figure 2 shows the percentage of respondents who, upon hearing a description of its elements and budgetary costs, say that the ESF budget ought to be maintained or increased (European Opinion Research Group 2006, 59).

The final two bars per country summarize support for EU external trade protection, based on questions from Eurobarometers in 1996 (44.2bis) and 1997 (47.2), asking whether the EU should make a key priority of: 'preventing the import of manufactured goods from countries where working conditions are unacceptable'; or 'protecting EU products from imports made from non-EU members'. The different wording and timing of these various survey questions complicate any systematic comparisons. These are, however, concrete examples of how EU management might set the terms of openness to trade, worded without framing of costs and benefits of interventions, and provide therefore some reference point for assessing support for redistributive measures.

In any event, as worded, both kinds of EU management are seen by majorities in the EU-15 as key priorities for the EU, but the patterns suggest more support for redistributive protection than for trade protection. Support for EU import restrictions where working conditions are unacceptable averages 58 per cent, and ranges from 45 per cent in Italy to 76 per cent in France and Luxembourg, and support for import limits to protect EU products averages 56 per cent and ranges from 31 per cent in Sweden to 73 per cent in France. In contrast, support for EU policies to jointly fight unemployment averages 85 per cent, ranging from 58 (Denmark) to 93 per cent (Portugal), while support for EU management to help EU's own poor and socially excluded averages 71 per cent (ranging from 56 per cent in Austria to 90 per cent in Portugal). Support for the ESF averages 71 per cent in the EU-15 (72 per cent in EU-27), ranging from 59 per cent in Austria to 88 per cent in Greece.

These snapshots suggest that while EU management of globalization via mechanisms of both redistribution and trade protection are popular, the former tends to be more so. Such a pattern clearly contrasts how actual EU competencies and policies setting the extent of globalization are more established than those setting redistribution for globalization. Public opinion harbors significant support for EU managed globalization; hence with perhaps more room for developing management via redistribution than via established EU-governed trade regulation.

MUTUAL INFLUENCES ACROSS KINDS AND LEVELS OF MANAGEMENT

This brings us to the origins of EU mechanisms for managing globalization. Those origins have much to do with factors articulated in the Introduction to this collection: Formal delegation of authority to the EU is strong in commerce and weak on social policy, for instance, and this helps explain the deeper EU management in setting terms of, rather than compensating for, openness. In addition, lack of convergence in national goals and capacities of member states with respect to social policy protections across the EU-27 further complicates already difficult-to-mediate divisions among member states over EU-level redistributive management.

However, the above portrait of EU redistributive management alongside management by other mechanisms and at different levels of governance suggests a different causal dynamic: that compensating for and setting terms of globalization at different governance levels are *causally interrelated*. That is, EU redistributive management is likely to be influenced by, and to influence, other kinds of management that set the terms and extent of globalization; and management via any mechanism at either the national, regional or supra-European level is likely to influence and be influenced by management at other levels. Such mutual influence may be significant, where management of different mechanisms and at different levels reinforce or undermine one another.

How and to what extent this is so involves many more (and more difficult to judge) relationships than can be mapped here, but focusing on the two categories of such interconnection clarifies such politics: (1) interconnection between EU management via redistribution and via setting terms of openness; and (2) between redistributive efforts at different levels of governance. Figure 3 summarizes these categories. For each, examples from developments in policy suggest the logic of the interconnections, while patterns in public opinion data provide more systematic information on the importance and direction of the interconnection.

Interconnection between mechanisms of managing globalization

The extensive literature on 'embedded liberalism' suggests that policies of redistribution affect and are affected by policies regulating the extent of economic openness. Such embedded liberalism includes examples of how two mechanisms of EU management of globalization affect one another: EU management by

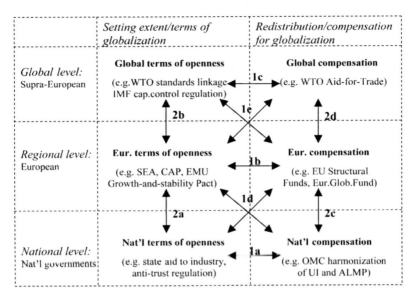

	Setting extent/terms of globalization	Redistribution/compensation for globalization
Global level: Supra-European	**Global terms of openness** (e.g.WTO standards linkage IMF cap.control regulation)	**Global compensation** (e.g. WTO Aid-for-Trade)
Regional level: European	**Eur. terms of openness** (e.g. SEA, CAP, EMU Growth-and-stability Pact)	**Eur. compensation** (e.g. EU Structural Funds, Eur.Glob.Fund)
National level: Nat'l governments	**Nat'l terms of openness** (e.g. state aid to industry, anti-trust regulation)	**Nat'l compensation** (e.g. OMC harmonization of UI and ALMP)

Figure 3 EU managed globalization across mechanisms and levels of governance

setting the extent and terms of openness, and such openness encouraging EU compensation or redistribution. The most familiar interaction in the literature is captured by arrow 1a: between a nation's exposure to globalization and its social policy provision. Debate continues over whether and under what conditions nationally determined openness tends to spur, constrain or have little affect on welfare states. A corollary to such study is whether existing social policies foster national openness (Hays *et al.* 2005). Although these dynamics are relevant to the broad politics of managing globalization, neither says much about the EU's role in such management. If the EU has a hand in constraining or benchmarking *national* social policies, however, these connections imply that EU redistributive management may affect and be affected by EU-mandated openness.

Studies of European integration identify strong interconnections between mechanisms of management at the regional-European level (see 1b in Figure 3). For example, scholars have analyzed how key integration moments involving terms of openness (e.g. European Economic Community in 1957, the Iberian enlargement, the Single European Act (SEA) in 1985, the Maastricht Treaty in 1992) unleashed pressures to expand the ESF and Cohesion Funds as 'side payments' to potential losers of such openness (Lange 1993; Thielemann 2005). Establishing the EGF on the heels of the French and Dutch 'no' votes on the EU Constitution arguably reflects such politics (arrow 1b from left to right).

Whatever the origins of EU's redistributive management at the regional level, the causal arrow may also run in the other direction (arrow 1b from right to left). Scholars debate whether Structural Funds solidify support for European integration, including economic integration (cf. Bachtler and Taylor 2003; Eriksson and Eriksson 2006). This may imply that such funds also solidify support for EU provisions that extend globalization, such as liberal trade policies – though as yet no evidence has been gathered directly addressing this possibility (more on this below).

Further, the supra-European level of EU redistributive and other mechanisms of management are likely interrelated. For example, efforts of EU representatives to develop 'Aid for Trade' assistance to developing countries are likely driven in part by hopes of relaunching the Doha Round of WTO trade negotiations in which developing countries are asked, with their increasing numbers and influence in that organization, to swallow liberalization amidst continued Western agricultural protection. If so, the EU is nurturing nascent supra-European compensation in the service of setting terms of supra-European openness (right arrow 1c, Figure 3).

Finally, redistributive management may also affect and be affected by EU regulation of terms of openness across different levels of governance. Debate continues over whether commercial, financial and monetary aspects of European integration unleash social dumping, or cause upward or downward convergence in *national* sovereignty in social policy-making (Streeck 1995; Scharpf 2002). This entails investigating 1d in Figure 3 (downward-right arrow). In addition, national compensation may affect support for and development of *EU* regulation of terms of openness – where social policy reform may have prepared a polity to embrace the EMU or SEA (upward-right arrow, 1d). Finally, regional-European EU redistributive management may also have influenced supra-European liberalization. Establishment of the EGF, whatever its origins, may buy support for EU Commission plans for making deeper concessions in the Common Agricultural Policy or other EU trade protections in order to relaunch the Doha Round. Such would be examples of how regional-level EU compensation may influence EU-led setting of the terms of openness at the supra-European level (upward-right arrow, 1e).

These anecdotal examples suggest the many categories of interactions between mechanisms of EU management of globalization. But how meaningful are such interactions? For instance, do redistribution efforts at different levels of governance provide equally strong political leverage to maintain or increase trade? Public opinion data provide some leverage to answer such questions, where we can compare how measures of redistribution policies at different levels of governance affect the degree to which publics in different EU countries support EU-level trade liberalization.

Figure 4 summarizes such analysis. The vertical axis of both scatterplots measures the percentage of national respondents very or fairly opposed to free trade (from Eurobarometer 67), roughly gauging sentiment towards limiting trade by EU management. The explanatory parameters on the horizontal axes are: for the left-hand panel, *Net replacement rates* for unemployment insurance, family assistance, housing assistance and social assistance to the long-term unemployed (net of taxes) (OECD 2004); and for the right-hand panel, *Structural Fund receipts*, average annual structural funds received by a member state, as per capita annual average budgeted for 2007 (EC 2007). The scatterplots also

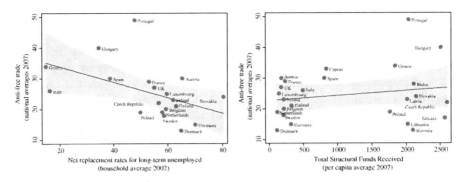

Figure 4 National social policy, EU Structural Funds and trade protectionism

include regression lines and 95 per cent confidence intervals to clarify the relationships between compensation and support for EU trade protection.

Following the discussion above, my expectation is that existing welfare compensation, at whatever level it is provided, ought to address globalization risk and hence lower citizen support for trade protectionism. The left-hand panel of Figure 4 shows that, consistent with conventional wisdom but now within an EU context, national net replacement rates tend to diminish average support for trade protectionism. This relationship is modest (R-square of 0.25; Beta of -0.49; and t-statistic 2.64) but holds up to controlling for per capita GDP, population and unemployment, and to other measures of welfare provision and support for EU protectionism from globalization.[1] The right-hand panel shows, however, that one rough measure of regional-level EU compensatory management – per capita receipts of Structural Funds – does not yield similar 'embedded liberalizing'. Receipts of EU structural funds have no statistically significant effect, correlating positively, if at all, with support for trade protectionism. Why this is so, while unclear, is perhaps that EU funds remain relatively modest to citizens' lives – even in new accession states receiving ample funds. But it is a hint that regional-European compensatory provisions might play out differently than do national provisions in shaping support for limiting globalization.

Interconnection between managed globalization's levels of governance

Within any given mechanism for managing globalization, management at one level of governance likely interacts with management at another level. Such interconnection can involve the way the EU sets the extent and terms of openness. For instance, EU decisions on the terms of intra-European openness can constrain national policies (downward arrow 2a, Figure 3) – such as the European Court's *Cassis de Dijon* decision and subsequent SEA's 'mutual recognition' constraining national intra-European non-tariff barriers (Alter and Meunier 1994). In addition, completing the SEA, via the principle of mutual recognition and loose rules of origin, may have had the unintended effect of facilitating extra-European liberalization, such as the 1994 Uruguay Round creating the WTO (Hanson 1998). If so, such politics exemplify regional-level EU setting of the terms of openness affecting EU activity in setting supra-European international openness (upward arrow 2b, Figure 3).

More importantly, interconnection across levels of management may also underlie development of EU redistributive management. This is true, most obviously, of how regional-European and national levels affect one another (2c, Figure 3). EU-level policies influence national welfare reforms in many ways (downward arrow, 2c) – supporting the well-established insight that supranational management yields 'semi-sovereign' national welfare states (Leibried and Pierson 1995; Leibfried 2000). For instance, since the European Coal and Steel Community, harmonization on a few aspects of social policy (e.g. equal treatment, occupational safety) has led to meaningful changes in member welfare states (Montanari 1995; Threlfall 2003).

Furthermore, national-level compensation may significantly influence the development (or lack) of EU-level social policies (upward arrow, 2c). Those lamenting the meager development of European social policy have commonly interpreted this to reflect not only political opposition by employers and others, but also how national social policy remains a cherished feature of national sovereignty – 'semi' or otherwise – something which neither social actors nor national politicians want to abdicate. In addition, national polities may be reluctant to support EU-level redistribution in part because diversity of national social models and cumbersome integration politics might yield 'lowest common denominator' harmonization of social policies that retrench generous welfare settings (Leibfried 2000; Scharpf 2002; Streeck 1995). In any event, many voters in the 1992 Danish referendum over Maastricht and the 2004 French referendum over the EU Constitution tied their 'no' votes to concerns about national welfare and pessimism over social Europe. And Sanchez-Cuenca (2000) found survey evidence that citizens were more likely to support deepening and speeding up of EU integration to the extent that they lived in less generous welfare settings. Burgoon and Jacoby (2004) found that European labor union representatives were supportive of building EU-level collective bargaining institutions in roughly inverse proportion to the generosity of their national welfare provisions.

Finally, regional-European EU management might have influenced the EU push for Aid for Trade provisions as part of the Doha Round. Long-standing EU practice and experience with providing Cohesion Fund and ERDF regional assistance helps consolidate political support among accession countries or weaker regions within the EU to accept painful economic liberalization. This may have yielded a practice of trying to duplicate such a dynamic in the WTO forum. By such logic, several generations of intra-EU side payments helped spawn EU plans to compensate developing countries for their liberalization compliance. Such politics, in any event, would be an example of how regional-European compensation helps spawn the pioneering development of supra-European compensation (upward arrow, 2d).

We can see from these examples that the interconnections between levels of governance at which EU management takes place can be as complicated as interconnections between mechanisms of management. But such anecdotes make it hard to judge how much management at one level might tend to be in tension with or spur management at another. Analysis of public opinion data, however, can shed some light on such issues by showing how actual provision of compensation at one level of governance might influence *support for* compensation at another level.

Figure 5 summarizes how national welfare correlates with support for EU-level activity relevant to compensation, and how receipts of Structural Funds correlate with support for national-level unemployment assistance. It considers the effects of the same measures of compensation at either the national or the EU level as in Figure 5 – generosity of welfare policies and Structural Fund receipts, respectively – for public support for compensation at the other level, as measured in a 2001 Eurobarometer (Eurobarometer 56.1). The left-hand panel shows how net replacement rates affect national average belief that a key EU priority ought to be 'fighting against poverty and social exclusion' (q.44.14, the same measure discussed in Figure 2, but for 2001). The right-hand panel shows how EU Structural Fund receipts correlate with support for 'national government providing a decent standard of living for the unemployed' (q.44.10). In addition to the bilateral scatterplots, the regression lines and confidence intervals show the significance of the relationships.

Building on the above discussion, one can expect either a positive or a negative connection between compensatory management on one level and support for such management on another. One possibility is that *ex ante* national-level assistance may actually diminish support for EU-level compensation, as citizens might see EU-level innovation as superfluous and a potential threat to national assistance. This may also hold for how EU Structural Funds affect support for national compensation – where citizens receiving more EU redistribution see this as obviating the need for national assistance. On the other hand,

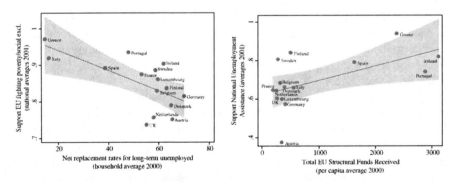

Figure 5 Actual national compensation (EU-level compensation) and support for EU-level compensation (national compensation)

compensation at the national and EU levels may be more complements than substitutes, where past assistance at one level inculcates expectations for, and bolsters political capacity to demand, assistance at another.

In fact, Figure 5 implies only one-way tension: national redistribution constraining EU redistributive management. The left-hand panel shows that generous national welfare correlates with lower support for EU-level welfare. The significant negative relationship (R-square of 0.43; Beta -0.66; t-statistic -5.32) holds up to more extensive regression analysis with controls and to alternative measures of support for EU-level compensation – such as support for European Social Funds, or making EU regulation of 'health and social security' (Burgoon 2009). The right-hand panel, meanwhile, shows how receiving EU structural funds *does not* significantly diminish support for national-level unemployment assistance. Receipts of structural funds, in fact, tend to correlate positively with support for national assistance. What underlies this pattern is unclear. But unlike national welfare provisions, Structural Fund transfers tend not to lower subjective insecurity – suggesting that they may be complements to national welfare (Burgoon 2009). In any event, these results suggest no tension between provided EU assistance and support for national assistance. Like the policy-making examples above, such patterns suggest that interconnection between levels and mechanisms of EU globalization management create both dilemmas and opportunities for such management.

CONCLUSION

The interplay between markets and political intervention has a long history in Europe, largely involving national political economy. The above discussion has tried to show that the most recent wave of globalization harbors policy and public support for EU interventions in a similar vein – both in setting the terms and redistributing the costs of economic globalization at the national, regional-European and supra-European levels of political economy. Discussion of these examples provides leverage to judge EU-led managed globalization as highly varied in its scope across mechanisms and levels of management, but also as meaningful and having a political future. Analysis of the interconnection between mechanisms and levels of management, furthermore, suggests how any given experiment in EU globalization management is likely rooted in and has strong implications for others.

Such a portrait of EU managed globalization remains, of course, suggestive. Further research can more accurately measure the extent to which EU managed globalization involves meaningful compensation for and setting the terms of economic openness at various governance levels. And better analysis of how citizens, labor and employer organizations, government officials and others take positions across mechanisms and levels of globalization management will clarify its origins. But the above analysis reveals EU redistributive management to be a meaningful part of contemporary political economy. It also provides a peek into the political limits and possibilities of redistributive management as a new kind of embedded liberalism.

ACKNOWLEDGEMENTS

The author thanks Daniel Nielson, Carles Boix, two anonymous reviewers and the editors for comments and suggestions on earlier versions of this contribution.

NOTE

1 This full model yields a significantly negative coefficient for net replacement rates: beta of -0.45, t-statistic 3.75 and R-square 0.44. Other specifications, yielding similar results, include for instance total welfare spending as share of GDP increasing chances that respondents say 'economic globalization is good for my country'.

REFERENCES

Alter, K. and Meunier, S. (1994) 'Judicial politics in the European Community: European integration and the path-breaking Cassis de Dijon decision', *Comparative Political Studies* 26(4): 535–61.

Bachtler, J. and Taylor, S. (2003) 'The added value of the structural funds: a regional perspective', Report on the structural funds, European Policies Research Centre, University of Strathclyde.

Burgoon, B. (2009) 'Social nation, social Europe: support for national and supranational welfare compensation in Europe', *European Union Politics* 10(4): 427–55.

Burgoon, B. and Jacoby, W. (2004) 'Patch-work solidarity: describing and explaining US and European labor internationalism', *Review of International Political Economy* 11(5): 849–79.

Ehrlich, S. (2009) 'How common is the common external tariff? Domestic influences on European Union trade policy', *European Union Politics* 10(1): 115–41.

Eriksson, J. and Eriksson, R. (2006) 'Do the European Union's structural funds affect the support for European integration in receiving areas?', Swedish Institute of European Policy Studies.

European Commission (2007) 'Regional policy: budget', available at: http://ec.europa.eu/regional_policy/funds/prord/sf_en.htm (accessed August 2009).

European Commission (2008) 'EU globalization adjustment fund website', available at: http://ec.europa.eu/employment_social/egf/applications07_en.html (accessed August 2009).

European Opinion Research Group (1997) 'Eurobarometer 47.2: women and cancer'.

European Opinion Research Group (2002) 'Eurobarometer 56.1: social exclusion'.

European Opinion Research Group (2004) 'Eurobarometer 61: CCEB2004.1'.

European Opinion Research Group (2006) 'Eurobarometer 261: European employment and social policy'.

European Opinion Research Group (2007) 'Eurobarometer 67: standard'.

European Opinion Research Group (2008) 'Eurobarometer 234: citizens' perceptions of EU regional policy'.

Garcia, M. and Lammersen, F. (2008) 'WTO Symposium on Implementation', available at: http://www.wto.org/english/tratop_e/devel_e/a4t_e/symp_sept08_sess1_oecd_e.pdf (accessed August 2009).

Hanson, B. (1998) 'What happened to fortress Europe?: External trade policy liberalization in the European Union', *International Organization* 52(1): 55–85.

Hays, J., Ehrlich, S. and Peinhardt, C. (2005) 'Government spending and public support for trade in the OECD', *International Organization* 59: 473–94.

Lange, P. (1993) 'Maastricht and the social protocol: why did they do it?', *Politics and Society* 21: 5–36.

Leibfried, S. (2000) 'National welfare states, European integration and globalization: a perspective for the next century', *Social Policy & Administration* 34(1): 44–63.

Leibfried, S. and Pierson, P. (1995) 'Semi-sovereign welfare states: social policy in a multitiered Europe', in S. Leibfried and P. Pierson (eds), *European Social Policy: Between Fragmentation and Integration*, Washington, DC: Brookings Institution.

Montanari, I. (1995) 'Harmonization of social policies and social regulation in the European Community', *European Journal of Political Research* 27(1): 21–45.

Mosher, J. and Trubek, D. (2003) 'Alternative approaches to governance in the EU: EU social policy and the European employment strategy', *Journal of Common Market Studies* 41(1): 63–88.

Organization for Economic Cooperation and Development (2004) *Benefits and Wages: Indicators*, Paris: OECD.

Polanyi, K. (1944) *The Great Transformation: The Political and Economic Origins of Our Time*, Boston, MA: Beacon Press.

Rodrik, D. (1997) *Has Globalization Gone Too Far?*, Washington, DC: IIE press.

Ruggie, J. (1982) 'International regimes, transactions, and change: embedded liberalism in the postwar economic order', *International Organization* 36(2): 195–231.

Sánchez-Cuenca, I. (2000) 'The political basis of support for European integration', *European Union Politics* 1(2): 147–71.

Scharpf, F. (1988) 'The joint-decision trap: lessons from German federalism and European integration', *Public Administration* 66: 239–78.

Scharpf, F. (2002) 'The European social model', *Journal of Common Market Studies* 40(4): 645–70.

Streeck, W. (1995) 'From market making to state building? Reflections on the political economy of European social policy', in S. Leibfried and P. Pierson (eds), *European Social Policy. Between Fragmentation and Integration*, Washington, DC: The Brookings Institution, pp. 389–481.

Thielemann, E. (2005) 'Symbolic politics or effective burden-sharing? Redistribution, side-payments and the European refugee fund', *Journal of Common Market Studies* 43(4): 807–24.

Threlfall, M. (2003) 'European social integration: harmonization, convergence and single social areas', *Journal of European Social Policy* 13(2): 121–39.

Zeitlin, J. (2005) 'Social Europe and experimentalist governance: towards a new constitutional compromise?', in G. de Búrca (ed.), *EU Law and the Welfare State: In Search of Solidarity*, Oxford: Oxford University Press.

Index

Page numbers in **Bold** represent figures.

INDEX

pollutants: regulating persistent organic
37
pollution: East Germany 46
Poret, Pierre 63
Portugal 141; EGF 138; immigration
125
Posner, Elliot 4, 8, 9, 12
poverty 147
power: normative and market 38
precautionary principle 39, 44;
environment 10; legitimacy 44
price stability 94; (ESCB) 32
Prodi, Romano 3, 40
production regimes 130
professional certificates: recognition of
124
Prospectus Directive 112
prostitution 124
protectionism 4–5, 103, 111, 125
prudential regulation 103
public consultation 107
public deficits 23, 28
public interest: EU 42; firm discretion
103
public opinion 4, 136; redistributive
management 139–42

race-to-the-bottom 38, 93
railways 111
recognition: mutual 93, 95
recovery 127
redistributive management 11–12; at
three levels of governance 137–9;
conclusion 142–8; introduction 135–7;
mutual influences 142–8; public
opinion 139–42; setting extent of and
compensation for openness 137–42;
support for EU **141**
regional integration: Lamy 60–1
regionalism 6; multilateralism 77
regulation failure: economic crisis 2
regulations 8–9; and competition 41;
costly standards 38; emulating 8;
legitimizing 38
regulatory arbitrage 108
regulatory influence: empowering
international institutions 38
regulatory politics perspective 41
Ricol, René 66
Rio Earth Summit (1992) 40, 43, 45
risk 44
Rodrik, Dani 91
Romania 123, 139; textiles 130
Rome: Treaty of 61, 63, 73

rules: liberalization 1
Russia 127; Kyoto Protocol 46

Sánchez-Cuenca, I. 146
Sarbanes-Oxley Act (2002) 104, 105
Sarkozy, Nicholas 47, 66, 85, 91, 112
Sbragia, Alberta 10, 14, 128
Scharpf, F. 117
Scheipers, S. 40
Seattle: WTO 57, 58
securities: mortgage backed 53
September 11th terrorist attacks 32
Sicurelli, D. 40
Singapore 78; 1996 ministerial
conference 59
single currency 110–11
Single European Act (SEA 1986) 56,
112, 143, 144, 145
Single Market 6; principles 124
Single Market Commissioner 110
Skoda 126
Slovakia 123, 126, 128, 130; autos 130;
US steel 122
Slovenia 128
social assistance 144
social constructivists 39
social dumping 144
Social Europe 138
social exclusion 140, 147
social globalization 3
social progress 90
social purpose 86
social risk 89
South Africa 74
South Korea 78, 80
sovereignty: concerns with euro 23–7;
euro 27–33; market globalization 22
Spain 53; immigration 125; production
127; public view of globalization 4
Stability and Growth Pact (SGP) 12, 29;
European Central Bank (ECB) 28;
fiscal discipline 20, 21
standards 38; common minimum 93;
exporting 43; international 8
state tied policy 14
steel 59, 125
Steinbrück, Peer 112
Stephan, H. 40
stimulus package: Merkel 30; Obama 33
stock exchanges 109
Stockholm Convention on Persistent
Organic Pollutants 49
Strauss-Kahn, Dominique: IMF 66
structural adjustment 89

158

Perspectives on European Politics and Society

EDITOR:
Dr. Cameron Ross, *Department of Politics,*
University of Dundee, UK

The collapse of Communism in Eastern Europe and the Soviet Union and the enlargement of the European Union provide new opportunities for academics to engage in scholarly debate on the new developments in European politics and society. The editors of *Perspectives on European Politics and Society* welcome articles on all aspects of European Politics, widely defined to include, comparative politics, political sociology, international relations, and modern history. The geographical scope of the journal covers all of Europe including the Russian Federation.

To sign up for tables of contents, new publications and citation alerting services visit **www.informaworld.com/alerting**

Register your email address at **www.tandf.co.uk/journals/eupdates.asp** to receive information on books, journals and other news within your areas of interest.

For further information, please contact Customer Services at either of the following:
T&F Informa UK Ltd, Sheepen Place, Colchester, Essex, CO3 3LP, UK
Tel: +44 (0) 20 7017 5544 Fax: 44 (0) 20 7017 5198
Email: subscriptions@tandf.co.uk
Taylor & Francis Inc, 325 Chestnut Street, Philadelphia, PA 19106, USA
Tel: +1 800 354 1420 (toll-free calls from within the US)
or +1 215 625 8900 (calls from overseas) Fax: +1 215 625 2940
Email: customerservice@taylorandfrancis.com

View an online sample issue at:
www.tandf.co.uk/journals/rpep

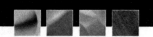